WHATEVER THE GODS DO

Also by Patti Miller

Writing Your Life

The Last One Who Remembers

Child

WHATEVER THE *Gods Do*

PATTI MILLER

A MEMOIR

VINTAGE

A Vintage Book
Published by
Random House Australia Pty Ltd
20 Alfred Street, Milsons Point, NSW 2061
http://www.randomhouse.com.au

Sydney New York Toronto
London Auckland Johannesburg

National Library of Australia
Cataloguing-in-Publication Entry

Miller, Patti, 1954– .
Whatever the gods do.

ISBN 1 74051 233 2.

1. Miller, Patti, 1954– . I. Title.

A823.3

Cover design by Greendot Design
Cover image from Bridgeman Art Library, London, 'Three Fin-de-Siecle Ladies Singing Berlioz' by Louis Weldon Hawkin (1849–1910)
Illustrations by What If Productions
Typeset in 10.5/12pt Goudy by Midland Typesetters, Maryborough, Victoria
Printed and bound by Griffin Press, Netley, South Australia

10 9 8 7 6 5 4 3 2 1

To Λ.R.
For you at last

I

One

I'm walking around the house, singing. The words and tune are not distinct, but the strong full-throated voice lifting and falling is clear and rich, more like honey than wine, warm and golden, appearing to melt into the light, to change form as it floats through the air. The notes harmonise with the chairs, curtains, cupboards, seeming to flow around them like bolts of silk flung out around the room. Afternoon sun streams through the study window, patterning bamboo on the walls and lighting the haphazard pile of books on the table. As I sing, my voice mingles with sun and shadows. I sing with my mouth wide open, with breath and flesh and bones.

This was my dream, my longing, not a statement of fact. It was written on a card and pinned on the wall of the study as a prop for imagining the future, the summer the singing lessons began and the summer Theo left for Melbourne.

'Bye,' he said quickly at the airport and pulled away from my clumsy arms. As if it wasn't the end of seven years.

The steward accompanying Theo onto his flight looked at me sympathetically. He had a story about us in his eyes – I was Theo's mother being forced to let my son go once again. As they disappeared through the departure door and along the corridor I heard Theo say to him, 'I'm going to see my dad. In Melbourne.'

I drove back home by myself. *It had all been for nothing*. If I had been able to sing a lament I would have wailed it all the way. But I couldn't sing – I hadn't even had my first lesson yet – and it was too hot and the certain stream of traffic pushed me off into the wrong lane so I missed the turn-off to the Blue Mountains where I live and had to backtrack, sweaty and a bit tearful until I found my way again.

Anthony was waiting at home. Over the years he had stayed a little to one edge in my slow dance with Theo. Always there, but not cutting in.

'It's over,' I said.

'Not over, just changed,' he said. 'Like seasons.'

It was a summer that makes me think now of paths crossing and heading off in new directions, of things changing form; a flock of starlings above the farm where I lived as a child, twisting and parting and rejoining, sometimes black against the blue, other times on a sudden turn, invisible, transforming seemingly at random from one shape to another. Sometimes, in a more precise mood, I'm reminded of a Möbius strip, those strips of paper folded like an infinity sign, crossing over in the middle, resulting in only one surface. It looks as if the strip has two sides, but if you take a pen and draw a line up the middle, you find there is only one and you end up where you began. I don't think I ended up where I began, I hope not, but there did seem to be a crossover of things that hadn't appeared connected. They looped away in either direction and I thought some things were over or changed forever and some were just beginning to arc out into empty space.

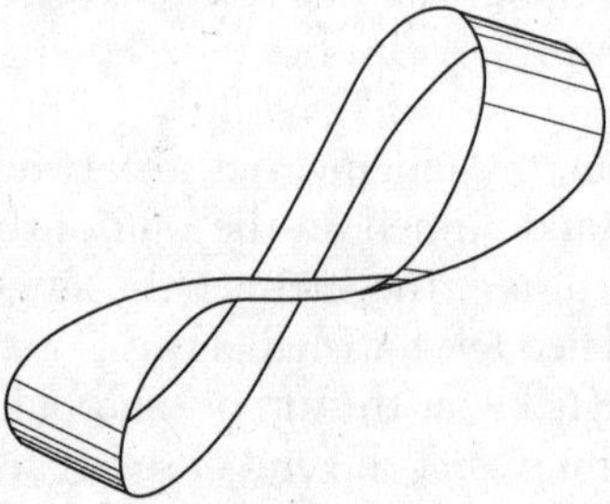

I have come to this beach-house here on the coastal lagoon, away from my home, to try and trace some of the arcs, perhaps find where some began, where some ended. It's not clear which arcs to trace, or even why arc-tracing is necessary; perhaps it is simply the old familiar desire to seize the moment; but it doesn't matter because I've discovered that why is not a useful question to ask in the beginning of anything, most especially in the beginning of stories. The work I do, my daily job, is helping other people recount their stories, the things that have happened to them in their lives, so I have learned that some questions are not helpful. I have heard more stories of other lives than I could ever tell and they lap over into mine all the time. It seems at times that I am made of other people's stories and perhaps the truth is, I need to find which are mine. These questions float around the edges of my mind, complicating matters, but in one way it is very simple; Theo moved away last summer, more than a year has gone by, and I want to tell the story.

The house I have come to has nothing to do with Theo or singing lessons, but it suits because it looks out on the lagoon and not on the crashing waves of the beach. Waves are too excitable, too obvious, for the currents I want to follow. The house has wide glass doors across the front of a single room and from them the gleam of still water is visible through the she-oaks that grow at the water's edge despite the saltiness of the lagoon. The lines of their shadows move a little as water birds and breezes briefly disturb the stillness. I go through the doors and onto the verandah and gaze down at the water. Fragments surface in my mind as I stand and listen to the unfamiliar water-bird sounds.

Dina stood on a stage, singing, with a band behind her. She had black hair, thick and curly, and wore a blue suede dress with appliquéd pink suede hands – one across one of her breasts and the other reaching down between her legs. She had made it herself; she was a skilled designer and made most of her own clothes. She had also made a jacket of pieces of silk and brocade, emerald and jade green, wrapped and tied in a most intricate way – like a kind of rock'n'roll kimono (she liked the Japanese aesthetic – the pure relationship between form and function, she said, but she couldn't help bending it to her own ends). She told me she liked imagining the design in her head and then figuring out how to make it work. She knew the look she wanted, the fabric and the colour and the shape, but said she never knew when she began how it was going to fit together, or whether it was going to work at all. I never saw Dina wearing the suede dress, but she showed it to me the summer before she died. She was Theo's mother.

I didn't know her as a singer. That was before I met her. I think she was performing in a country–rock band when she first met Kit, Theo's father, but by the time they married several years later she had stopped singing professionally and become a designer. I had heard her sing, though, an earthy, slightly mocking voice, as if she didn't take it seriously. She simply opened her mouth and sang as if it were nothing. When I heard her, there was always a pang of longing or hunger – as if I was missing the thing I most wanted, the thing that would fill the hole I suspect is just under the false bottom of my soul (well-made, nicely covered, no-one would notice, it seems as if you are whole, no gaps anywhere). So I'd stand back and listen and, if it was a song I was meant to join in with, 'Happy Birthday' or 'Auld Lang Syne', I'd mouth the words.

'Happy birthday, dear Theo,' Dina had sung, head back, hair tied in a ponytail, wearing white shirt and blue jeans, just like any other mother. This would have been the last time I heard her sing. She was thirty-seven, Theo was two.

Will Theo remember the sound of her voice, the aroma of her body, one birthday when the combination of voices and the fall of light through the windows echoes that day exactly? Nothing is remembered alone, each image tugs at another, and because of my work on other people's stories I am struck over and over by the intricacy of memory's labyrinth. One sound, one scent, one madeleine cake, and the door of the labyrinth swings wide. But it's not until you enter that you start to find out what is linked to what, so how or why the singing lessons are part of Theo leaving, except for the fact that they both happened the same summer, I'm not sure. They are patterned together in my memory and connect to a myriad of other images and stories; childhood memories of birdsong; my father's singing and his death; Dina's living and dying; the ebb and flow of blood in my body; dreams of loss and longing; even other people's stories set in countries I've never been to. They are made up of many small pieces, like one of Dina's dresses, or the notes of a song.

Somewhere before the beginning of the story, the absence of a singing voice must be understood – the cramped silent tuneless-ness inside. When you can sing, it's probably hard to imagine the absence. The stoniness of it.

Before the singing lessons, I hadn't sung in earshot of anyone for years, had barely hummed a song even when I was alone. The last time anyone had heard me sing was when I crooned lullabies to my younger son, over and over. In the dim light of the winter moon I'd sat beside the cot with him, the angel-faced child who never wanted to sleep. It was three a.m., the time when souls slip in and out of the world and those not being born or dying have no healthy business being awake. Tired beyond reason or com-passion after months of jagged nights bleeding into long days,

I took relief in imagining the brief peace and quiet that would reign if I flung the crying baby out the window. I sang in a sugary murderer's voice, 'Someone's sleeping, Lord, Kumbayah, Someone's sleeping, Lord, Kumbayah'. When he was old enough to talk he told me not to sing any more, but I can't blame him. I barely sang before that. I couldn't ever remember singing without being afraid someone might hear my thin voice. I didn't want to hear it myself and, anyway, I had nothing to sing. There were no song-shapes inside me.

The Vedas say singing is the voice of the soul: *whatever the gods do, they do by song*. My voice was sugar water with oily lumps of something undissolved in it. The lumps might be congealed longing but I was afraid of poking at them in case they broke open and their taste was bitter.

It seems like a given to me, but I suppose there needs to be an accounting for the longing to sing. I've often made the mistake of thinking other people want the same things as I do, but I don't believe I'm alone in this particular desire. I saw a play a few years ago, *Picasso at the Lapin Agile*, in which a fictional Picasso said, 'I'd give it all up if I could sing songs about love'. I sat up, startled. It was the first time I'd recognised the longing, only realising it as Picasso said the words. He said them with such desire, knowing he could never have what he wanted. In the darkened theatre I'd felt an excitement I hadn't experienced for years, a kind of urgency mixed with a faint embarrassment that what I had been yearning for was such a commonplace. Everyone knew about it and I hadn't even realised.

How far back do I go to trace its origins?

A Fairy Tale

I must have read the story of the king and the nightingale early on. As I remember it, the nightingale sang for the king every evening under his window. Its voice was exquisite, so lovely there was nothing to liken it to except itself. It transported the king's soul – I imagined it travelling upwards on a golden cushion to heaven, and gently drifting back into his body when the song was over.

The king longed to see the bird that made such a sound, believing it must be the most beautiful creature on earth. For a long time he yearned until one day he saw the bird (did he wait up at night, or did his courtiers catch it for him? I can't remember), and as everyone knows, the nightingale is a very ordinary, smallish brown bird. The king was very disillusioned and became unhappy, so to cheer him up his courtiers brought him a pretty mechanical bird that could sing very nicely. It was brightly painted and most appealing, much prettier than the nightingale – indeed, there was no comparison. The king set it up in his room on a gold stand and ignored the real nightingale.

The nightingale disappeared, brokenhearted, and for a while the king enjoyed the mechanical bird. But in time he became unaccountably ill and sad. The courtiers wound up the mechanical bird to sing for him, but the sound irritated him. His health declined and the courtiers became worried.

'Find me the nightingale,' said the king.

The kingdom was searched, and all the while the king grew weaker. Eventually the nightingale heard that the king was ill and came to his window one evening and began to sing. As the king died he heard the exquisite sound and was happy. His soul was transported upwards to heaven as he breathed out his last into the sound of the nightingale.

That might not be exactly the way the story goes – I think the mechanical bird might have broken at some stage, and probably other details are wrong – but it doesn't really matter. The point of the fairy tale is clear – singing is the voice of the soul, and if it is a true voice, it can save us from all sorrows. Or at least release us for a few moments.

And it's not only in fairy tales. History recounts that in the eighteenth century, King Philip V of Spain engaged a castrato with a voice of great beauty to sing him the same aria every night for fourteen years to relieve his melancholia. Every evening, year in and year out, the voice of the man-angel soared through the palace and lifted his soul out of the swamp. Released him into the clear air to breathe gently for a minute or two.

The summer Theo left was unusually hot and stormy. Sheets of lightning opened up the sky above the cliffs like bright windows into the void, giving everyone primitive shivers at the power of the gods. The heat and electricity and humidity made me intensely aware of my body, its moist density and its flickering currents. Some days I felt the soft lips between my legs tingling as I sat in my class discussing stories, or stood washing up at home (no seduction possible in either case); other days there was only a cold stony pebble, no matter what enticements were offered.

Unarguable dry absence drifted into my body and it felt as if I had forgotten – no, as if I never knew – the urgency of desire. Sometimes my moon-cycling blood became a trickle, sometimes it flooded, dark red and thick. When it flowed I felt like a lumbering animal and nothing else was of any interest or import.

The problem is that, even now, I'm finding it difficult to know what was important and what wasn't. Theo leaving and the singing lessons were, that much is clear; both made my heart thump too loudly, an ordinary enough indication. But it's also difficult to see where various arcs began. The starlings seem to appear out of nowhere at times. With Theo, for instance, I'd probably have to go right back to when I first met Dina. And that means I'll have to tell the whole story of what happened to her, because if she hadn't died, then Theo would just have been someone else's son.

And with the singing lessons, well, who knows how far I'd have to go back to find the real beginning? The nightingale was not in my experience; in fact, I still have not heard a nightingale, or even a recording of one. Maybe the magpies singing in the drought were the beginning for me. I definitely heard the magpies before I read the king and the nightingale story.

I had just woken up one morning during the long drought of the sixties. Even as I woke I could feel the heat and desolation of our farm through the boards of my room. Out in the paddocks my father had planted wheat but it had come up patchily in thin spears and withered in a few weeks; dams became boggy mudholes and then dried up, leaving cracked depressions; soil blew away and dust storms blew in to fill the house with inches of fine red dirt from farms out west. My older sister kept saying, 'It's past a joke,' as she *shovelled* dust from the house. The patch of lawn my mother tried to grow in the house-yard died and the ground was baked and dusty. Pellets of sheep manure were strewn under trees where the scraggy, dirt-brown mob stood in the shade trying to conserve moisture, but they grew bony and died or were sold for next to nothing.

We prayed for rain every day and sometimes clouds drifted over and promised, but after a while you did not believe the promises of clouds. The body nearly burst with the effort of willing it to rain, the soul stretched with praying, but nothing made any difference. The beloved landscape had become ugly and I felt the guilt of hating it.

Then one morning in bed, just as was I waking, I heard magpies carolling in their joyous, thrilling way and for an instant the paddocks were rolling green, the sheep and lambs were snowy white, the creeks and dams were glittering with water. In that moment the grey-brown world outside was transformed. Spring was here, stocks and sweet peas were scenting the air, the wheat had plump juicy heads, rain lay in puddles on the road. The magpies were singing and the land was beautiful. I don't remember anything else that happened that year – I don't even remember what year it was. All I remember is the sound of the magpies and the momentary belief in a transformed world.

Transformation does not have to begin with beauty or cataclysm. It's often a mundane thing. 'How little a thing is needed for us to be lost or to be saved', said Guy de Maupassant. It was the nineteenth century, when writers were allowed to sum up the meaning of their story in one line. I like the way he does it, slipping it in two-thirds of the way through the story so that you don't really notice it until afterwards. And then you start thinking of all the 'little things' a life might turn on; momentary epiphanies of birdsong; slow upheavals over a lifetime. In the story, the characters' lives turn on losing a borrowed fake diamond necklace which they both think is worth a fortune. They spend the rest of their lives in dire poverty, repaying the fortune, unaware that the necklace was worth nothing in the first place.

It has made me wonder what 'little things' led me into Theo and Dina's life. What led me to singing. Some days the 'little thing' exhilarates, other days there is nothing more frightening, so I carry de Maupassant's line around with me like a talisman as if, by knowing about it, I can always take the arc that will save me.

Of course it doesn't work that way. Look what happened to Dina. She bent down one winter morning to pick up Theo's toy bird from the floor and an aneurysm in the tissue surrounding her brain burst and that was pretty much it for her. You couldn't call that a 'little thing', certainly, but it was underneath her life all the time – she was born with an abnormally thin wall in one of the blood vessels in the sub-arachnoid cluster behind her right ear – ready to change everything in an absolute way without any warning. Or practically none.

I'd rather things were announced. Angels and trumpets. I grew up with the Annunciation as an ordinary kitchen calendar idea – every year my father bought the Columban Missionary calendars, which featured reproductions of great religious paintings and there were always plenty of Annunciations. Some years ago, just after Dina died, I found a print of the Annunciation by a Renaissance artist whose name I could not decipher. The angel has his finger up in that annoying gesture some people adopt when they want to make a point, and the Virgin Mary also has her hand up as if she can't quite hear what he's on about. The angel stands humbly outside the Italianate room where Mary is praying and they both look rather wimpish. The only reason I bought it was because of the angel's rosella wings, his scarlet, blue and green feathers, and because, as I said, I'd always liked paintings of the Annunciation – the drama of the moment (this is what you've got to do) and the often implacable angel and the astonished Mary (Who, me? How on earth? The mother of whom, did you say?).

I have another Annunciation print, a Simone Martini, which I cut from an old calendar – not a Columban but from the Uffizi Gallery. It appears to be painted on gold and there are elaborate carved gold arches over the angel and Mary. It made me laugh because they both look so annoyed – the angel's head is bent forward at that bossy 'you do have to do this, you know' angle and his gaze is fierce; Mary is turned sideways with her shoulder hunched against him, her face averted at a 'I don't wanna' angle and her mouth downturned so she looks like a sulky teenager. I don't blame her for being pissed off, because the angel's words are actually carved into the surface of the painting from his mouth to her ear so there is absolutely no chance of her not hearing them. (I mean, you might want to know what you're supposed to be doing here in the world, but not right away. Not-knowing has its freedoms. You can fool around distracting yourself but once you know, that's it, you've got to do it.) Mary looks as if she thinks she's much too young to find her truth. She still has her thumb marking her place in the book she was reading before the angel showed up. She'd really rather just go on with that this afternoon, thanks.

Would it be heretical to say I know how she felt? I sometimes feel I've spent my life with my thumb in the book saying to the angel (mine stands there shrugging and rearranging his wings, annoyed that he's been given just an ordinary woman with no chance of god-babies he can announce), 'Look, just go away for now, I really don't want to deal with that today'.

Not that he has even tried to make any spectacular announcements, he's just planted common restlessness, the usual feeling of missing out on something. It's a low level buzz of irritation that won't go away until, finally, I have to do something about it. Slowly, one day, one winter or summer, things change under the lumpy surface until it splits and a series of events start unfolding that, after a while, you think you initiated yourself.

Annunciation

It had nothing directly to do with Theo leaving and certainly not with singing. In fact it was completely silent. It happened, or rather, I observed it, the winter before all this began, when I was staying by the sea.

It was late in the afternoon after I had finished a weekend class and was feeling unsettled, (sometimes other people's lives lap over mine until I feel dissolved), so I went for a walk along the beach. There was a man flying a kite near the lagoon and, having nothing better to do, I stopped to watch. When I came upon the kite it was already flying long horizontal infinity signs back and forth across the sky. I don't know whether this was a beginning or a bold change of pace halfway through, but then it flew straight up and looped around and back down its vertical path, then glided gently down almost to the lagoon surface before curving upwards and into a sensuous jazzy dance across the top of an imaginary vertical dance floor, rolling and slinking and flirting, joyous and tempting, then suddenly diving in a death-wish straight down to the sand, jerking out of it at the last moment and dancing lazily over the lagoon like a dragonfly skitting and buzzing on a summer's day, playing with light and air, then another long slow climb upwards, nosing this way and that, testing the limits of the upper air before performing long slow arabesques across the top of the sky. It went on and on, intricate and patterned, an airy ballet in the sky. It seemed to be inscribing the blue air with a secret hieroglyphic code that remained hanging for a millisecond before it disappeared, but it was still there in a kind of ghost-writing to give shape and meaning to the new lines as they unfurled. There could not have been any overall plan – how could you choreograph a dance in mid air? – but each movement followed gracefully from the one before, counterpointing, extending, so that the whole seemed inevitable, a form delineated by the natures of air and kite.

Afterwards, I knew things had changed. There had been yearning all along, but for something nameless and shapeless. Somehow (shall I discover how?), watching the kite made an arc just long enough to move me off my track so that I couldn't go on the way I had been. I felt bereft for quite a while – it was not as dramatic as despair, more like a helpless knowledge that what you have done before is not the right path, but not knowing where to go now.

It was the moment before the apple was eaten, before you fell in love, before the darkness was divided. It is the place pulsing with mystery and chaos where hormones send the first (or last) ova down the fallopian tubes, or where the cells mutate into a faulty construction of capillaries in the cerebellum; where a woman conceives that she will sing a song or write a story; where a father and son decide to move to another city on another coast. I imagine that it quivers, hums.

I wait now in the house I have come to beside the lagoon and wonder where the story of that summer can begin. I have to look at the many arcs and find the origin of their curves through space and time. At the bottom of the yard, at the water's edge, there is a brush turkey scratching at his mound. The mound is made of leaves, small branches, twigs, decaying garden refuse and is already several metres across and more than a metre high. The eggs must be in it already, because he rakes aside leaves and twigs and sticks his beak in to see how warm it is. Then he scratches and digs some more and tests again. He is well ahead of me.

Two

Origins

In the writing class I most often ask for a first memory. It's difficult to know which memory is first – the conscious mind has a vested interest in what is remembered and what is forgotten – but whatever is chosen as a first memory can be like the image beginning a film. It stays there underneath, shaping the way the rest of the film is seen. Damon introduced himself to the class and announced he was originally from the Igorot tribe in the highlands of the Philippines, a people who 'resisted the Spanish for three hundred years and fell to the American missionaries in thirty'. He had a broad handsome face and long straight black hair and everyone was slightly in awe of his amused eyes and the fact that he had a doctorate in philosophy from Manila University.

He read his first memory, looking up from his notebook to hold our eyes as his story unfolded. He was two years old, standing under an apple tree in his village trying to pick the fruit. The apples were small and tempting but out of his reach, even when he stretched up on his still unsteady feet. His brown body was plump and naked as he reached upwards. He looked around and saw a pile of sticks someone had gathered against the wall of the house. He grabbed a stick and stood back under the tree, then reached out and hit at the lowest apple. Suddenly, he experienced his first ever consciousness of being, an overpowering awareness that he was in the world and that the world had existed before he was in it. He was here, a separate being, in a world on which he could act. He was a small plump boy standing under a tree with arm upstretched. All the rest of the world existed, dust under his feet, leaves over his head, dappled light on his skin, and he could observe all of it. It was his original knowledge of being, of knowing that he existed.

'The fruit of the tree of knowledge,' I said later, during the tea break.

'Yes,' he said with a smile.

'So apples grew in the Philippine highlands?'

'Yes,' he said, still smiling.

Origins of the Singing Lessons – a brief history (i)

Sometimes when I visited my mother in the country, I'd go to church with her to keep her company. I liked some of the hymns, the Alleluia ones full of spiritual patriotism and glory, and the ones that pulsed with longing, a hungry sense of desire for something, God, I guess. I mouthed the words so softly not even my mother standing next to me could hear. Although I had never heard her sing, she had an ear for music and would know how terrible I sounded. Her father, who died the year I was born, was a musician, a trumpet-player, who played the musical accompaniment at the silent movies before 'talkies' were invented, so she grew up with music around the house. He played trumpet with the sweetest tone I ever heard, my mother always said.

Origins of the Singing Lessons (ii)

My father only ever sang one song. Over and over. His voice was like a truck on a flat gravel road, the same note all the time, and always the same song: 'Home, home on the range'. It was clear that it was his song about the farm, even though we had sheep and cows rather than deer and antelope playing. 'Where seldom is heard, a discouragin' word, And the skies are not cloudy all day.' When I listened to his flat voice singing those words, they were about the blue sky over the farm holding us in. Everyone else laughed at his singing and said he was tone-deaf (for years I thought it was stone-deaf and imagined oval riverstones blocking his ears), but I liked it. The sameness of it was reassuring, like a chant. He read aloud in the same flat, burry voice. That's what I liked, I think, the way his voice didn't change. He read like a muddy brown river and I could just sink into it and be carried along. It was the sound of something that had been there forever.

Origins of the Singing Lessons (iii)

Occasionally over the years I would say, aloud, 'One day I will find a very patient singing teacher and take private lessons then come out singing and amaze everyone.' I said it laughingly so my family and friends knew I didn't mean it. So they didn't know how deeply I meant it.

Origins of the Singing Lessons (iv)

I was given a book, *The Clear Voice Suddenly Singing*, for Christmas the summer Theo left. I read: '*I became aware for the first time how much the singer reveals of himself, how undefended an act of singing can be; how impossible it is to fake almost anything*'. Nerves in my stomach jumped. Although I had not sung in front of anyone, I knew the words were true. Sometimes you know something is true before you have tried it; the words hit some truth-registering organ undiscovered by science. I started to have that sick-in-the-stomach feeling that happens before you do something dangerous. It happens when you know it's too late, when there's no going back. I've felt it just before birth contractions start convulsing the body, just before I open my mouth to say something revealing, just before a story begins.

It's true, you just have to sing and you get your spirit back. It was the last line in the book. The words registered as an urgent instruction. I had to do it. I closed the book and jumped off the bed where I had been reading all afternoon. There was no doubt that singing was the highest art, the deepest well of the self, the most powerful link to the sacred. I was full of superlatives, my chest was expanding with them.

I told Anthony, burning with the thrilling sensation that comes when you know something is going to change your life. He looked up from reading the paper on the back verandah and nodded pleasantly. 'If you say so.'

'You're not listening. It's my soul I'm talking about,' I cried. 'If I can't share my soul's longing with you then there's no point to us.'

This sounded rather extreme even in my overwrought state, but I couldn't retract a word of it. At that moment I meant it.

He looked a little rattled. It had been a peaceful sunny Sunday afternoon. He put the paper down and tried to listen.

Origins of the Singing Lessons (v)

'Singing lessons for beginners and the terrified. Don't let your fear stop you!' One of the gods must have sent a pushy ad-writing angel down to put it in the classifieds of the local newspaper just for me. I was sure it had never been there before.

I circled it and then wished I hadn't because my family would know I'd been seriously considering it. She can't sing, they would say, laughing at the thought of it, and I would laugh too. She can't even hum movie themes.

But there was no-one home to see me circle the ad except Theo, and he was absorbed in his Lego, creating more and more elaborate spaceships. He had added extra gun turrets and missile launchers on both wings and built another command module at the back and, just in case, attached a cunning little escape pod underneath. He was ready to fight off unexpected attack from all sides. He was ten years old and his laughing black-haired mother had died when he was three. Nothing could defend him against the miasma of loss that still floated up around him without warning in the middle of any sunny day.

He had been coming to stay with me on weekends for nearly seven years, nearly a whole cycle of existence. The body cells replace themselves entirely in seven years, which meant there were none of the body cells left that Dina knew. And none of the cells left that he knew her with. But his memory of her was chemical, it had somehow stained the nucleus, soaked into the chromosomes and reproduced when the cells divided.

Or perhaps it was only the stories he remembered.

I told him the story Dina told me of how she tried not to laugh when he was a naughty two-year-old painting his highchair with jam.

'Where did she tell you?' he asked.

'She was standing on the back step, right there. She was laughing.'

He looked animated; he had just thought of something. 'And was she wearing her hair like this?' He lifted both his arms and tried to hold his short hair back and up as if he had a long ponytail.

'Yes!' I exclaimed. 'She was!'

'And was she wearing a white shirt? With buttons?' He was very excited now.

'Yes. I believe she was. And jeans.'

'I think I remember her that day!' he cried triumphantly. His eyes were lit with joy, his face wide open.

I didn't remind him that I'd told this story a dozen times before. Or that his father had a photograph of Dina with her long black hair in a ponytail and wearing a white shirt. She is holding Theo, a little baby, lovingly to her cheek.

I continued looking through the 'Tuition' section of the paper. There was an ad for French classes further down the page. I had always wanted to brush up my French, learn to speak it fluently. Wouldn't it be wonderful to converse in French? I circled the ad with a bigger, more certain circle, then put the newspaper down.

No. Ring the singing teacher.

I picked up the newspaper, strode into the study and sat at the telephone.

I don't need to do this. It won't make any difference and it will just be embarrassing to reveal how badly I do it. I'll never be any good at it and anyway all I want is to sing around the house. I can start doing that when there is no-one else about. Why humiliate myself at what will probably be expensive lessons?

I punched the numbers in quickly.

'I want to know about the singing lessons for terrified people.'

I was going to book a lesson. I knew it before I rang, before I circled the ad, before I picked the newspaper up. A train of events had already been put in place, the decision was made a long time ago, I was merely carrying out the mechanics of its unfolding.

'What day?' he asked.

I put the receiver down afterwards, astonished.

I rang my mother and told her I had booked singing lessons.

'What are you doing that for?' She laughed to cover the panic in her voice. She didn't want me to make a fool of myself. She had the same tone in her voice when I announced my plan to sing solo at the primary school concert when I was eleven. It was before I had any idea I couldn't sing, but her tone was enough to dissuade me then.

'I just want to be able to sing around the house,' I said. 'I'm not thinking I can be a singer or anything. I just want to sing, that's all.'

'Perhaps I should come with you and learn to sing too.' She laughed, but she meant it somewhere underneath. I could hear the longing.

'No, you can't,' I replied, laughing. 'You have to find your own teacher.'

Origins of the Singing Lessons (vi)

'I am going to take singing lessons,' I said to Theo.

'Uh-huh,' he said. He looked up from his spaceships and smiled vaguely in the way I did when I wasn't really listening to him. It was the polite 'I know this matters to you' smile. I wanted to make him listen, tell him that his mother was a singer in her early days, that she travelled around the outback with the Theatre of Light and Air in the seventies and had sometimes teamed up with Aboriginal bands singing country and western songs. But I didn't because his mother was dead and it would have sounded as if I was trying to take her place. Ten-year-olds don't miss much, even if they are polite.

Origins of the Singing Lessons (vii)
That evening I told my son, Mani, who had a voice like an angel until it broke, that no-one realised how important this singing lesson was to me. He grinned uncomfortably. 'Yeah, well, I think it's stupid too.'

In the End
Damon died of cancer a few years after coming to writing class. It might be too far to jump from a two-year-old's epiphany under the apple tree in the Philippines to dying in Australia fifty years later, but I only hear fragments of lives at class, so beginnings and endings can come right next to each other. An ancient culture undone by the force of American evangelising, cells mutating silently inside a body, a cluster of fine veins stretching and thinning, these slow transformations seem sudden because their progress is left unrecorded. Damon read to us his stories of childhood, of the old men telling the future from the intestines of chickens, and of the weeks of chanting and singing the funeral rites when a relative died. One day I looked at the pages he had been reading from and there was nothing on them.

Three

A Short History of Theo Leaving (i)

For three nights I dreamed of the farm where the magpies sang. The first night I was watching a violent storm through the kitchen window. We used to love watching storms as children, but in the dream Theo was out in it and I couldn't make him come in. Suddenly the whole verandah and back section of the house came crashing down and he was nowhere to be seen.

The second night the dream was about a home-made video starring my two sisters and myself. We were mucking about in the back yard at the farmhouse, which is now derelict. We were shooting the video for our mother, but I realised she wouldn't want to see how broken-down the house is now. She would want to remember it the way it was.

The third night Theo and I were standing near the wood-heap looking down across the farm towards the back paddock. It was very grassy and green from all the rain, but the fence had been shifted by the new owners and the cow yard and shed were gone. I sobbed with a terrible grief that the evidence of my childhood there was disappearing forever.

'Are you thinking of when you were a little kid?' Theo asked.

A Short History of Theo Leaving (ii)

Kit came to see me with an announcement to make. It was after the winter kite-flying by the sea and before the hot humid summer. Kit was as big as a heavyweight boxer and walked with a limp after falling through a ceiling he'd been building. I don't know that you could call falling through a ceiling a 'little thing', but that was the way it worked for Kit – he had been an actor, and a builder between acting jobs, but he had given up both and was now studying to be a lawyer.

I could tell by the conciliatory tone Kit adopted that the announcement was a major one and one I wouldn't like.

'I want to leave the Mountains. I think Melbourne might be good.'

I thought at first he was discussing possibilities, asking me what I thought, but he had already decided. He intended to take Theo nearly halfway across south-eastern Australia, more than a thousand kilometres away.

'Why?' I asked.

'I want to make a fresh start,' he said.

'But you've done that already. You've started your life again. You're almost qualified as a lawyer already. You don't have to go to the other end of the country.'

'No-one will know about Dina there. They'll just meet me and take me as I am. I don't want to be "poor Kit whose wife had a brain haemorrhage and died" for the rest of my life.'

'What about Theo though?' My heart started to beat harder. My body was always such a traitor; it gave me away every time.

'He'll be fine. I'll look out for him.'

'But will you? You already get so immersed in your study or whatever you're doing, you don't notice how he is. He has to go to after-school care every day because you're studying and he hates it.' I knew I had leapt over a boundary but I'd been gathering to make the leap for a while. I sat neatly on my lounge, trying to find the right place to put my hands. Do they go along the arms of the chair or on your lap when you think you know better than someone else how to bring up their own child and you're going to tell them so? I folded them under my chest then quickly unfolded them and put one on my knee and one on the arm of the chair. A deep breath.

'He never has any friends around either. And he never goes to any friends' places. Kids need someone to make arrangements for them, phone up other kids' mothers, drop them off at each other's place. You're always studying; none of the other parents knows who you are. They need to know who you are so they can arrange visits with you.'

I kept my eyes on Kit, waiting for the moment he would explode. I would see it in his eyes first and in the muscles around his mouth. There was more to say, and worse. 'And Theo is picked on every day at school. He's become a victim. I've seen him turn an ordinary game into a problem, even with the kids next door when he's at my place. Then he gets like a cornered animal. The other kids just zero in on him – they have an instinct for it. They need to see he has someone who will stick up for him. And he needs to feel sure of himself. If you did something with him, bike-riding or something, he'd feel more confident. It really makes a difference with boys. They would stop hurting him.'

I was way outside the bounds of friendship by now and my heart banged with the risk of it. The skin on my face had tightened, felt smooth and hard like a mask. But I went on and on, making my speech, because I'd already broken the taboo against telling people what to do with their kids and there was no point in backing out now.

'That's it then,' I said in the end. 'You can walk out now.' A weak smile.

'I know,' Kit said.

What? He was supposed to argue with me, defend himself.

'I know I've let him down.'

He was supposed to tell me to mind my own business.

'Things will be different now. In Melbourne.'

The force of my accusations dissipated as if they had hit something completely absorbent. The room echoed a little with the harsh sound of my voice but that was all.

'What about Theo and me?' I said finally.

'You guys can talk on the phone. He can come and visit at the end of the year.'

'It won't be the same.'

'No, it won't be the same.'

That was it. I had kissed his wriggling two-year-old tummy as I buttoned his shirt; he had made me a crooked blue papier-mâché bowl at school for Mother's Day; I'd changed his sheets in the night when he'd thrown up all over them after too much blue-iced birthday cake; he'd held my hand every time he crossed the road; I'd yelled at him for nagging me all the way home from the fireworks and said he should be grateful I'd taken him at all on a cold night; he'd brushed my hair into funny styles as I sat on the back step; I'd bought him sets of space Lego; he'd told me how the other kids had him cornered in the playground at school; we had cuddled on the lounge watching television and he'd gone to sleep in my arms a hundred times.

What were we going to do now?

A Short History of Theo Leaving (iii)

The morning Theo was leaving, he climbed into bed with me as he always used to when he was little. He was ten years old, near the end of childhood. Kit had already gone to Melbourne to look for a house so Theo had stayed the whole summer holidays with Anthony and me and Mani.

'Here's a bear hug,' I said and I gave him a tight engulfing hug, almost squeezing the breath out of him. He giggled and puffed, pretending he had been squashed to death.

'What about a baby hug?' he asked.

I gave him a soft little cuddle and murmured nonsense endearments.

'And a father hug?'

I gave him a big firm hug, similar to the bear hug but accompanied by deep, gruff 'My boy' exclamations which made him laugh. Then there was a short silence.

'And a mother hug?' His voice was shy, his throat vibrating slightly as if the unsayable history we shared was caught there like a moth under a curtain.

My pulse beat with his. We had stepped a long way into each other's hearts. There was no going back.

I cuddled him tenderly, kissing the top of his head. 'My darling boy.'

A Short History of Theo Leaving (iv)

It cycles through my mind. The last scene: undramatic, anticlimactic.

At the airport he was sturdy, no-nonsense. He had a backpack with toys and pencils for the plane. The steward introduced himself to me and to Theo.

'Time to say goodbye,' the steward said and looked away as we had one last, uncomfortable hug. Theo's body was already straining to be gone. The steward, the one with the story about us in his eyes, took Theo's hand and looked at me understandingly. As they disappeared through the departure gate, I heard Theo say, 'I'm going to see my dad'. Or something like that.

I was sturdy, no-nonsense as I walked away. Seven years.

Four

The light wakes me and I get up and breakfast on the verandah. I see a pelican standing on a pandanus leaf on the lagoon, his wings held out wide. He just stands there, not flapping, each feather outstretched. I suppose he is drying his wings. Here, where I sit and watch, there is the pelican, the water, the verandah, solitariness. I am conscious of how many elements there are to each day, each story. Nothing seems excluded. The problem is that setting anything down in words is always an act of exclusion.

For a start, the body is always there. My heart pumps, lungs flap in and out, cells divide or die, hormones flood or trickle, ova dreamily float down the tube unaware they could have had another destiny. It's something I never used to think about. Body parts.

I found in a magazine here a diagram of the human body with the parts drawn in proportion to how often the mind was aware of that part. It's a comical drawing with a large face, small torso (except for a big stomach and largish sex organs), thin arms and legs, and practically nonexistent elbows, knees and toes. The largest parts of the body, by far, are the hands. I think the researchers must have tested the wrong people. Without having done any investigating apart from undisciplined observation, I'd have to claim the mouth occupies a central proportion of my conscious attention.

The mouth is in there most of the time – eating, kissing, smiling, arguing, talking, (not singing), munching on sandwiches, discussing books, sucking a breast, biting a hand (not lately), licking an ear, pleading for a hearing, pursing shut, quivering.

When I look at the mouth of a baby, the squashed bow of its lips closing over a nipple, even now, years after I last held a child to my breast, there is the small contraction of desire. The mouth of a baby sucking painfully hard; smiling with the sweetness of pure being, screaming at mind-shattering pitch and intensity; it's the mouth of the world, devouring time. And so tender and implacable, like a bud.

I touch my lips. So soft. And so cunning the way the red curve – I like to wear lipstick -conceals sharp teeth, slightly serrated and crooked. Then there is the soft moistness just inside the lips. It's arousing just to run my fingertips gently inside them, around and around, not forgetting to move slowly around the fleshy corners. Naturally it reminds me of other lips, the labia opening in sympathy with the mouth, enclosing fiercely in lovemaking, stretching wide to expel life. I remember giving birth with a smile as wide as my pregnant belly, but my mouth didn't feel as if it were stretching, simply expanding to its natural size.

It's a long time since my body held a baby inside it and felt that secret power of holding an entire human being in your belly. Has anyone ever really confessed to it? Some shadowy sorrow moves under my ribs, something arriving or leaving, and there is nothing that will content me.

The first time I saw Dina she was pregnant with Theo. I'd already met Kit in a writing class but had only heard about Dina so invited them both to a friend's book launch in Sydney. I was sitting at a desk with a pile of books, selling the occasional copy, and the sun was streaming in through the glass doors. The light shafted through a glass of red wine and made a ruby on the white paper tablecloth – it was one of those rare silken days when for a few hours life seems to flow out with grace and you feel at ease in the stream, not flapping your arms wildly to stop from drowning or to gain attention. On such days you know that you will remember what happens, and that it might matter for the rest of your life. Kit walked in the door and beside him was a woman with black hair and red lips, small but striking. She was wearing olive green jersey silk over her pregnant bulge. She looked like an exotic doll, miniature and perfect, next to his large builder's labourer frame.

'Hello there – Kit has told me about you.' Her voice was deep for such a curvy feminine body. She smiled, red lips and pale skin, and bought a copy of the book. Her face was rounded with pregnancy – in fact I had an overall impression of roundness and was surprised to see how slender she actually was the next time I met her, after Theo's birth. Her eyes were dark brown and very pretty – Theo inherited them exactly and is regularly offended by exclamations about their prettiness.

'Well, I hope it was good things.'

That was all we said to each other, I think. She bobbed away with Kit – she was at the stage of pregnancy when the body moves like one of those weighted inflatable toys that sway about but can't be knocked over – and disappeared into the crowd. I didn't see her again for a couple of months, but Kit came to class not long after the launch and told us he and Dina had had a baby son.

The week Theo left, I dreamed of a baby being born. I was the midwife, not the mother, and there was a surge of happiness as the plump vernix-streaked body slid safely out into the world. But then I saw that its umbilical cord was looped around its neck. It was thick and bluish and still throbbing with the mother's blood. I had to do something quickly. I took hold of the bloody cord, thinking it would be easy to pull it over the baby's head, but it was slippery and tangled, and as I tugged at it, it tightened into the baby's neck as it struggled to draw in its first breath. The greasy blood-smeared cord, thick as a finger, pressed deeper into its throat. The baby was gasping, its eyes popping. I slid my finger under the cord at its neck and loosened it, and suddenly it untangled enough for me to stretch it out and over the head. The baby was freed, the cord coming out of its navel still throbbing innocently. I looked around for clamps to clip onto it so that I could cut through it. The details became hazy. I woke as the dream midwife was trying to find the scissors.

The terror of the near-strangled baby was still in my body as I lay in the hot bedroom. You can see how I might have interpreted the dream – the dream symbolist was pretty obvious with his imagery – but it was also the morning of the day of the First Singing Lesson. Anxiety had seeped in under everything since the telephone call. Aching head, tense shoulders, vague nausea.

I wrote, read, walked in the bush – not for long, it was too hot – but nothing distracted. It irritated that it mattered so much. Why should a singing lesson terrify me?

I was the bold child who had the whole world at my command – what should I care?

The Queen of Beat

I am eleven and the farm is just beginning to become dull. There's nothing to do – I hang about near the car-shed and the petrol drums, hoping someone might be going somewhere. I start to bang on one of the 44-gallon drums with my hand and it makes a commanding boom. It is empty but I can still smell petrol in the heat. I bang the drum next to it and it makes a slightly different noise. The drum is heavy and high, up to my chest, and I have to lift my elbows out straight to hit the top with the flat of my palm.

I beat slowly and evenly, just one single beat after the other. The sun is directly above and the dust is warm under my bare feet. I put my shoulders back and my head up, standing upright, beating solemnly with my palms.

I begin to beat faster with a hard-soft rhythm. Boom, *boom*, boom, *boom*. In my shadow it looks as if I have feathers in my hair as I move my head up and down. My pulse beats through my blood and my rib bones expand. I hit faster and faster, watching my hands thump on the steel, the sound like an echoing heart-beat. The pounding noise rolls across the farm, and it seems to be urging something to happen.

I lift my head back, throat bare, eyes open. Suddenly, from over the rise across the paddock, cattle come charging down the hill. First there are two or three cows and then the bull and then the whole herd, heifers and steers and calves. I beat faster and they gather pace, galloping towards the fence, bellowing loudly, their hooves pounding on the hard summer ground. Udders swing awkwardly under them and their horns sway as they toss their heads. I stop drumming and they stop in their tracks. That's odd. I begin drumming again, slowly and evenly as I had begun. The cattle begin rushing forward again, faster and faster, bellowing as they come, the dust rising and swirling over their reddish-brown hides.

I stop again and they stop, but still bellow. I feel my heart beating all over my body; I am controlling them by the drumming! The sound of the drumming has called them from beyond the hill – they are in my power. I begin again, a little afraid, but there is a fence between me and them so I think I'm safe. This time I beat the drum slow and steady and the cattle jostle up along the fence, bellowing, pawing the ground with their hooves, making a huge racket.

'What the hell is going on!' My father rushes out of the house. In the sudden silent heat I can feel my heart pounding and body sweating.

Nothing was going to help me face the many-headed singing teacher. He had the treasure I sought, he existed beyond the borders of myth, he knew how to talk with dragons and angels. By the time I was driving up the highway to my first lesson nothing was out of the question.

I found his house, which was very ordinary – for a mythical being's residence – neat and brick with a gate to unlock, a long tiled verandah to cross. Arm outstretched, I was just about to knock on the door when it opened.

There he was. The Singing Teacher. He gave an impression of other-worldliness, or at least of belonging in another century. He had long wavy hair, tied back, and a high cheekboned face. He greeted me in a friendly way and said his name was Edward and that he wasn't psychic, he'd heard me unlatch the gate. Apparently the singing room was around the back of the house. I followed him down a path to the garden which looked out over the bush towards the cliffs, and into a room that contained two chairs. Of course it contained other things, but that was all I noticed.

I sat down, bolt upright on the edge of one of the chairs. I tried to lean back but my body felt exposed. There didn't seem to be any way of arranging my knees, my arms, my hands. I felt like I was in a confessional and ought to kneel. I clasped my hands, fingers folded in a not-quite-praying gesture and confessed, 'I will be the worst student you have ever had.'

He said all the right reassuring words, but mine were a simple statement of fact, not a fishing expedition. Pretty soon, he would know the facts too.

He plucked a note on his guitar and asked me to sing it. My mouth wouldn't open. It had somehow turned to half-set concrete. I tried again and managed to get my mouth open but no sound came out. Same on the third attempt. At the fourth, a thin sound wavered briefly.

'La.'

'Okay,' he said. 'Try again.'

My stomach was watery by this time and my mind rushed to and fro, almost whirring and clicking like a computer trying to find the right program. I felt the strange separation that comes when someone else inside you seems to be observing your mind, noting its reactions, as if you were not your mind. It becomes an entity, with another you watching it. There must be a path, I reasoned, the same as when you want to pick up a pen. Your mind simply thinks it and your hand does it. It must work like that. But there was only blankness, a sensation of coming up against a thick fog. There appeared to be no link between mind and voice box. The same thin watery sound came out.

The teacher told me to listen this time, and try again.

I tried the old childhood method of dealing with a problem – pretend he's not there. I focused my gaze at a point above his shoulder, trying to absorb the note he plucked on the guitar, trying to direct my lungs, voice box, throat, mouth to reproduce it. I pushed with all my will but there was only white marshmallow in my brain with no path through for carrying the messages. The separate entity of mind was annoyed that its directions had no effect, that will and desire were powerless. My face, neck, body, were hot.

He must have seen my panic; his eyes registered something – helplessness. He clearly had not had anyone this bad before.

Suddenly he told me to rub my ears.

'I'm sorry?'

'Rub your ears and remind yourself to listen, and then rub your throat and sigh.' I did as he said. It was an intimate thing to do in front of a stranger, rubbing one's throat and sighing, but after all, he was my confessor. He would cure my secret longing.

It seemed I had been sitting there for a very long time but I dared not look at the clock in case he thought I was impatient. My legs were sweaty, slipping on the chair, my hands damp like a mortician's. My mouth, my aching jaw and teeth and tongue were all made of the same inflexible grey stuff. Every sound that came out was squeaky and off-pitch. He looked at the clock. Of course he'd had enough.

'Do you believe you can do it?' He stood up to open the door.

'No,' I answered. 'But I believe in you. I will do whatever you say.'

I walked out the door and up to the car, light-headed. It was as if I'd been through a flaying, skin covered in red welts, and survived, and now the world was different. The air was moist and warm, gum blossoms on the trees along the road were creamy-white lace on blue-green leaves.

Adrenalin started to pump and I laughed out loud, surging with a kind of perverse pride. I drove down the highway, surprised that people were still going about their business in the usual way, surprised that I still knew how to drive.

'It's changed my life,' I declared when I got home.

Some years ago I had a car accident on Kangaroo Island off the southern Australian coast – I was sightseeing there with Mani.

The car slid on the ironstone pebbles covering the road and skidded out of control. It slalomed down the hill like a crazed skier and then crashed off the road and smashed into a clump of gums and yakkas. A yakka stump was rammed under the engine and a branch of a gum tree broke through the back window. We were stuck; the car wouldn't move, its bonnet and side panels smashed in, but we were unhurt, not even a bruise or scratch. A passing helicopter pilot rescued us and off we went with a fine story to tell. But when I arrived safe and sound back home, I started having attacks – sudden arrhythmic heartbeats, needle-pricking pain on my skull, a frightening vulnerability coursing through me. Sometimes dizziness hit and I crouched terrified in the bathroom, on the blurry littoral of blacking out.

'How are you?' Anthony would ask.

'Frail,' I would say, and smile weakly. I couldn't explain how an image harassed me. It turned over and over in my brain when I lay down to sleep and flashed into my mind in the middle of the day. It wasn't the crash – tearing metal, jerking bodies, or anything like that. It was the unbelievable moment, my fingers tight on the steering wheel, when the car drifted irretrievably sideways out of my control. Under that moment gaped vast realms where will and desire are powerless.

Telephone Call (i)

'Hello?'

'Hello, darlin'! How are you?' My voice sweet (oversweet, like a mother to a child when she has ground to make up), Theo's faintly anxious.

'Good.'

'Do you like your new house?'

'Yep. It's good.'

'And your room? What is it like?'

'It's good too.'

'What's your new school like?'

'It's excellent.'

'Really? And what about your new teacher?'

'She's excellent. And she has an excellent accent. She's from America.'

'Wow! Whereabouts in America?'

'She said Minnesota. It's in the middle of America.'

'What does she look like?'

'Sort of blonde hair.'

'Old or young?'

'Sort of young. Younger than you.'

'Is she nice?'

'Yes, she's excellent. She smiles a lot.'

Her smiling broad face, inherited from Minnesota Dutch or Norwegian ancestors, blue eyes, cherry-sprigged dress. What right did she have? She hadn't even known Dina.

Kit came on the phone. He said he'd told the teacher about Theo's 'situation' and she had promised to keep a special eye out for him as he settled in.

'Good,' I said.

Telephone Call (ii)

I rang my mother to tell her I'd had my first lesson.

'Has the opera offered you a contract yet?' She laughed.

I explained again, firmly, that I only wanted to sing around the house.

Opera Singing

Elizabeth came to the writing class to write the story of her singing and of her rare and debilitating disease. She had trained to be an opera singer, first at the Conservatorium of Music, then with a renowned teacher. She was very promising, with a strong, warm voice and a richness especially suited to German lieder. One day she collapsed and had to be rushed to hospital. She continued with her lessons and began to perform but the same thing happened again. Chronic illness had come and it ruined her career before it had barely started.

One of the bizarre effects of her particular illness was that it gave the skin a brownish tinge, so she always looked tanned and healthy. 'Difficult to gain sympathy,' she said, and laughed. She had the typical strong frame and deep chest of an opera singer and the wide-boned, firm-jawed face of a woman constitutionally able to take on the world. She came to class each week dressed confidently and even flamboyantly, emerald green and peacock blue, but it was clear she had lost what she wanted most, for in her bright blue eyes there was a kind of bruising evident, an effect like trampled morning glory. I had the will, she wrote, and I believe the natural gift, but when my body let me down, my dream moved entirely out of reach.

Five

Stories About Dina Before Everything Changed (i)

'No people are uninteresting,' I said. We were all sitting around the table on the back verandah. Our place was in a valley so there were no spectacular long-shot views, misty and eucalypt-blue over the escarpments, but a close-up grey and green tangle of gums and banksias sloping down to a creek. Sometimes I'd long to be able to see further. An aspect too soon stopped has always made me feel cramped – I imagine it comes from growing up out west where the horizon was always at least a few miles away.

'How patronising is that!' Dina leaned in from a conversation at the other end of the table, glass of wine in hand. (Why can I still see this moment so clearly? It's like a snapshot in my mind, the angle of her head, her challenging eyes, her half-full glass of white wine, Phoebe Snow singing in the background 'Strut and fret our hour upon the stage'. It doesn't *mean* anything.)

'I wasn't being patronising. I was quoting Yevtushenko. And anyway, I listen to people's stories all the time and it's true.'

'Bullshit. Lots of people are dull.'

'I don't mean that everyone is *amazing*. But everyone experiences being here in the world from the same point. That sense of where the hell are we, you know, that's the common mystery and I like it. I like knowing about how people experience that.'

'Mystery is just another word for illusion. Who wants to listen to all that ordinary rubbish?'

We argued for a while in a Sunday-lunch-with-a-couple-of-glasses-of-wine fashion until we worked ourselves back to some common ground. We still didn't know each other very well, not even what we each did for a living, so she hadn't realised she was criticising my work. And she had indulged in more excess than I had, at least more drugs and rock'n'roll (probably around the same amount of sex – uncharacteristically for our times and milieu, we had both been in long monogamous relationships), so probably had a lower tolerance for ordinary life.

As well as singing in a country-rock band she'd had various jobs, including working in a brothel – as a receptionist. She still did sometimes, I gathered, although I didn't ask directly. I was a bit shocked but acted blasé. I could not imagine myself sitting at the front desk in a brothel (do they have front desks?), listing services, taking bookings and fees. The men would surely include you in their possible shopping list, or at least imagine that you had once been available. And Dina had a baby too. And what about Kit, what did he think? Anyway, that was what she did in the downtimes between real jobs. And she wasn't a singer any more. Too hard to make a living. It was difficult to understand exactly what she did the rest of the time, but it was something to do with designing events. She had helped arrange the Paris Opera exhibition at the New South Wales Art Gallery, and an extravaganza for the opening of a north Queensland resort – an events organiser, I suppose. She still worked, too, with a friend, Cathy, designing and making clothes – lots of Dina's clothes bore Cathy's label, Live Fast. For lunch on our back verandah she wore linen trousers and her stunning flowery riding boots. Dina was always the person you noticed at any gathering. Her clothes mostly weren't outrageous, except for the suede 'hands' dress, but she always dressed in a way that expressed her being in the world on that day in that place. The aesthetic eye was always pleased by her.

We talked a little about our childhoods too, mine on the farm out west waiting for something to happen, and hers in Christchurch in New Zealand waiting for something to happen.

'Why is it that some people always want something else to happen?' she said.

Christchurch was such a quiet and proper city that she had left as soon as she could, headed for Sydney. She had lived in San Fransisco briefly, and Tokyo too, singing in a nightclub there – and taking too many drugs, she said. There was a brief stint in Adelaide, then back to Sydney.

'You seem to me like someone who hasn't really found what she wants to do yet,' I remarked.

'Yep. I'm thirty-six and I still haven't found what I'm lookin' for.' She sang the last few words. 'I've gone out and had a look and experimented, though – I haven't just waited for things to knock on my door.'

Both of us offered pieces of ourselves – not what we thought but our memories, feelings. With Kit it was always ideas, what we were reading – I suppose because we met in writing class. Kit and I were both fascinated by the edges between things, the littoral, the place where things changed into something else . . . 'between the seawind's hum / in airshot cliffs and water's bright/ network of overlapping light', our shared favourite poet wrote. Sometimes it became too esoteric, rarefied, and I'd feel as if my head was floating off my shoulders. Then I'd wish we could just gossip about shoes. With Dina the move between metaphysics and shoes was always natural and elegant.

'So why did you move to the Mountains?' I asked. 'It's pretty quiet up here. Just a string of villages with bowling clubs and soccer teams.' That wasn't quite true. Every other person in the Mountains was a painter or a poet, it seemed, and the area had a romantic past as a honeymoon destination, but otherwise it was like any country town with its share of highway petrol stations, faded Schools of Arts, tired grand hotels. It was a place where things had once been better.

'Theo. Times change, I wanted to have a baby. I'd wanted to for ages. I wanted a peaceful place for him to grow up. Where things don't change so much and people know who he is. You know, he can go into a shop and people will say, "That's Dina and Kit's boy."'

I think we talked about babies then. I don't recall Theo being at the lunch, the split-level conversation you have to have when there is a baby or little child present, so he must have been sleeping inside on our bed. Dina treated me like the wise woman about kids, I remember, because although she was a couple of years older than me, I'd had two sons, one of them a teenager already.

Stories About Dina Before Everything Changed (ii)

I visited Dina at the house she and Kit had bought with the insurance payout he'd been awarded after he was run over by a truck during the filming of a post-apocalypse style movie. Kit had played one of the violent ferals rampaging across the countryside – because he was so big and solid he was always offered roles as a violent thug or a mentally deficient delinquent – and for one scene in this film he was chained behind the wheels of a massive armoured truck. The chains slipped and with the crew and other actors looking on in white-faced horror – he said he could see their faces against the blue of the sky – he slid under the double wheels and the truck ran right over him. Most of his internal organs were squashed and he spent several months in hospital, everyone amazed that he was still alive. It does make falling through a ceiling seem like a 'little thing', except he did shatter his thigh bone that time and the pain left him screaming even after the ambulance man had given him a double dose of morphine. There's more, but clearly, sudden and violent upheaval was not so unusual in Kit's life.

So, here they were in their ordinary house on the high side of Terrace Falls Road with a view out over the mountains. It was almost a nondescript house except for the overgrown terraced garden stretching down to an orchard at the back; gardenias, glowing white in the dark green undergrowth, azaleas and dogwood and camellias crowding over hidden stone walls. Dina was keen to build a verandah on the back of the house so they could sit there and look down over it. Presently, Kit was knocking down the wall between the kitchen and lounge-room to let 'the cook' (he was the main cook) share in the light and the view from the picture window across the front of the lounge-room. Dina had draped thick cream calico curtains around the window with an elaborate knot of fabric looped across the top so that the unfinished room already looked calm and stylish.

Dina's dog, a white Oxford bull terrier, stood nearby. He was old and walked in a sedate old man way and stood solidly as Theo tried to push him out of the way.

'Theo and Jock squabble over me,' Dina said. 'They both follow me around the house all day.'

'Who wins?'

'Theo. I'm amazed at the way Jock lets a baby push him around.'

'Aren't you worried the dog will bite him?'

'Jock wouldn't touch him. He knows Theo is the love of my life. He's just a jealous old lover.'

'Like me,' Kit said from the kitchen.

'Yep, Theo is my love now. Anyway, look at this. I've just started an upholstery course. I'm going to reupholster it myself.' Dina indicated a vinyl-covered curved lounge which stretched halfway around the room. It looked a bit like one of those large curved lounges in hotel foyers in movies. I was more than suitably impressed with her intent – I lack the skills to make or remake anything physically and the practical world has always seemed particularly resistant to transformation.

'I wish I could make things. I need some curtains for our place.'

'I'll make them for you.'

'I wasn't angling.'

'No, that's all right. I wanted to experiment with something for our room anyway. What about I get some more calico and dye it, and wrap it, sort of plait it across the top and have the curtains falling down from there to the floor?'

She picked Theo up from near the back door where he had been busily taking Kit's tools out of his toolbox and I followed her as she carried him on her hip into the bedroom.

'See, this is where I want to put them. This is about the size of your window, isn't it?'

I didn't look – I was more taken with the large, real tiger-skin rug – head and all – nailed to the wall beside the double bed. It took up most of the space, its head lifted in a last endangered-species roar.

'I bought that at a garage sale at the brothel,' Dina said. 'It's really old. I thought it would be all right. I mean, it was killed fifty years ago.'

It was such a beautiful and violent and sensual thing that I hardly knew where to look.

'It's terribly sexy,' I said.

'Yep.' Dina grinned. 'I sometimes think it really is a bit of an overstatement. It's so huge in this room. And I do feel a bit guilty about it. It was killed for its beauty.'

'But what else would you do with it? You can't just throw it away.'

'I don't know. Sell it. I'd rather make things than buy them anyway. I've been making this mirror.' She showed me a large mirror leaning against the wall that she had started to frame with padded satin and silk. There were curious surreal shapes, fish-like and bird-like, sewn on here and there all the way around it. I've written about this mirror before, in a fictional story, so it is hard to remember now what the mirror was really like and what I have made up, but what is absolutely true is what Dina said about it. We were standing in the sunny room, our backs to the uncurtained windows, Theo bouncing on the bed, Jock standing forlornly at the door knowing none of this was anything to do with him.

'I've been feeling strange, actually. A horrible sense of foreboding. I really couldn't shake it and then I realised I just needed to do something creative, that I was frightened of losing it. And it's working. I feel much better now, just by making this mirror.'

And I remember what I said too. I said it so enthusiastically, so warm with the pleasure of affirming the eternal stream, the irony of it makes it seem as if I invented it, but life is like art sometimes. 'Isn't that so true? Creativity will save you every time.'

Stories About Dina Before Everything Changed (iii)

We had been seeing a fair amount of one another when Dina and Kit invited Anthony, Mani – nine years old at the time – and me over in the middle of the day for a traditional fifties Sunday roast dinner. Our teenage son was invited too, but he had his own life by now and was only ever on the edge of our story with Kit and Dina and Theo. It was the first time I'd had a traditional Sunday roast since the Sunday dinners with my parents, who never gave up the dinner in the middle of the day habit, even after they left their farm and lived in town. Around one o'clock every Sunday on the farm, just as the news was coming on the wireless, we would all sit around the old wooden table in the kitchen. Whenever I hear the ABC news fanfare I still taste the potatoes and peas and gravy, feel the lino underfoot, see the jars of pennies and piles of papers and the clock and the statue of the Virgin Mary on the mantelpiece above the wood stove, see the grabbing for tomato sauce and white bread (no madeleine cake) as my brothers and sisters jostled for elbow space.

At Dina's there was a damask tablecloth and napkins, heavy silver cutlery and roast lamb with mint sauce and all the trimmings. It was a neater, more middle-class version than my Sunday lunch memories, but it was near enough. Dina had even found one of those bride-and-groom salt and pepper shakers, the salt bride in her wide white hat, the pepper groom with little holes in his head. A set of coloured canisters graced the servery which stood where the wall had been, three ducks flew up the wall behind us, Dina was wearing a fifties-style dress, gathered in at the waist, her hair up in a ponytail and her usual bright red lipstick. Mani obligingly played hide-and-seek with Theo, jumping out from behind the still-vinyl lounge and making him laugh at his sudden reappearance – the mystery of here, not-here, the most astonishing joke. Apart from the fact that Dina was rolling marijuana joints at the kitchen bench and that 'Blue Hills' wasn't on the wireless, it seemed a perfect re-enactment of innocent fifties life.

Not that any of us could remember the fifties. We had been babies then, so our first memories were from the sixties. (One of my earliest memories is scratching the numerals 1960 on a flat stone – I must have just learned about dates – and I can remember realising that this time would never happen again.) I don't think we talked about the past, though. I do remember something about Labor politics – Kit was a party member then – and being surprised by Dina's knowledge of and forceful opinion about some policy issue – I can't recall what. I don't want to be vague but it is hard to recall conversations at a Sunday dinner that no-one knew was going to be the last one before it all changed. Other details might have gotten mixed up too. Perhaps it was this day that Dina showed me the mirror.

Six

I do some singing practice straight after breakfast. First there's the song a singing teacher I met recently has written: 'May your heart be blessed in song'. It's like a hymn, a blessing. Then the so-fa scale. Practising scales makes me feel like a proper singer and I sing a little louder alone in the beach-house. I can hear the sounds of wildlife outside, a kind of accompaniment. So many new bird sounds and water sounds. Fish jumping and plopping back into the lagoon, hooting, quacking, squawking water-bird calls, bellbirds chiming all the way up the valley, the sudden splash of a black duck landing, a rustle of the brush turkey at his mound, clacking sounds, trumpetings, clicks of beaks, a short harsh sound between a hoot and a chopping quack that I know no word for. But there are some familiar sounds too – magpies warbling like happiness itself, crows cawing as they pluck out the eyes of newborn lambs, peewees crying like they always did across the hot dry paddock stubble, the sounds of childhood in the sixties. Here amongst the sarsaparilla and paperbarks and casuarinas, they seem unreal.

Sounds of the Sixties (i)

The sounds of water, raining, flowing, burbling, were sweetest. As a child I could tell how much water was in a corrugated iron tank by sound: I'd knock on the rungs with my knuckles and where the tone changed from flat and hard to high and ringing, that's where the water stopped. Below the water line it sounded unfriendly, as if I wasn't going to be allowed to do something. I knew the hard noise was because the waves of sound were muffled by the water, and water was always a good thing but I guiltily preferred the purer sound of the empty tank.

Sometimes I'd hear a frog in the nearly empty tank, the

strangely reassuring croak echoing around the corrugated iron. Bullfrogs down at the Macquarie River a few miles from our farm sounded like double-bass drums, *bou-oum, bou-oum*. It seemed to vibrate in my chest. Our usual frogs on the farm went *kerar-ark, kerar-ark*. When my father heard the frogs croaking he would say 'sounds like rain's coming', and so the song of frogs was the sound of good things to come. The frogs are singing, all will be well, all will be well in the world. I wondered how they knew rain was coming. Or was it that they called the rain with their singing?

I looked for the frogs around the artesian well, peering under the corrugated iron cover, catching glimpses of the dark water below and amazed by all that water under the ground from rain millions of years ago. Such old water, too old to drink. Frogs didn't hop across the open ground but hid under the iron or under the rocks around the edge of the well in secret places, damp and cool, and they stopped singing when anyone came close so they were difficult to find. Their secretiveness was partly why I liked them – they only sang out when they thought no-one could find them. When they were caught they mostly sat silently on my palm, pretending they weren't there at all then suddenly leaping off when I wasn't watching. But sometimes (perhaps they got nervous sitting there so quietly out in the open and needed to assert their frog reality) they would unexpectedly croak – *kerar-ark, kerar-ark* – and it always sounded so perfect, frog and frog-song exactly matched. You couldn't ask for more than a green frog croaking in your hand.

Sounds of the Sixties (ii)

There were more bird sounds than anything else. Besides the peewees and the magpies and the desolate caw of the crows, there was the raucous squawking of galahs flapping and overbalancing on the telephone wires; the whirr and flutter of the plover trying to distract from its eggs that it had foolishly left in the open paddock; the witch-laugh of the row of kookaburras on the tree outside the school every morning – mocking us we thought; the scary hoot of the mopoke at night warning of death and the other world; and in the sunny day, the 'sweet pretty creature' chirrup of the quick willy wagtail for which I'd make up different words each time I heard it. I wasn't very good at mimicking its actual sound.

Sometimes we had competitions at home for the best mimicking. Crows were the easiest (*aarrk, aaark aaooooorrr*); the boys were best at birds that required a whistle; and, despite it seeming straightforward, no-one was very accurate at the kookaburra's peal. It required a fair degree of abandon to get the laugh right.

On our rare trips to Sydney, once when I was seven, and again after the drought the magpie sang, I waited to hear the sound of bellbirds. In the Blue Mountains, just past Kurrajong, my oldest brother told us we must wind the car windows down on a particular corner on Bellbird Hill to hear their lovely song. (This precise piece of knowledge – knowing when to wind the windows down – impressed me greatly.) Quick, wind the windows down and be quiet. Silence in the car, eight kids and none of them speaking. There, there it was! Where? I didn't hear it. There, there, don't you hear it? The clear silvery sound, a flute-bell ringing in the moist summer air. Exclamations and then shushing to listen again. The sound rang sweetly, a clear piping note calling, echoing, reminiscent of something – here it is, here it is. 'By channels of coolness I hear the creek falling, And down the dim gorges the bellbirds are calling.' In there, just off the road, were coolness and gorges, a phosphorescent green underworld, tree ferns and fronds, a place of infinite possibilities. We never actually saw the bellbirds; we drove past the dim gorges in the car and down to the plains and endured the long hot haul across the suburbs, but one day, I promised, I would turn off the road and look.

Sounds of the Sixties (iii)

My younger brother and I discovered you could make the meaning of a word disappear and just leave a sound. All you had to do was pick a word and say it maybe ten or fifteen times and its meaning just evaporated.

I had been reading but I'd promised to go and swing on the pipe over the creek with my brother and he was saying 'When?' over and over to annoy me. He suddenly stopped and said, 'Hey, isn't "when" a funny word? Listen to this. When, when, when, when, when, when, when, when, when, when.'

It had turned into a sound, just a sound. I couldn't tell exactly where the change had taken place but somehow it had separated from its meaning. *Wen*. A sound a baby might make, or maybe a Chinese word we didn't know the meaning of. A sound made of a pursing of lips and a rush of air from the voice box and a movement of the tongue to the roof of the mouth.

We tried it with other words and it worked. Every time, the word started off real and then within a few seconds it had turned into a sound without meaning. It was like the discovery of a door into a space that you hadn't known existed, one you could create yourself. It didn't last long because within a few seconds the sound and meaning melded back together again, but still, being able to prise them apart so neatly and quickly made us feel extraordinarily powerful.

Every now and then, after that first discovery, one of us would say out of the blue, 'Hey, isn't "play" a funny word?' And then we would do it again for a while.

Sounds of the Sixties (iv)

ABC radio broadcasts were the soundtrack from the outside world. On the farm I heard stock reports, cricket, the news and the Argonauts Club. I have no memories of listening to music programs. At school it was health and hygiene, social studies and folk singing. The teacher put the wireless on and then pottered about outside while we students obediently did as the wireless voice said. The ABC voices always knew everything. They were solid with no gaps, polished, rich, sure voices. I think my (false) idea of how a voice ought to sound was formed by their confident English-accented certainty.

Then, one day, my older brother bought a transistor radio and a guitar. He listened to rock'n'roll songs on the trannie and began to learn them on his guitar, until one Sunday he refused to go to church because he wanted to stay home and practise a new song. My father said he had to go to Mass but my brother accused him of being like a Communist, trying to make him do something he didn't want to. It was the worst possible insult in our family. Then he just sat on his bed and starting playing 'Under The Boardwalk'. Over and over, slowly strumming the chords. My father didn't know what to do and grabbed him by the shirt and started pulling him and the guitar fell on the floor with a loud clatter and my mother came hurrying in. It was sorted out, more or less, but things were different after that. The reported world had lapped into our farm.

One afternoon, my brother walked out with his guitar and sat on the vinyl banana chair on the parched grass out the back and played 'The House of the Rising Sun' for us. I thought it sounded just like the wireless. Some days, not very often, he let us listen to the Beatles and the Beachboys on the little green trannie. I liked it better when he brought the trannie outside in the summer evenings. We all lay on blankets on the grass away from the suffocating heat inside and watched the stars and satellites move and he'd let us listen to the late-night ghost-story program. I still remember the shivery phrase 'the sound of a footfall accompanied by the scent of rotting magnolia flowers' from one of the stories. My brother could easily decide to turn it off or go inside if any of us irritated him so we lay very quietly, pretending we weren't really listening.

Sounds of the Sixties (v)

The Catholic church we attended in town didn't have much in the way of singing in the sixties, but there was the chanting at Saturday afternoon Benediction – the Exposition and Veneration of the Blessed Sacrament (these kinds of phrases have been ordinary to me since I was at least seven). The priest wore heavily embroidered gold and white vestments and sprinkled holy water on the congregation from a brass bowl and swung burning frankincense in a brass thurible (and these kinds of words, lovely in a dry landscape). Near the end, the altar boy put a white-and-gold shawl around the priest's shoulders and, with his hands wrapped in the shawl, the priest held up a large golden monstrance. It had spiky rays coming out from it (it looked like a sun) and a circle of bread – the True Presence – in the middle with a tiny glass door over it. He swayed the monstrance back and forth while the congregation bowed their heads and considered the presence of God. None of the ordinary people around me – the bookie's wife, the corner-shop owner, the farmers, the barber – none of them thought that any of this gold embroidery or incense or chanting was in the slightest bit odd or even exotic.

The best part of the ceremony was the Divine Praises which the priest chanted and which we all chanted back. To get the best effect – by yourself and out of earshot if you don't want to be thought strange – the Divine Praises ought to said out aloud and in a deep rhythmic voice. You don't have to believe in God or anything – it's the sound that matters. The second praise should be said lower and a bit muffled.

Blessed be God.
Blessed be God.

Blessed be His Holy Name.
Blessed be His Holy Name.
Blessed be Jesus Christ, true God and true Man.
Blessed be Jesus Christ, true God and true Man.
Blessed be the name of Jesus.
Blessed be the name of Jesus.
Blessed be His most Sacred Heart.
Blessed be His most Sacred Heart.

Should I include it all? It really needs to go on. Perhaps it was the sturdy trochaic beat that soothed, or perhaps it was that, after a while, the voices rising and falling sounded like rain on a tin roof, drumming and receding, the most comforting sound possible if you've grown up through a drought.

Blessed be His most Precious Blood.
Blessed be Jesus in the most holy sacrament of the altar.
Blessed be the Holy Spirit, Paraclete.
Blessed be the great Mother of God, Mary most holy.
Blessed be her holy and Immaculate Conception.
Blessed be her glorious Assumption.
Blessed be the name of Mary, Virgin and Mother.
Blessed be St Joseph, her most chaste spouse.
Blessed be God in His angels and in His saints.

Sounds of the Sixties (vi)

There was a sound that came some wintry nights and sang along the creek and up into the hills and far up into the sky. At times it rose higher, almost to a wail, and then sank again to a deep comforting hum. I lay still in the bed, feeling the heaviness of the bedding, and listened to it. If I lay still and straight in the dark there was only the weight of my blankets and the humming.

I wondered if it could be the sound of angels streaming through the night, collecting used souls. Or giving out new ones to those being born, creamy silver soul discs, oval shaped, held in their arms. Perhaps the sound was their wings beating slowly, then quickly. Or was it God's voice singing out to them, hey there, hey there, keeping them on track because angels could lose their way, especially in Australia, where there was so much desert to cross. I believed that one day they would find me and want my soul back, but not for a long while. I thought of Aborigines with no houses around them, listening before I was born. They had lain in the dark, with no walls or roof, just the black sky and the Southern Cross and the silvery cutout of the moon to let the light from outside the skin of the world shine in. As they lay on the ground under kangaroo fur blankets (rancid-smelling, like sheepskins), they could have seen souls slipping out of the dead to join the humming.

My brothers explained it was the sound of the wind in the telephone wires, but I wasn't convinced because it only happened at night. If it was wind, I reasoned, the wires would wail in the daytime too. It was the sound of God sending angels down from the sky and over the hills, through the dark and along the creek past our house.

Seven

Sacred and Profane Stories of Sex and Singing (i)

The unusual, for the Blue Mountains, heat of the singing lessons summer was like a drumbeat. It was there all the time. Every morning, it seems in memory, hot and humid air rose from the overheated city on the plains below and a languid anything-might-happen atmosphere drifted over our usually sedate mountain town. Every late afternoon, cumulus clouds darkened and a sound and light show stormed across the cliffs dumping tropical rain on the steaming footpaths and streets and tangled bush. Grass lapped around our ankles. Sweat ran down under arms and between breasts and legs. It should have been great weather for sex.

Sacred and Profane Stories of Sex and Singing (ii)

In the writing class Josef read out his first memory, a story about his aunt. He was a little boy, six years old, standing in the garden with her one Polish summer. She was a young woman and very pretty; he described her long slim legs beside him – it was hot and her legs were bare and tanned. A bicycle pulled up and was leaned against the fence; the little boy saw the spokes between the palings. Silver spokes, white palings. A handsome man came into the garden holding a brown paper bag and stood in front of Josef and his aunt. Josef moved a little nearer to his aunt; he could feel her cotton dress, the softness of it brushing the hairs on his arm. The man opened the bag and held it out to Josef's aunt, then leant down and offered it to Josef. He peered in to see juicy red plums nestling in the bag. Their round redness and scent mingled with the closeness of his aunt and something in the way the man had walked towards her. In sixty-seven years Josef had not forgotten the plums.

'I can still smell them.' He looked up, his first erotic moment still shining in his eyes.

Sacred and Profane Stories of Sex and Singing (iii)

Dina told me she ran away from home once.

'Like all teenagers,' she said.

'I didn't,' I said.

We were sitting on the back verandah with cups of tea, Joni Mitchell singing in the background. 'A Free Man in Paris'. When she sang, her extraordinary voice turning 360 degrees inside a word, like a brown hawk suddenly ascending or descending, it meant anything was possible. It seemed a long time since we had first heard her sing that song. From near the end of the century, we were just starting to see the curve of time. Everything seemed a long time ago that afternoon.

'Just for the weekend, it turned out.'

She and a girlfriend had hitchhiked north from Christchurch in a truck, 'Hitchhiker' playing on the truckie's transistor (or so Dina said), the truckie wondering if he was in with a chance, the girls wanting the whole world to start happening now. They were heading for Auckland.

'God, Auckland! That was as much as we could imagine! It was a country town in the sixties.'

She wanted to sing in a band. 'Be a rock'n'roll star. Or something.' She had the long black hair and red lips already; she could sing all the songs on the wireless. 'Dusty Springfield. Little Patti,' she said with a grin. 'Leader of the Pack.'

'When we got to Picton we sneaked onto the inter-island ferry across to Wellington. We walked around the deck pretending we were going to England. I met this boy, eighteen or so.'

'How old were you?'

'Fourteen. It was the first time I'd seen a penis.'

'And then what happened?'

Sacred and Profane Stories of Sex and Singing (iv)

Mostly I don't want to hear talk about sex. Even twenty years ago – when I ought to have been more tolerant – Jules, I think it was, left a note by our double bed: 'Had a wild time in yr bed. Fanny flooding. No time to change sheets. Thanks', I'd thought, what made her think I want to hear about *her* fanny? I crumpled the note and threw it into the bin before stripping the bed and stuffing the sheets in the machine with an extra cup of washing powder. Even after that fastidiousness, I still didn't feel like lying in the bed.

I don't mind reading about sex – I loved the erotic passage in a novel I read recently about a young Japanese couple making love all in one deliciously long sentence. And the story Kit wrote (fiction, I hoped) about a man and the woman house guest in his lounge-room who caressed and licked his penis when he got up from his wife's bed for a drink in the middle of the night. But if people start talking or reading aloud about licking and sucking fannies and caressing curved thighs and throbbing penises, all I can do is laugh anxiously and wish they would shut up. I try to look accommodating but my lips go a little thin.

Sacred and Profane Stories of Sex and Singing (v)

My father used to say, 'The body is the temple of the Holy Spirit'. I heard him say that many times but I didn't know what it meant. I am not sure whether he did or not. He didn't explain because he was a modest man who did not talk about the body or sex. When he was old, not long before he died, my mother and I lifted his heavy body into a sitting position on the side of the bed so he could use the urine bottle. I looked away, but as we were helping him lie back down again, his loose pyjama fly came open and I saw his soft curled penis nestling against his white-haired balls. I felt shocked and sad. Partly I felt like Noah's sons, that to have seen the instrument of my origins was wrong in an unarguable mythic sense, but it was also an intrusion on my father's privacy. If he were in control of his circumstances, he would never have allowed himself to be exposed like that. When he said 'temple of the Holy Spirit', you could see a white bird, a dove from the picture of the 'Descent of the Holy Ghost upon the Apostles' or 'The Annunciation', nestling inside my father's chest, his ribs the golden columns of the temple.

Sacred and Profane Stories of Sex and Singing (vi)

When male bass voices sing particular notes in harmony – anything below low G – the sound vibrates around my pelvic bone. I feel the pelvis like a large hand cupping the body, holding it, the notes of the bass voices resonating with the curved bone. It must be to do with the oscillation of the sound waves, their length and height, entering the density of flesh and bone vibrating at the same natural rate, like a curtain rod in the house suddenly vibrating to hum with a particular truck engine out on the road. It's disconcertingly intimate. I'm not the only one – I've talked about it with other women and they laugh and say, yes. It's a sexual thing, a vibrating in the pit of our bodies and it can happen any time men sing those low notes, but more so if it's live, not a recording. It feels primeval, like the beginning of time, as if the cupped bone and the sound are the ground of physical being. I imagine caves and earth and the chests of men humming the world into existence. The men sing and the beginning of time, the origins of human beings, of men and women, seems to be inside our bodies.

Sacred and Profane Stories of Sex and Singing (vii)

Just before coming up to the beach-house I watched a documentary video of the voice box that my new singing teacher lent me. The documentary-maker had used one of those tiny medical cameras in the end of a tube and stuck it down the person's throat as they were singing and so was able to film the throat and uvula and larynx close-up. I was startled and a bit embarrassed (I was watching it with other people) to see how very like vulva and labia the larynx was; the thick soft red folds; the glistening moistness; the rhythmic pulsing of blood, the exquisitely fine quivering of the flesh. How does such an organ create sound? A soft wet fanny in the throat?

A sound sings in through the ear, down the canal and vibrates the tympanic membrane which sets off the hammer, anvil and stirrup. These dainty little bones transmit the vibrations to the oval window into the inner ear wherein lies the cochlea coiled like a spiralled seashell. It is the seashell that hears. The fanny in the throat sings and the seashell at the bottom of the canal hears and the universe came into being from a mathematical equation. It's the way things are.

Sacred and Profane Stories of Sex and Singing (viii)

The trouble was, it wasn't working. Sex, I mean. Like my father, I'd rather not mention it, but I'm trying to be truthful about what changed, what crossed over, what finished, or seemed to, that summer, and the rhythms of oestrogen and progesterone have to be part of it; the chemistry of days and nights. Sex should have been sensational with all that humidity, but one day, flatly, it just wasn't there. The absence happened without warning, or none that I noticed (and what is the use of a warning that can only be read afterwards, except to make us feel the sharp cut of 'if only'). No desire, no tingling, no throbbing. It wasn't just in bed either. I stood in the shower, walked up the road, listened to stories, and the absence was there. My body felt physically altered, as if the sensitive lips and folds had been surgically removed and replaced with old tyre rubber. At the same time it felt as if I was fading and flattening, as if all the rosy pinks and scarlets and golds of intimacy had faded to a cool grey-blue as I lost the roundness of being. It was like suddenly stepping out of bright hot life into the plane of a television screen where everything still looked alive but there was no heat, no smell, no dampness.

Sacred and Profane Stories of Sex and Singing (ix)

We stood out the front of my house, Dina and I. Kit was putting Theo, asleep in the baby-capsule, into their old Valiant and Anthony was leaning on the car talking to him, both out of earshot of us. It was late afternoon after a long Sunday lunch, salad from Anthony's garden and his Mexican pie and a couple of glasses of wine. Our talking, mine and Dina's, had got around to sex, I can't remember how. It could have been the same day we were exchanging 'first times' (mine with a blond, blue-eyed boy on a mattress on the floor of a ski lodge, awkward, unpleasurable. The earth didn't move that time, nor without quite a few more attempts. And later he slept with my beautiful schoolfriend – even after he broke his leg skiing. I was in the next room, on her verandah, actually, and could hear it all.)

'I know people are thinking about It when they see us together.'

'What?' I said.

'How big Kit is and how small I am. I'm sure they're thinking, how do they do It? That he must surely squash me.'

'Well, only if he's on top,' I said. It seemed the only thing to say, but I blushed a bit anyway.

Dina grinned. 'That's what I say.'

We both looked at Kit. He caught us looking as he shut the Valiant door and raised his eyebrows. We both laughed.

'What?' he asked.

'Nothing to do with you,' said Dina. She winked at me. 'Just talking about our sex lives.'

Eight

Voice as Epiphenomenon
or
The Mechanics of Singing

Those parts of the body most closely associated with singing production include the lungs, the trachea, the larynx, the nasal cavities and the oral cavities (mouth). These structures form a versatile and intricate sound production system.

Two absolute requirements for the production of sounds of any kind are a source of energy and a vibrating element. The primary source of energy for singing production is air provided by the lower respiratory tract, in particular the lungs. They supply the sound vibrators (the vocal folds of the larynx) with power in the form of a fairly smooth unmodulated flow of air. We should note, however, that the conversion of a flow of air into sound may take place almost anywhere along the vocal tract, which is that portion of the singing mechanism lying above (and including) the vocal folds . . .

. . . The Histology of the Vocal Fold:

1. The epithelium, which is squamous. It can be regarded as a thin and stiff capsule which maintains the shape of the vocal fold.
2. The superficial layer of the lamina propria (Reinke's space) consisting of loose fibrous components and matrix, which can be regarded as a mass of soft gelatin.
3. The intermediate layer of the lamina propria, consisting chiefly of elastic fibres and likened to a bundle of soft rubber bands.
4. The deeper layer of the lamina propria, consisting of

collagenous fibres and somewhat like a bundle of cotton thread.

5. The vocalis muscle, which constitutes the main body of the vocal fold and is like a bundle of rather stiff rubber bands.

. . . The singing mechanism is an extraordinary sound-producing mechanism. Think for a moment of the vast array of sounds that can be produced by this remarkable acoustical mechanism. The repertory is staggering, and yet, in spite of its versatility, the singing mechanism operates as nothing more than a variable resistance to the flow of air, and in that event the voice is hardly more than an epiphenomenon!

This is copied word for word from *Speech and Hearing Science: Anatomy and Physiology*, Third Edition, by Willard R. Zemlin, except that as I understand it, singing and speech have the same physiology and anatomy, so I have substituted 'singing' wherever Zemlin had written 'speech'. The other words – epithelium, lamina propria, vocalis, squamous – a benediction chant of the holy sacrament of science that I wouldn't dream of changing.

Looking at the photographs that Zemlin used to illustrate the mode of vocal fold vibration – single frames from a high-speed film – I'm struck again by their likeness to the labia. Although Zemlin is too much of a scientist to remark on the symbolic correspondences of form, surely he couldn't help noticing it? Singing, sex, vibration, they all belong in the same breath.

The Second Singing Lesson

It didn't start well. On the way I was delayed by an overturned semitrailer blocking both sides of the highway on the bend just outside town. The cab was twisted in front of the trailer in a way that made it look like a huge creature with its neck broken. Boxes had split open and toys were spread across the road. What must have happened to the driver in the mangled mess flicked like a snake's tongue around the edge of my mind. Suddenly life was very different for him; me, I was just on the way to the weekly mortification session. I considered turning around and driving back home. I looked down at my boots clamped on the brake. Dina's flowery boots.

At the singing teacher's house, a pipe had burst and his studio was flooded so we couldn't have the lesson there. I said I could just go home, but he said we could use the kitchen. I followed him down the hall.

'Sit down.' He gestured to a chair with its back to the window and picked up his guitar. 'This week I am going to tape the lesson so that you can listen and practise at home.' He explained how singing came from the body, from breathing and the air going over the voice box, and how it all needed to be exercised – the chest and voice box and throat – just like any other part of the body. He put the tape in and turned the cassette player on as he talked.

The rationality of his explanation was momentarily reassuring. I'd never really considered voice as a function of the body before. Wasn't it made of feelings, the bare soul, Edith Piaf, Joe Cocker, Phoebe Snow, giving you their hearts?

'So first off, loosen your jaw. Let it hang. Like the village idiot.'

I did as he instructed, feeling the stiffness of my jaw as it clicked down. My shoulders were already hunched, restricting my breathing. My body had begun its mad list of directives to try and stop this silly singing business.

'Now. La la la la la,' he sang.

I opened my mouth. Thin scratchy sounds disturbed the kitchen briefly.

We struggled on. He said I imagined the pitch higher than it was, that I needed to learn to listen, and I said, but it was like me trying to listen to Russian or Greek, that there was nowhere in my mind that knew how to listen. He didn't know what I meant. He had lived in music all his life, it coursed through him. I wasn't deaf, how could I not hear? No amount of words about it were going to help anyway, I knew that much. I remember at one point the fridge started to hum and I was relieved to hear another sound in the bare kitchen.

He tried again with one note at a time, but in a sequence, going up the scale each time. There was something logical about the way each note followed the one before it and my mind latched onto the rising pitch as something it could discern. I tried again but it was no use. Why was my mind treating singing as so fundamentally different to speaking? There must be only the slightest physiological difference. I sighed and slumped in the chair like a teenager, staring at the floor. The flowery boots looked too big and bright on me.

'But I can hear that you are getting better,' the teacher said.

'Yeah?'

I watched the clock behind the teacher's head creep around to two o'clock.

I left quickly and drove home via the back road, along the ochre cliffs. The air shimmered above the valleys as if it was the middle of the afternoon in a desert. When I got out of the car and walked, my gait was lumbering, like a large animal. I sat on the back verandah; there seemed no point in going back.

Still, I Did My Singing Practice

I waited until everyone had left the house (I wished everyone would leave the street), then I shut the doors and windows, put a kitchen chair down in front of the tape recorder and sat on it neatly like a good girl at school. I faced into the wall rather than the window, so the sound wouldn't travel as far.

I'd never practised music before. My family wasn't musical and we had no money for lessons. We were the ragtag kids at school whose arms had high-tide marks where we had finished bathing and who never went to piano or tap or ballet. We scorned and pitied the neat kids as they went to lessons and then had to practise while we did as we pleased every day after school, never having to sit down and practise anything. We were lucky, we said.

Dina told me her mother gave piano lessons. There was always music in the house. Students came and took their lessons and Dina heard them stumbling through their scales as she lay on her bed. A soft wind came through the open window and the lace curtain seemed to undulate in time to the notes of '*Für Elise*'. For her it was as easy as walking and talking. She had learned before she could remember learning – music and singing were native languages.

Nine

Conversations (i)

'Sing a note for me,' Anthony said, smiling.

'No.'

'Go on.'

'No. Not in front of you.'

'Why not?'

'You're mocking me.'

'What did I say?'

'It was the way you said it.'

'Come off it. All I said was "sing me a note". I'm showing an interest.'

'No you're not. You think I'm being silly even trying to sing. You think I'm so hopeless it's a joke.'

'You're being ridiculous. Come on, you don't have to be afraid of my judgment.'

'Yes, I do. You can sing anything. You'll think how bad I am. You don't encourage me, you think I'm hopeless.'

'Well, if you won't even sing one note, you are.'

'See?'

Conversations (ii)

I walked up the street to the post office and tried to practise notes as I went. Walking along, singing. I was a sunny-day woman walking along singing a song. Ah, ah, ah. Just strolling along. La-da-da. It sounded thin and sugary but still, a few days later I told my friend Anna that I walked up the street singing like a normal person. She said normal people didn't walk along the street singing. She said, 'Think about it – if someone was walking towards you down the street and they were singing aloud, what would you think?'

Conversations (iii)

Eventually, I went to the Chinese herbalist to see if he could give me anything for the absence of desire. It might be the cause of all suffering, but life without it was desolate.

'Maybe it's just anxiety. Theo leaving. And the singing lessons seem to be stressful,' Anthony said.

'It's never happened before,' I said. I felt stubborn, resistant to what I suspected must be beginning to happen. 'Not ever.'

'I'm having trouble with my libido,' I said to the herbalist. (I'd remembered that word, libido, otherwise I wouldn't have said anything. Desire was too intimate and dangerous to say.) 'And my periods are coming either too often or too little.' He gave me dozens of brown paper bags filled with bark and sticks and fungi and as I was walking out with them clutched to my chest I happened to bump into JK from the writing group.

'Darl,' she said, 'what are you up to?'

'Just picking up my Chinese herbs.'

She raised her eyebrows behind her cat's eye glasses but I didn't explain. I particularly didn't want to talk about the sex thing to her, not after reading her account of having sex twelve times in one day. Can't have been that mind-blowing if they were still counting, I'd thought sourly.

'Okay. So, how did the singing class go?'

'Terrible. It was mortifying to do something so badly in front of someone who's so good at it.'

'Fuck 'em, darl,' JK said.

It sounded so easy that I burst out laughing. Yeah, who cares? Fuck'em. Then I'd be able to sing.

Conversations (iv)

Theo rang and told me about Jake, his new friend from down the road. His father is Egyptian, he said, and they have a swimming pool and they are really rich.

'What's he like?'

'We're opposites,' he said. From the tone of his voice it was apparent he was repeating a remark he had heard and liked. 'He's big and I'm small, and he's dark and I'm kinda light, and he's the toughest kid in the class and I'm . . . not really.'

'So how do you get along, being so different?'

'Easy. We both go to karate and we are both into Lego.'

'How's karate?'

'It's excellent. I go three times a week.'

'That's good. And what kind of Lego does Jake like?'

'Oh, everything. Space. Aqualego. Technics. He's got heaps of Technics.'

'What's Aqualego? I've never heard of that.'

'You build underwater stuff.' He was casual with a faint note of scorn for my ignorance.

'Does he have space blocks?'

'Yeah, but mostly Technics.'

'I made a Technic robot once. It walked right across the kitchen.'

'Yeah.' He'd heard my great robot achievement story before and I'd run out of Lego stories of my own so I changed the subject.

'I've been to two singing lessons.'

'Can you sing now?'

'Not yet. It'll take a while. I'm pretty bad.'

'Mrs March says I'm a good singer.'

'Who's Mrs March?'

'My teacher. From Minnesota.'

'That's good. Your mum was a good singer.'

'Yeah.'

'So, well then, is Mrs March still excellent?'

'Yeah.'

Monosyllables were Theo's favoured punishment. I should not have mentioned his mother. I'd stepped over a fine line, tried to tighten a thread and he wasn't going to have it. He had never let me get away with that. One day a couple of years ago I was visiting Kit, wearing Dina's flowery boots which he had given me when he was sharing all Dina's clothes out amongst her friends. They were the ones she'd worn that day on the verandah that Theo thought he remembered, the ones I wore to my singing lessons. They were covered in wildflowers, pointy-toed, elastic-sided, like RM Williams riding boots at the Mardi Gras. I knew as I put them on that day that I was fishing for something. Anyway, Kit had put the coffee on and asked Theo to show me his new soccer gear while I was waiting. I took Theo's hand and he held it stiffly, his hand not curving into mine.

I admired his soccer outfit and especially the studded boots, and then looked around his room. On the shelf over his bed there was a photograph of Dina, her dark eyes sparkling. I sat down on the bed and looked up at it. Theo ignored my gaze.

'Your mum,' I said.

'Yeah.'

'She was beautiful.'

'Yeah.'

I looked at him but he was busy pulling the axle out of a plastic wheel. I looked down at the flowery boots. There was a white smudge on the toe where the flowers had rubbed off.

'These were your mum's.'

Theo looked at the boots briefly and then went on with the axle operation.

'Thought they looked stupid,' he said.

Ten

The Day It Happened.

Theo saw it. It was June 16 and they were going out to lunch at a friend's place a couple of streets away. Kit and Dina and Theo were all smartly dressed. Theo wore little blue overalls and a hand-knitted jumper – I know that because we had to rush over and collect him after it happened. He had been standing near the lounge, scrubbed-face solemn as he watched the frown on his mother's face. Dina said she had a bit of a headache from dashing around to get ready and Kit went to fetch a Panadol from the bathroom.

'Come on. We have to get going. We're late already, Mish will be waiting,' he probably said.

Dina bent down to pick something up. I don't actually know what – I've imagined nappies, Theo's toy bird, or it could have been just to lace up her Docs. It doesn't matter because what happened next erased all that. Suddenly the lounge-room and Theo would have seemed unreal, like 3D laser images. Then, abruptly, the pain in her head would have become extreme, her neck would have stiffened and she'd have felt dizzy. Unknown to her, the dangerously thin membrane wall she had been born with in the sub-arachnoid cluster of blood vessels nestling fine and spidery behind her left ear had suddenly stretched and burst, flooding blood across her brain. The hypothalamus, which monitors body activity, registered something was wrong and directed her heart to speed up, pumping even more blood across the cerebral hemispheres. The pumping blood filled the skull cavity instead of carrying oxygen to the various lobes, including along the central sulcus (Fissure of Rolando it is also called in the physiology book, making it sound like romantic terrain), a kind of fold between the frontal and the parietal lobes where the motor regions are located. Without oxygen the brain cells that direct muscular activity began to die and her body spasmed with unco-ordinated electrical impulses, her limbs and torso twisting and flailing. It was as if someone was giving electric shocks to various parts of her brain. What Theo saw was his mother fall, then buck on the floor like a crazed animal, her eyes staring straight ahead. Kit heard the crash and came running. Dina was lying on the floor and Theo stood wide-eyed, not crying, not speaking.

'He didn't say a word,' Kit said later.

Setting this down now is like being in a hall of mirrors. There are so many versions of what happened and from so many different times; there is the account Kit gave; the doctors' reports; the medical books' explanation of the physiology of a haemorrhage; a fictional description for a character for whom I borrowed Dina's illness; the version I'm trying to report here where I am sorting through the various pieces. The version that can never be told is Dina's. There is no voice for her; she was silenced. It's a fact that I slap hard into at times and then I feel beached. There is no getting around that this is not her story but mine.

In my work, when I read the stories of a life, I'm listening for the tone and timbre of a voice recounting its own experience of being. There is no deeper mystery. It is the sound that carries through all human time. Here on my own where there are only the sounds of the lagoon and its birds, pieces of many of the stories often come back to trouble the stillness of this place.

A List of True Stories

U's mother killed herself when U was two – and forty years later her only daughter also suicided.

As a child during the war, T watched human bodies being eaten by fish in the Chindwin River.

J's father used her for sex after her mother died.

R's parents left him, aged three, and his baby sister to fend for themselves in a Berlin flat.

C heard both her parents being tortured to death by the Japanese during the war.

G was raped by his teacher in a Christian orphanage.

Y's mother forced her to eat her own vomit.

Just after the war ended, N saw her fellow villagers in the Ukraine drive a road grader over an unarmed eighteen-year-old German boy.

D regularly and carefully sliced her own arms when she was a teenager to divert herself from the pain in her mind.

B's husband spent four years in Changi POW camp and had nightmares for the ensuing fifty until Alzheimer's gave him peace at last.

I don't know what to do with all this suffering. I have no idea. And there's plenty more where these stories came from. There's blood spilled, dreams crushed into greyness. Neither writing nor singing have any power to prevent it. What use are they?

There's a splashing down at the lagoon. I put the list away and take up the binoculars which I've discovered on the bookshelf in the beach-house. I have never had binoculars before and I keep them near me, fascinated by the sudden change of perspective they give. It takes a few sweeps of the area, rushing through a blur of green and blue, before I find the source of the sound. There is a white crane standing in the water on the edge of the lagoon with a fish wriggling in its beak. 'The Crane is my Neighbour . . . silent he was and yet he seemed to sing.' I can see the bird close up, the whiteness of the feathers on its slender neck, its unbearably thin legs, its long beak and the silvery flapping fish. I can even see the reflection of the crane and fish in the water. Both the crane and fish are beautiful, perfect. Soon the fish, gulping, dying in the air, will be itself gulped down the elegant neck. I am spying; the crane cannot know I am watching it so closely, and I feel some shame, but it is overtaken by a sense of benediction. It is grace given, to observe the world.

I remember what T, the one who saw fish eating human flesh (she was Burmese from Mandalay and it was World War II) said to the writing class one day: 'Every time I write, I cry.' After she said it there was one of the strangest silences I have ever heard – everyone was stilled and her words seemed to vibrate in the air. I suddenly thought of 'the ring of truth'. She'd said the secret thing and it hung there like a pure note from a Buddhist gong or a bell-bird's call on a sultry afternoon.

The point is, Dina didn't die. Not then. She lay unmoving for a minute after the initial haemorrhage and Kit lifted her rigid body onto the lounge and rang the ambulance. He came back and kneeled by her side and Dina whispered something to him and then her body began bucking again. Kit rang us, crying, 'Dina is having a turn! Can you come and take Theo right now?' (That's what he said: 'a turn'. I remember thinking what a strange old lady-ish word to use.) Dina was rushed up to Blue Mountains Hospital by ambulance and then flown by helicopter to Westmead Hospital down on the plains. There, a surgeon removed a piece of bone from the front right side of her skull to relieve the pressure of blood on her brain. I can't even imagine the nerve it would take to saw (chip? snip?) through skull-bone and lift a piece out and put it in the metal kidney tray like it was a leftover from the design. And then to sew the skin back together, knowing anyone could poke their finger right through to the brain, soft and squishy under the thin skin sagging down without the bone to stretch it taut.

Eleven

The Science

About twenty per cent of strokes occur from haemorrhage — a sudden bleeding — in the brain. Sub-arachnoid haemorrhage is usually caused by the rupture of an aneurysm, a weakened blood vessel wall – often an inherited trait. A condition called arterio-venous malformation (AVM) is an abnormal connection between arteries and veins. If it occurs in the brain and ruptures, it can cause a stroke.

Although most people who suffer sub-arachnoid haemorrhages survive the first stroke, many experience rebleeding or a dangerous complication in which the blood vessels go into a spasm and deprive the brain of oxygen.

Researchers are working to discover the cycle of events involved in cell death after oxygen is lost. One hypothesis begins when blood is cut off in the brain and substances known as excitatory amino acids are released. They open channels in the membranes that cover neurones (brain cells) and allow large amounts of calcium to flow in. Calcium reacts within the neurones to release harmful substances. Of particular interest is nitric oxide, an oxygen-free radical which is important for maintaining elasticity in blood vessels but, when released in brain cells, damages their DNA. Another hypothesis focuses on an enzyme called PARP, which ordinarily makes minor molecular repairs. Confronted with substantial injury, however, PARP over-responds and takes up ATP, the major source of energy in cells. The cells die. Within minutes of a stroke, the zone of initial cell death is surrounded by additional damaged and dying brain cells; this process can continue for hours.

Elevated levels of a substance called lipoprotein(a) may reveal the possibility of an unruptured aneurysm, which can be confirmed with an MRI (magnetic resonance imaging) scan. Whether such tests should become part of a regular screening process will be determined with more research.

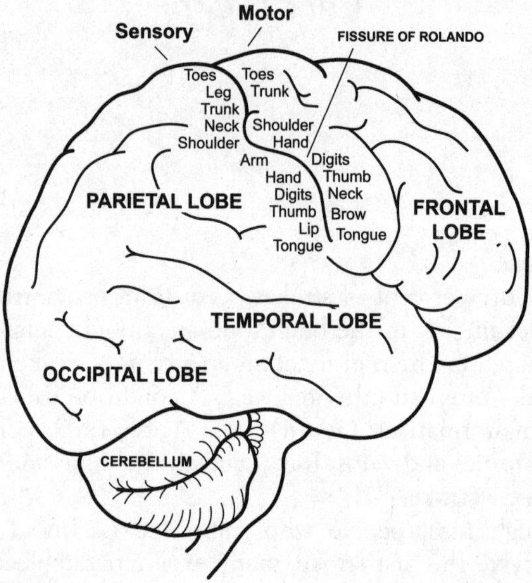

You can see from the diagram that if the regions along the Fissure of Rolando were deprived of oxygen and the cells died, you wouldn't be able to swallow, talk, sing, walk, make love, turn the pages of a book, caress a cheek, do anything that requires conscious movement of muscles. If other lobes were not damaged, the neurones processing sensory perception would still function; you could still see and hear and feel and taste – that's if you could open your mouth and swallow. You could still have will and desire. And you could still think. You could even think about thinking.

The brain itself is made of squishy grey and white stuff that is probably quite tasty to eat (it sounds gross, but my only direct experience of actual brains is that as a child I used to eat crumbed sheep's brains fried by my grandmother). Still, despite its unimpressive appearance, and depending on the various lobes all working and communicating with one another, it can design an erotic dress, figure out the notes of a song after hearing it once, or try to come to terms with the Buddhist philosophy of impermanence.

The Buddhist Philosophy of Impermanence

It was three days after the haemorrhage when I first visited Dina. I didn't want to but I thought I ought to. It would look bad if I didn't. At the same time, I was curious, with that superstitious curiosity reserved for horror. I wanted to know every detail, watch the dreadful event over and over, avid for every new angle. It fed a strange horror-hungry part of the psyche, but there was also a magic immunity being built. Fate does not like being ignored and if I really acknowledged its awful power, maybe it would leave me alone.

I parked in the new hospital grounds and watched other people arrive with flowers and grapes. There was no point in me bringing anything.

I followed Kit's directions and took the lift up to the third floor. The ward sister at the nursing station stopped me.

'Who are you visiting?

'Dina Griffen.'

'You know she looks very different, don't you?'

'Yes.'

'And that she is still unconscious.'

'Yes, I know.'

'I'll show you where to go, then.'

The nurse and I squeaked our way along the wide polished hallway into a large bright room. There in the high-tech hospital bed lay a body I would not have recognised as Dina's if I had been walking by. All her beautiful hair had been shaved off and you could see even under the covering of bandages how the right temple was caved in. There was a faint prickle of black hair covering her scalp, a three-day growth, so that she looked like a skinhead who'd been in a really bad brawl. There was a hole in her throat with a little plastic frame inserted and a tube taped into it and there were tubes going into her nose and arms as well. She was wearing a blue hospital gown, the sort that is open at the back, which took the colour from her already white face. She would have hated the way she looked. I gazed guiltily on her unprotected face.

Twelve

It's the middle of the day and although no-one else is visible through the thick screen of sarsaparilla and trailing vines with purple flowers, I can hear the sounds of human activity from other houses along the lagoon. 'Killing Me Softly With His Song' plays on next door's radio. Accusing. Plaintive. I have to stop what I am doing. With no more than a pang of longing, I am eighteen, living in a terrace in Napier Street, Darlinghurst, just behind Taylor Square, with Sara and Ester and Sara's Chilean boyfriend, Andreas. Dina lives nearby although I don't meet her for another fifteen years. I must pass her on the street.

I have just left school and the farm and moved to Sydney. I'm aware of being a stranger, sure that everyone is looking at me. I buy sunglasses at the chemist to hide from the gaze of all the unknown people.

I waitress at the Professors' Club at Sydney University and learn to catch a bus up Oxford Street to Central and then along Broadway to Parramatta Road. I alight at the park stop before the university to walk along the path worn by students and through the side gate into the university grounds, proud of knowing about the side gate, a small relief from the rawness of being a stranger.

Harry comes around to visit, arriving with a roar on his Triumph, lean and sexy and ten years older than me. We don't have sex but I let him put his head in my lap and his hands inside my pants. I am thrilled when he writes a letter (the spelling and grammar aren't so good) saying he is in love with me and that he shouldn't see me any more because I'm too good for him.

Andreas rarely emerges from Sara's bedroom. He is darkly handsome and has a heavy accent and an anguished look – it's no wonder everyone is in love with him. He barely says a word to me except early one morning when he arrives home after tripping on acid all night and asks if I want to go down to the park at Tamarama Beach with him – he says it's magic. We ride there on his motorbike and wander around looking at the Moreton Bay figs, shadowy and strange in the early morning. He's still tripping and is blown away by the sorrow of the twisted roots and branches, exclaiming in his beautiful accent and drifting from tree to tree. He sits down and tells me that he was a revolutionary in Chile and escaped torturers by using a knife he had hidden on him. I am so ignorant of world events that I've not heard of Pinochet, but willingly believe his story.

The only other time I talk with Andreas is when I see him outside in the street on my way to work for the afternoon shift. He has been tripping again and this time looks haunted. He asks for a loan of twenty dollars, a third of my weekly waitressing pay. I know I'll never get it back but I'm glad to be part of this world where revolutionaries can ask me for money in the early afternoon.

The singer has finished her song, it's nearly a quarter of a century later. Why wouldn't you want to be a singer when you carry the key to 3D memory? Like a sorcerer or a laser archivist, you conjure up the past; Sara and Ester and Andreas and Harry; the haunting air of dawn under the Moreton Bay figs, and more, the first bite into an oyster and blushing, the first time getting a taxi home at three o'clock in the morning, the first feel of semen inside your thigh.

The memory surfaces in the middle of the day and none of it is to do with Dina except that she lived nearby.

The truth is, I didn't ever know Dina very well. She has entered my life since she died via the labyrinthine paths of dreams and other people's memories, and the things she made. There are photographs too, taken by other people of events I was never at. And there is Theo, her god-boy creation. Her brown eyes gleam out of his creamy-pale face, but they're not really hers, only a facsimile. I've known her mainly in reflection, in a set of mirrors. And then I realise the last thing she made the summer before her brain exploded was the mirror, the one with the surreal fish-bird creatures on it. How elegant life can be on rare occasions, though probably only when it's enacting tragedy.

I dreamed I saw Dina at a garden party. She was standing in a glasshouse (a glasshouse!) wearing a large sunhat – not the sort of thing I ever saw her wear – and a Spanish-style off-the-shoulder dress with large scarlet flowers on it. I didn't know it in the dream, but I realise now that the flowers were the same as the flowers on the dress she was buried in. (It was the dress she was wearing in the Happy Families photo taken in the back yard at Terrace Falls Road). She had a glass of wine in her hand but she looked as if she were going to sing. As I walked towards her, or drifted, or however it is that a dreamer moves, I realised gradually that it wasn't her, it was just someone who looked like her.

I only actually knew her, the three-dimensional walking talking laughing Dina, for three years before she died. It wasn't long. I didn't know her as a schoolgirl. I didn't know her as a dancer or singer, I didn't see her meet Kit. I wasn't at their wedding. Why then does it feel as if I know her as my child, my sister, myself? Why does it feel as if she lives inside me?

Thirteen

I dream again of a baby, this time a strange, frightening baby. Even though it's only a few months old, it's rangy and muscular and walks as well as talks. It keeps complaining that I am not a good mother, that I am too rough. I think that the baby's attitude is unjustified and malicious, and am determined to prove it wrong. Other people stand about, persuaded by the baby's articulate and uncompromising argument. My anxiety makes me clumsy and I bump into the baby and dislocate its shoulder. It falls to the floor in great pain (I feel it's putting it on a bit) and everyone sees that the baby's point is proved. Trying desperately to help the situation, I place the complaining baby on its stomach and push hard on its shoulder to pop the bone back into its socket. To my horror, a little piece of bloody flesh squishes out from under the shoulder blade. The dream fades to black like a movie.

About Blood (i)

Some nights over the years when Theo was staying, he had nosebleeds. He would start crying quietly and Mani, who still shared his room with Theo, would yell out, 'Mu-um! Theo's bleeding'. Theo never cried out loud, never drew attention to himself except in passive, self-punishing ways.

I'd come running in and there would be blood smeared and dripping down Theo's face and pyjamas and on the sheets; tears rolling silently over his so-pale cheeks. I would be nearly dancing about with the horror of it, blood vessels breaking, blood surging where it shouldn't, the absurd bright redness of it – who'd have thought there was so much blood in the little boy – my heart pumping in awful recognition, but at the same time I was very calm. I'd get ice and hankies, cuddle Theo's trembling body, find some old pyjamas of my son's and change Theo – rolling back the too-long sleeves – find clean sheets, strip and remake the bed, soak the sheets in cold water.

After both boys were tucked back in, foreheads stroked, cheeks kissed, I'd sit down feeling stained and a bit queasy. Sometimes I'd ring my mother, who had been a nurse, and talk about it. 'Better a nosebleed than anywhere else,' she'd say, and we'd both be silent a little longer than was comfortable.

About Blood (ii)

A Maltese woman in the writing class said that she loved to walk around the house singing opera at the top of her voice, 'Because opera is controlled screaming.' She was a beautiful woman with a twelve-year-old daughter as beautiful as she was. She once said that if anyone harmed her daughter she would kill them; she would cut their throat. She said it in a way that you knew she meant it – she would actually find and kill anyone who harmed her child. I don't think she was bloodthirsty but she was the only woman I had ever met who has sworn to spill another's blood if the circumstance arose.

About Blood (iii)

In the writing class Michel read his story carefully, trying to make sure his English was clear. He was a boy of eleven on an Algerian wharf during the war for independence. Hundreds of French–Algerians were milling about on the wharf, all trying to get on boats of any kind to escape across the Mediterranean. There was noise and urgency and Michel had no idea where his mother was. An Arab–Algerian arrived on the wharf and suddenly the frantic atmosphere changed in a menacing way.

Rumour was the Arab had been involved in smuggling guns, probably for both sides, and he too had to escape the rebel Arabs. But he had leapt into the fire. The boy watched the crowd as it metamorphosed into a mob and gathered around the Arab, crying, 'Traitor, traitor'.

A large woman pushed the Arab on the shoulder and he stumbled a little, pleading, 'Leave me in peace. For the love of God.' A weedy man was aroused to shove the Arab in the face, hissing, 'Leech, leech'. The boy's heart beat fast. He recognised mortal fear in the man's eyes, although he had never seen it before.

Someone noticed the boy in front of the crowd and pushed him away. Hands bundled him backwards until he couldn't see the Arab at all. He tripped and fell heavily on the wooden planks of the wharf. There was a horrible cry, 'Mon Dieu, mon Dieu,' which gargled and choked at the end. Michel saw a bloody knife with a beautifully carved handle thrown down through the forest of legs and he watched it skitter across the planks and disappear under a coil of rope. The mob moved as one to the edge of the wharf, then there was a loud splash as something heavy was heaved into the sea. Michel saw nothing, except where the knife had gone. In a few minutes, unnoticed, he crawled across and reached under the rope.

The writing group sat, pens in hand, ashamed of pallid suburban childhoods. Michel reached into his pocket and pulled out a knife with a beautifully carved handle and put it on the carpet in front of his chair. I stared at it, somehow surprised that it had no blood on it.

About Blood (iv)

Over the summer Theo left, I brewed the Chinese herbs in the kitchen every evening. The herbs were said to increase 'blood energy'. (In western medicine I guessed it must be to do with stimulating hormones to encourage menstruation and libido, but 'blood energy' sounded accurate enough.) The process was something of a ritual and I felt like one of the weird sisters in Macbeth – flapping clothes, wild red hair, bat's wings, eye of newt – it made the flesh on my skull creep.

I peered into the brown paper bag of herbs first, a thrill pulsing somewhere. There seemed to be a recognition, a memory, at the sight of the dried fungi, the sticks and leaves and roots mixed together in the bag. There were black rubbery licorice-smelling slices too, and little white chunks of something that looked like dried tofu. I tipped the lot into a Chinese pot – it was a blackened ceramic pot with a spout and a handle on either side like two stumpy uplifted arms, then I added three-and-a-half cups of water and swirled it around and put the pot on the gas stove (it needed a little fire of sticks and heather, a dim hut, a spell or two). The first time Theo was still there and he watched me, fascinated and a little suspicious. The pot steamed away on the stove for more than an hour, filling the house with an acrid, evil smell. Anthony complained, saying it made the place smell like a witch's den. I said, at least he didn't have to drink it. The mixture brewed down to a single cup of thick black potion that tasted even worse than it smelt and caused an involuntarily shudder as I sipped it. It felt as if I was drinking black blood.

Fourteen

There is something here at the beach-house making me feel closed in, cramped. The sarsaparilla and coachwoods crowd around and I suddenly realise the claustrophobia is because I can't see enough sky. I walk out the back where there are fewer trees and there is some release. I keep walking, following the road along the lagoon and then take the path down to the beach. It's a long beach, the lagoon dividing it about two-thirds of the way along, and there are tree-covered headlands at either end. I sit, hunched against the autumn evening, and watch the waves for a while. They are subtle waves, not roaring and dumping but slapping softly and making intricate patterns as they run up the sand.

I keep going over the necessities of the summer of the singing lessons. It's clear now that in telling about Theo leaving, the story of Dina has had to unfold. One wave on a diagonal to the beach slaps into another and a new, absurdly complex pattern is formed. This is the way it is. But what of the singing lessons themselves? I'm not sure, but I'm beginning to see they were more than an effort to distract from my losing him, and certainly more than a vain attempt to link myself with her.

Lesson Three

Night thoughts: you are getting no better, you are only going to make a total fool of yourself again. Give up. The world can do without it. The obsessive determination to learn to sing was releasing its hold, as if I'd taken a drug that was losing its impact. 'In Xanadu did Kubla Khan/A stately pleasure-dome decree.' But the caves of ices were melting and the damsel with the dulcimer had put it down and was leaning on her elbows waiting for something else to happen.

When I woke again the night thoughts were dismissed. I arrived early for the lesson in the afternoon, waiting by the door, letting the heat soak in. Sweat ran down under my arms. There was silence all around; not even the cicadas could break through the weight of heat.

The teacher came down the side of the house singing, 'Sing right fol rol, the diddle all the dee.'

In my present mood the meaningless words irritated intensely.

'Hello there; sorry I'm late,' he said gaily.

We went into the studio and I sat myself on the chair while he picked up his guitar. My stomach tightened as usual and I was conscious of a bunched fist of urgency in my chest. He plucked the note and I took a deep breath and looked away out the window at the bush.

'La, la, la, la, la.'

My voice disappeared thinly in the heat, strained and wavering.

Teacher sighed a little. 'Try this.' He stood up in front of me. 'Put your hand here on my chest.' He indicated the bare skin at the top of his chest, the triangle of smooth brown skin between his unbuttoned shirt and throat.

I put my fingers lightly on his skin, gazing conscientiously at my own hand.

He began singing. The vibration of his throat and upper chest buzzed through my fingertips and palm. I suddenly realised his body was the instrument, that singing came from the bones and muscles and orifices of the body. He breathed in and lungs and ribs pushed the air back up through the vibrating voice folds (all of them: squamous; rubber bands; gelatin; cotton thread), and his mouth shaped the sounds as if it were eating fruit. It came from the body; no amount of ideas or theories or even will was going to help me.

'Now you do it. Try closing your mouth and humming the notes.'

I closed my lips and tried to make the sound inside my mouth. The sound was thin and I trailed off.

'Yes,' he said, 'but you are not letting go. You have to learn how to let go, surrender.'

Let go! I felt my skin burning. I hated the idea that thinking stopped you from feeling, that your mind had to surrender control before you could express your heart. I wanted to defend myself, sarcastically say I *can* think and feel at the same time you know, but the accusation cut sharply. What if he was right; what if I did control too much with intellect? And worse, what if I did let go and there wasn't anything behind it? Just a blank, unfeeling flatness observing the world. What if I was nothing but the facade of mind? In that moment it felt utterly true. The truth about me had been revealed: I was entirely empty behind my well-made skin of thoughts. In the heat of the day a weird desolate coldness seemed to settle in my guts.

It was aeons later but only a second. I was still standing in the room, hot and bloodless, my skin cut away in front of him

'Okay. It's okay. We'll get there.' It sounded as if he was talking to himself. He wasn't even looking at me. 'Let's try something else. Let's try this nursery song. Row, row, row your boat.'

I stared at him. I couldn't sing a note and he wanted me to sing a whole line.

'Row, row, row your boat,' he sang.

I tried it, feeling more empty and foolish than I'd ever felt in my life.

'Merrily, merrily, merrily, merrily. '

'Flat. Try again.'

'Merrily, merrily, merrily, merrily.'

'Again.'

Life is but a dream.

That night I dreamt the words 'slough of despond'. There was no story or images this time, just the words. It was melodramatic given I was only trying to learn how to sing, but that's the way my imagination inclines at night. It grabs its chance for Gothic extremes when the conscious mind is half asleep, pulling out images of eternally slipping mountainsides, girls with bunches of hair sprouting from their shoulders, caged lambs in dungeons, bombs exploding inside my head.

Being Bad at Singing

Why is singing so frightening, so threatening, when speaking isn't? It's still just air flowing over vibrating gelatinous, cottony and rubbery folds. Why does being bad at singing feel like a failure at something fundamental to being human, a fundamental lack? Like having no heart or no soul. It's not the same as not being able to write well, or paint well. Singing badly, singing off-pitch, having a thin voice, wobbling on the note – the humiliation is irrational and overwhelming. Like being forced to strip naked on a stage.

The Difference Between Speech and Singing

Sound is created by air vibrating the vocal folds. When speaking or singing, there is always an underlying 'note' or pitch to each sound. The pitch is defined as the average rate of vocal fold vibration and is measured in cycles per second, or Hertz. For pitch to rise the vocal folds must vibrate more quickly – they do this by stretching and becoming thinner. Throat muscles tense and thereby stretch and thin the folds which raises the pitch. Pitch is lowered when the muscles draw the cartilage in and so relax the folds. It is the same for speaking or singing.

In purely physiological terms there is no difference between speech and singing, i.e. the vocal folds perform in exactly the same way for each act. But if we think of the differences between singing and speech acts, then we can conceive of the likely differences in some of the physiological manifestations.

In speech we use words rapidly. In singing, the phrases are longer, more drawn out. So the breath depth and timing is different. Therefore the vocal folds are vibrating for each vowel for longer periods.

In singing we also use what we call different voice 'qualities'. When we sing in different voice qualities the folds themselves are still working in the same way, but the rest of the throat above the level of the vocal folds will change shape according to the 'quality' being sung. Technically, we say that voice quality depends on vocal tract shape ie supraglottic differences.

Alison Winkworth
Department of Speech Pathology and Audiology,
University of Queensland

Singing requires the production of prescribed pitches of a prescribed duration. In speaking, people create their own pitch and duration of sound. This is the fundamental difference.

Janet Rodger
Pacific College of Music

> In terms of physiological differences between speaking and singing, there really are none beyond the fact that singing is a heightened form of speech.
>
> There are no special muscles or organs that become engaged just for singing, they're all used in speech as well. The vocal folds sustain specific pitches in singing more than in speaking, but function in the same way. Increased resonance in the voice makes singing more beautiful, but it isn't required. When you look at the fact that everyone has a normal 'shower and car' voice that sounds very much, if not exactly like, their speaking voice, then it's easier to see. People with highly developed skills as singers (opera singers, for example) have simply trained the same muscles used in speech to function at a higher level of energy for singing.
>
> Kevin Robison
> Director of Music, Pacific Conservatory
> of the Performing Arts

In Zemlin's *Speech and Hearing Science* there's lots more technical detail about the 'Bernoulli effect' and how it draws the sides of the glottis together which the air has to force open ('the stream of air is chopped up to make waves of sound'); and also detailed descriptions of the different modes of vibration in chest and head 'qualities', but none of it alters the fact that there is no fundamental physiological difference between speaking and singing. Physiologically speaking, if I can speak, I can sing.

Not Singing

Dina couldn't speak or sing. After two weeks she remained in a coma, a still shape in the bed, a strange pale cocoon, Mrs Dina Griffen printed neatly on her patient ID card to distinguish her from the other pale cocoons. I'd never thought of her as a Mrs before. It made her sound like someone else, like a nice suburban mum. You wouldn't imagine Mrs Griffen in a suede hands-on-breast-and-crotch dress singing in a Tokyo nightclub.

The second time I visited Dina, during the second week, a wave of friends came at once: actors, designers, singers, and it was like a party in her room. Cathy, Mish, Bob, Chrissie, Pia, Monica, Roger. (Mish and Bob and Cathy were the only ones I'd already met). They were good-looking, well-dressed in an artistic way, vibrant, although a bit more subdued than usual. It was a strange sort of party with the guest of honour unconscious and not looking so stylish.

Dina lay unmoving. Her hair had grown a little, a black fuzz, and the bandage had been reduced to a dressing over the incision so you could see clearly the sunken curve of her temple. She was wearing her own opal-patterned night shirt instead of a hospital gown, but there were still tubes going into her throat and nose and arms and her skin was still pasty and greasy. She had not roused at all from her coma, but every now and then one of us saw her eyeballs moving under her eyelids.

'Look, look,' we cried to each other. Soon she will wake, soon she will be back.

A nurse came in and out to check the tracheotomy tube or the catheter or the rate of flow of the naso-gastric tube which went in through one nostril and down the oesophagus into Dina's stomach. When she was in the room we were quiet, or talked amongst ourselves.

When I arrived this particular day Cathy was already there. She was dark-haired like Dina but taller, and wearing a black wool dress which I knew was one of her designs. (The 'look' of all this seems important – it's like a play in my mind now, the antiseptic-smelling set and the elegant actors, the bit-part nurses.) She was sitting with Dina, stroking her hand, her fine bony hand. I sat down on the other side of the bed.

'Hi, Dina,' I said selfconsciously. It was like being caught greeting a blank-eyed store dummy.

'Hello,' said Cathy. 'I'm Cathy.'

'Hello. Yes, I know, I met you briefly at Dina's. You were just going one day when I called in there.'

'How do you know Dina?'

'I'm a local. I live around the corner from Kit and Dina.'

'Uh-huh. I'm a designer. Dina worked with me. For years.'

I didn't want to say 'yes, I know' again so I nodded. Some kind of hierarchy of friendship was being established. We continued chatting awkwardly, looking at Dina as if she was part of the conversation. The muscles of her face were slack so that her mouth fell downwards at the corners, her whole face set in severe, inward falling lines. I didn't want to look. She couldn't look away, couldn't stare back, couldn't rearrange her face to more appealing lines or poke out her tongue at me. And the horrible greasiness of her skin.

Monica, the torch singer, and Pia, an actress, arrived together in a flurry of scarves and lipstick and kisses. Cathy and I stood up and moved back from the bed. Somehow we already knew some of the etiquette of hospital visiting. Pia and Monica both kissed Dina's cheeks – it was difficult to avoid tubes and bandages – and then sat and held one of her hands each. Their 'Hi, Dinas' were not as awkward as mine, both of them carrying off with some kind of grace the weirdness of addressing someone who could not answer. There was a kind of stubbornness too, though, in their manner, in everyone's manner, an edgy refusal to accept that lovely, slightly wicked Dina could be blighted like this. It could not happen to one of the beautiful ones.

Chrissie had already made a poster of photographs of Dina: the jeans-wearing, ponytailed one with Theo to her cheek; a publicity shot from the opening of the resort, Dina elegant in black, her hair in a French roll; the Happy Families shot of her and Kit and Theo seated on a bench, Kit's arm around her shoulder; a wedding photo taken on the headland at Tamarama, only ocean and sky behind her. Threaded between the photos were phrases, 'We love you, Deen', and 'Come on, girl', and flower doodles and glitter. There were vases and vases of flowers and dozens of cards around the room too; on both bedside tables and on another table the nurses had had to bring in especially. They weren't the usual hospital offerings, carnations or sweet williams, but large exuberant flowers, tiger lilies and proteas and giant orange and purple gerberas, and a huge blue bowl of floating dark red camellias.

There were presents too; Paloma perfume, sexy-smelling soaps, cassette tapes – kd lang and African Sanctus – and bits of dyed fabric for her to look at when she woke up. Pia had brought chocolates which we ate, telling each other that Dina would forgive us when she found out.

Dina's wedding rings were stolen. There was a diamond ring and a plain gold one. They had been taken off her hand and placed in her bedside drawer. I don't know why – I suppose it was part of surgical preparations before the operation on her skull. Anyway, someone stole them. We thought at first, snobbishly, that it must have been the cleaners on the wards, but Kit suspected that it was a boyfriend of one of Dina's visitors who had a cocaine habit. Kit had been staying calm, discussing horror with doctors and surgeons and nurses in his steady way, but the stealing of Dina's wedding rings enraged him. 'She was powerless,' he said. 'They stole from a woman who was utterly powerless.'

Fifteen

Wolves (i)

I walked about the yard with Theo in the early weeks after the haemorrhage. He held his body stiffly away from mine as if he didn't want to be carried, but if I put him down, tears started to flow. I wouldn't know he was crying unless I looked at him because he didn't make any sound, just tears rolling down. So I'd pick him up again and we'd continue our awkward walking. His plump legs splayed out around my hip and one hand sat above my breast as if for balance. It made me feel shielded – as if no-one else was allowed to approach me. I carried him and talked to him, pointing out the wattle blossoms, the creek running over rough sand, the rosellas on the seed tray, the spider's web. We listened to the whip-cracking song of a whip bird and the oodle-ardle-wardlings of the magpie, and I chattered on. He didn't want to play in the yard by himself – he said there were wolves down the back.

He was taken to visit his mother two or three times a week. Kit thought it was important that Theo saw her and understood that his mother had not just abandoned him. I have no sensible idea of what a two-and-a-half-year-old might have made of this shaven-headed, very still mother with a hole in her throat and tubes dangling everywhere. Kit explained that she was 'sick', and Theo listened silently, but the sight of her, even to us with a larger range of images to fit her into, and without the desperate need for her to be our mother, was nightmarish. There well might be wolves down the back yard.

Wolves (ii)

One Saturday midway through the summer, the singing teacher had a gig performing at the opening of the new post office at my local shops. I caught the faint shadow of embarrassment in his eyes as he told me and looked away quickly. I said I would see him there and then wished I hadn't.

I wondered what he would sing. I thought minstrel ballads – I could see him travelling from far towns, traversing woods filled with wolves and robbers and listening to tales in marketplaces. When I walked past the post office on Saturday morning, he was plugging leads into amplifiers and adjusting the microphone.

'Hello,' I said quickly.

'Hello,' he said. The shadow flitted through his eyes again.

'I see you exist outside of the singing room,' I said.

'You too,' he said.

'Yeah. See you in a while.' I went into the post office and by the time I'd emerged he was singing with a small crowd in front of him. He sounded nervous. I went to the supermarket and the greengrocers and then to buy some fresh rolls at the cafe, criss-crossing back and forth through the sound of his voice. He sang laid-back songs from the sixties and seventies: Cat Stevens, the Beatles, Bob Dylan, Simon & Garfunkel, Joni Mitchell, Carole King – the songs that were on the radio when I was a girl.

When I was a girl. The pang of lost youth pulsed around the shopping centre. Our music had become shopping centre songs. It wasn't just me. Most of the people buying their weekly groceries were around my age, finally realising that we were not the chosen ones any more. The saggy-bellied wolves of mortality were circling the castle walls.

Wolves (iii)

The wedding was the year before I met Kit and Dina. I've seen the photographs and the wedding invitation though. The invitation has symbolic maps of a man's and woman's heart printed on the front. The whole upper right side of the woman's heart is labelled as 'Land of Love of Dress' – I guess that suited Dina. Her ivory silk wedding dress was strapless and body-hugging – Kit said she took his breath away when he turned and saw her coming up the aisle – and he had been living with her for ten years already. In the photographs her dark hair is pulled back a little from her face (well-arched eyebrows, bright red lipstick) and then falls in tumbling curls onto her bare shoulders.

In the wedding party photo, her attendants, Cathy, Katie and two others I didn't ever meet, are all wearing ivory silk as well, but each one is of a different design and length so that the effect is stylish and very elegant. When they came out of the old sandstone church, they stepped into a white Corniche convertible belonging to their one rich friend and went for a spin along the Bondi waterfront. Kit said Dina's train floated out behind them as they Rolls-Royced down Campbell Parade with passers-by cheering and clapping as if they were in a Hollywood movie. Then there were the photographs at Tamarama headland – there's one of Kit looking handsome in a tux, standing on a sandstone shelf holding Dina in his arms as if he was carrying her over a threshold and Dina's train is billowing out across the ocean and sky, a few clouds in the blue to balance the ivory white of Dina's dress.

Afterwards they went to Katie's place where a dance floor and speakers had been set up – Kit had spent the day before assembling the dance floor – and the party was in full swing. There were performers: an a cappella group as well as Monica the torch singer, and her brother Ignatius, the lounge singer. They all sang using the high back steps as a stage. Dina didn't perform any more but she still knew lots of singers and Kit's friends were actors, so the partying went on until the next day. Everyone danced and drank sambuca and champagne and toasted Kit and Dina's future together, which no-one supposed would be any different to their past.

There ought to be a song about it. A sad love song. Ivory silk and lilies, pale indigo sky and kisses in the back seat and dancing in the wind on the cliff top. But who would want to write a truthful end to the song?

Nothing much rhymes with haemorrhage, except, roughly and unrhythmically, damage and savage, ravage. The wolves were already circling in Dina's head, and no-one knew.

Sixteen

Here I Am (i)

On weekdays when he wasn't visiting his mother in hospital, we took Theo to the local child-care centre. Kit wanted him to have the constancy of people and a place he was used to, and the staff there bent all the rules to give him child-care whenever he wanted it. I took him on the days he stayed over at our place. I had taken my own younger son there seven years earlier, and most of the same people worked there, so it was a familiar return. I sat on the little chairs as I used to when I went to pick up Mani, and ate afternoon tea with the kids and named the shape of the biscuit I was eating, just as I had before.

I'm not sure if Theo met Jason at child-care, but that's when I first heard of him. Jason played chasies with Theo all the time, he had lollies whenever he wanted, he had new Lego every day, he went for rides in the car and didn't have to wear his seat-belt. There was nothing Jason didn't have or couldn't do. He went everywhere with us, although he was always just out of sight. He came and played in our back yard and accompanied us shopping and to the swimming pool and even came on holidays with us once. I was not expected to see him or speak to him, only to acknowledge his presence somewhere just out of my vision – and to allow enough food for him on some occasions.

Theo and I were on our way to child-care one day, both of us quiet for a bit as we tackled the steep part of the hill and climbed the steps to take the short cut through the churchyard. Jason had been around for a few weeks and conversations about him usually began on the way to child-care or when we setting out for a ride in the car. As we came into the churchyard where the hill flattened out a bit, Theo started.

'I wanna go to Jason.'

'Not today. I don't know where he lives.'

'Round corner and round corner.'

'I don't know how to find his house. I don't know which house is his.'

'I show you.'

'But what does it look like?'

'I show you. I know.'

I plodded on for a bit, thinking fast. It was not good enough that I didn't know how to find the house. Adults could always find houses, they just went around corners and around corners and got there. I had to come up with a better reason.

'Well, we can't go today. He's gone to his grandma's, so he's not home.'

Theo fell silent.

When we arrived at child-care he asked me to stay with him for a while but I said I was too busy. I had work to do at home.

One day Theo told us Jason was having a birthday party and he wanted to go. He cried and cried. He stood silently in front of his father at home, tears rolling down his cheeks. Next day he told me Kit wouldn't let him go to Jason's birthday. 'You take me,' he said.

I couldn't. Although Jason had insisted on going everywhere with us for a long time, he was a boy made of need; an airy parallel boy with a perfect little boy life. He existed in elaborate fictional detail, eating, talking, playing. His perfection naturally included having a mother. Jason's mother was always at home and she gave him cake for breakfast and let him watch television whenever he wanted.

Here I Am (ii)

This evening at the beach-house I watch a television documentary on the siege of Stalingrad. It uses original footage and interviews with old men and women who had been fierce young soldiers and street fighters in the black-and-white days of 1942. One of the men tells how they used the bodies of dead Germans for traction when their jeep wheels were slipping in the icy slush. Another man says they had piled up the frozen bodies of fellow Russians to make a shelter because bullets couldn't penetrate a frozen human body. An elderly doctor describes how the side of the Volga was so littered with corpses every evening that he could not avoid stepping on them, on their splayed legs, their outstretched arms, and how, sometimes, a voice would cry out from beneath his feet, 'Look where you're walking, you idiot. I am here.' More than fifty years later I sit in the lounge-room, envious that I have no such stories to tell.

Here I Am (iii)

All summer Ursula had been coming to writing class. She sat by the front windows, straight-backed and full of a suffering that she would not impose on anyone. She was German, with a fine high-boned face, tall and very beautiful. Whenever I saw her I felt uncomfortable, as if to meet her eye I must somehow become a stronger, braver person.

She had been a teenager living in a German children's camp during the fifties; her father was still in the army and her mother had suicided when Ursula was a baby during the war. Ursula was befriended by an older boy, about eighteen, and they went for walks along lanes through maize and rye fields, talking philosophy and exchanging delicate secrets. He was her first friend for she'd had a very solitary childhood, and she opened her heart to him. One evening in their youth meeting, without warning, he deliberately betrayed one of her confidences, exposing her to ridicule in front of everyone. The mortification and pain of betrayal almost dismantled her. But he too had shared a confidence with her – he had an intense, neurotic fear of mice. She paid a local boy to catch some for her and bring them to her in a shoe-box. She took the shoe-box and went to his room and knocked on the door and gave it to him as if it were a present. He opened the box, thinking she had forgiven him. His high screams filled the dormitory. He had a nervous breakdown and was taken away from the camp and she never saw him again.

She looked up from her reading, betrayed and betrayer at the same time. There was hurt and compassion in her eyes, but no guilt. She was the woman whose daughter had also suicided, a woman in the middle of her life without a mother or a daughter. Her eyes looked like bruised flesh but she was self-sufficient, standing alone in the world. Here I am. Even if she wasn't so tall and beautiful, I still wouldn't have dreamed of putting my arms around her.

Here I Am (iv)

When my father died, two of my older brothers and one younger sister and I visited his body in the funeral parlour. I nearly laughed at the box of tissues placed on the side table when I first went in, although I had cause to use them later. I stood there, gazing at the waxy face of my father in the coffin, wondering about his life dedicated to God and religion, and whether he had found the confirmation of the Truth he'd always been looking for. I wondered if he was anywhere.

A few years back we had been sitting in the kitchen at the oval formica table (a piece of fifties furniture Dad had bought when I was a baby – I used to play under it) and he had said out of the blue, 'It doesn't go on forever, does it?' It's another of those snapshot scenes – I can see his felt hat pushed back from his head, the wispy bits of hair sticking out, his brown arms on the table, sleeves forever rolled up, the sad faded blue of his eyes. I'd sat there not wanting to understand what he meant, I didn't want to talk about this now, but he made it clear.

'No-one knows what it's like on the other side, do they?' he said.

I had blithered on about love but from the tired look in his eye, he knew I had no idea what I was talking about. Dad and I never could talk to each other, the timing was always wrong.

I am here, Dad. Where are you? Are you anywhere?

Nothing happened. I looked at my sister and brothers; they had their heads down. I looked down at the gaudy patterned carpet and then at the plastic roses and tacky crucifix behind Dad's coffin. Minutes passed and my mind wandered. Suddenly, when I wasn't thinking anything much, I became aware of a pervading feeling of something warm and uplifting. It was gentle and enveloping, like warm summer air, and quite still. I have to say it was a feeling of love. It wasn't in me, it was in the room. I swear to this, and I swear it was my father. I had never felt anything like that before – certainly not when I saw Dina in her coffin. I didn't mention it to anyone until three or four days later, when my next oldest brother and I were painting my mother's fence and it came up in our general conversation – we had got onto death, as you might expect.

'So, you felt it too,' my brother said with a surprised grin.

It made me uncertain that when it's over, it's over, and it has made me curious.

Here I Am (v)

Dina came out of the coma in early July, three weeks after the haemorrhage. She opened her eyes and seemed to see Kit. The doctor said it might not have been the first time. She might have drifted towards the surface unseen, felt the lumpish weight of a body slowed to idling around her, a fog of pain in her head; perhaps a shard of memory, antiseptic light burning her pupils. Then let her eyelids fall back into her body, a Gregor Samsa creature without a carapace, needing to remain in the dark.

But the eyelids lifted again and there was a face. She recognised Kit – he saw that she recognised him. I don't know what he said to her, what he explained, what she understood. I've never asked and I don't want to imagine such a conversation, such a monologue. It seems too private for anyone to overhear how he phrased his sentences.

Kit rang and told us: 'She opened her eyes! She's conscious. She's back!'

It was the moment waited on, imagined, but it seemed a lifetime already since the haemorrhage. Adjustments had been made; now there had to be a tremor of readjustment. The still quiet Dina was the one we'd grown used to. She was awake now. She would see us, gaze on us.

'Come and talk to her,' he said. 'She can't speak, but she can hear.'

'Yes, of course, yes.'

But I was busy with classes, so it wasn't until early the following week that I made time to see her. Made myself see her. The desolation of the mid-afternoon hospital car-park gnawed as I entered the shiny new foyer of the hospital. Take the lift up to the third floor, squeak my way along the corridor. This is a strange pathway to know; the way through the labyrinth to Dina's damaged brain and body. My stomach twisted. *She will look out and see what is in my eyes*.

I walked into her room. Kit was already there, holding her tightly bunched hand. She was propped up, not sitting, but her head up far enough to look around. As I sat down her eyes flicked towards me, too fast to see anything, then back to Kit. Someone had tied an emerald scarf over her head gypsy-fashion, so that she didn't look quite so bizarre, although the tracheotomy tube was still there in her throat and the naso-gastric tube in her nose. She had been awake for four or five days.

'Hello, Dina. How are you?'

Her brown eyes flicked towards me again, the polite stupidity of the question reflecting back in her flat gaze. Could she see what was in mine?

'Not so good, I guess.'

Her mouth, her lips, seemed to twist a little, perhaps a smile, then her gaze shifted back to Kit. Her face was thinner than before and because she could not move many of her facial muscles without great effort, the lines were severe.

'I have to go,' Kit said to her. 'I'm picking Theo up from child-care.' Then he looked at me. 'Talk to Dina. She understands, don't you, Deen? And she can move her fingers, mainly on the right. Chrissie and Cathy were here before and she stroked their hands. Tell her about anything; what you've been doing, the goss, the weather, it all helps fill in the blanks.'

He looked back at Dina. 'See you tomorrow, Deen.' He leaned over her and kissed her on her lips, which looked strangely rubbery and unyielding. Dina used to have such cupid's bow lips, such a sexy smile, such an earthy laugh. Her lips did not move and it struck me that it must be like kissing a corpse and, because it wasn't a quick peck but a proper kiss, I looked away studiously at one of the cards on the bedside table.

'Oh, and she can indicate no or yes by blinking. One blink is yes, two blinks is no.'

'I brought some books. I guess I could read to her.'

'Yep. Or just talk. Talking is good.'

After Kit left Dina closed her eyes without looking towards me at all. I sat for a while wondering what to do, then I touched her hand.

'Do you want to go to sleep, or shall I read to you?'

She didn't move. Her eyelids stayed shut. I suddenly realised she couldn't answer my question. The 'or' made it impossible for her.

'Sorry. Do you want to sleep?'

She blinked once, twice, then looked at me full on.

Suddenly, here it was. The whole story. It was as if she dropped the veil of decent misery and let me see what was really there.

Here I am, this is the way it is. Unutterable despair. There was a coldness around her, a miasma of hopelessness. It wasn't so much in her face – she could not move enough of her facial muscles to indicate feeling – but a misery so profound it emanated from her. Her life had blown up from the inside without warning and there was no redemption anywhere in sight.

I had no idea what to say or do. I wanted to run back down the stupid squeaky corridor.

'You're feeling pretty fucked, I guess?'

She blinked once. I grinned, feeling a little absurd relief. She did understand me. A straw in the rapids. Trying to stay afloat was probably a waste of time.

I sat there and talked too much. I rattled on about Theo and my work and the weather and the book I was reading, *The Name of the Rose*. The labyrinth in the monastery was his metaphor for the way language worked, I said.

I can hardly believe now that this was my conversation with a woman who'd just had a brain haemorrhage – probably not even terror excuses me. But, despite my self-absorption, I find I can remember well those early days and the first time I saw her awake. Much better than later on. There's a vividness to the detail of her face, its pastiness, the skinhead look of her, but most of all, the vertigo of her despair. I don't think I'd ever encountered actual despair before, and so I hadn't known how cold and flat it was, how it pulled inward like an implosion or a black hole. Now I can see that there is nothing anyone can do about despair, but at the time I chattered on, trying to protect myself, make a thin fence of words against it. And against her seeing what was in my eyes.

Oh thank Christ it's not me.

Here I Am (vi)

I drank the black brew of blood-strengthening herbs down, nose pinched, gasping with the taste of it. Still there was no blood. The swelling of breasts, the extending of my belly so I couldn't stand to wear jeans, the floating indecision where I'd dither about what colour notebook to buy, none of it came. There was no-one else at home and I had work to do, manuscripts to read, but there was only flatness. The dryness of my body felt like a drought, the absence of what is needed for anything to grow, and there were no magpies singing.

I went outside and down the yard into the bush and stood in the summer heat, among the grass and the dried banksias, but did not feel connected. The bush had its own reserves of moisture in narrow valleys and pools. Me – I was a stony gully. I did not want to tell anyone else. Even explaining to the Chinese herbalist had felt shaming. It wasn't my fault but in losing desire, I had somehow lost part of 'I am', and that was something to be ashamed of. It seemed that although I had no choice I felt culpable. It wasn't just the physical loss, the terrible silence of desire, but the absence of some warm lantern that always lit the world for me. It had been there inside me for as long as I could remember, somehow intimately connected to sexuality, my secret light that made the world rosy and glowing. I had not even noticed it, took it as a natural part of being, until it left. And now in the middle of the afternoon, I feared it might never come back to me and then I would not know how to live.

I wonder now if Dina felt ashamed of what had happened to her?

Seventeen

How still and pale the lagoon becomes in the evening. As the sun leaves, the water turns pale silver and the shadows of the casuarinas make their black Chinese writing inscriptions. It seems like a manuscript in code. All I need to do is work out how to translate it.

Lesson Four

The singing teacher and I sat there facing each other politely. Hopeful enthusiasm seemed like embarrassing naivety by now. It appeared we had reached the flat plain of nowhere else to go.

'Let's give it another shot,' he said.

I did try. It was scratchy and flat and my throat was dry. The teacher tried to hide the involuntary pained look, the tightening of muscles around his mouth and eyes.

'Again.'

'La-la, la-la laaa.' My voice wobbled with the strain of going up and down, like a ewe calling her lamb.

He told me to try some high notes, to start anywhere and just keep going up and up. I tried it and felt better because I didn't have to get any notes in particular. Then he said to make some low notes, any low notes. I opened my mouth but suddenly had no idea how to make a low note, apart from speaking.

'It sounds like a talking voice if I try to make that note. Am I supposed to do that?'

'That's right. It's like talking lyrically. That's where you are meant to sing from.' He explained about chest voice and head voice and how it moved from one to the other, and that it was normal at first for there to be a point where the voice cracked.

He played a note in the middle of the scale, explaining that I should sing it with my middle voice.

'I haven't got a middle voice.'

'You will have. It doesn't just cut off.' He sang up and down an octave of notes and I could hear where it changed.

'I can hear the difference, it's just that I don't believe I can do it.'

'When are you going to have faith?'

'What?'

'Which lesson are you going to have faith by? Decide.'

I was unsure if he had been asking a rhetorical question or not. It was like being asked when was I going to believe in God. I stood there nonplussed, then suddenly, a tiny clear thought broke through the boiled-milk surface of my brain; he was saying that faith starts in the imagination. A pinprick light came on with the thought. One must imagine having faith first, it's how everything works. Believe and then jump.

'Low, low, high, high, low,' I sang. A step happened as I sang, a tiny step over the abyss of fear. I had not fallen! For the first time I'd let go and sung without thinking about it.

I made more mistakes and laughed nervously, but it didn't matter. I had understood the principle and workings of faith!

'Well,' he said, 'you are getting some of the notes.'

'If I have, it's just luck.'

'You're getting them right maybe half the time. That can't be just luck, can it?'

Even though I knew it wasn't true – I understood he was saying it to make me feel safe – I glowed like a child.

Later, when Anthony asked about the lesson, I didn't tell him about the beginning of letting go. It seemed too momentary. A few seconds of faith was precious, but it wasn't enough to say aloud. It could have blown away in the breath of speech.

My father had faith. Or tried to. It became very wobbly later on in his life when anxiety about everything hit him so that it was even difficult to trust that the next breath would come. I remember him praying the rosary when we were kids, 'Now and at the hour of our death. Amen.' There was always a slightly higher pitch on 'death' before the firm 'amen'. When I was older I argued the case with him about the rosary. 'What's the point of mindlessly saying the same thing over and over?' I said scornfully. I hadn't heard of meditation or mantras or no-mind yet. Then there was Mass in the little corrugated iron church in the paddock on Sundays, and once a month in town. It was better going to the town church because of the white marble altars and the statues and all the unknown people. There was more chance that something else might happen. In the little tin church it was hard to imagine the round white bread was really changed into God. There were no stained glass windows, no marble statues, no incense, not even an organ; change on such a grand scale probably needs the help of smoke and lights and song.

I don't know if my father truly believed in transubstantiation – or if anyone does. It's a magical change where the form stays the same but the substance is different – not any old different, but God Himself. It takes a largish leap of faith from reasonably solid ground into very thin air. It's the art of sheer extremity, like a circus performer defying the laws of gravity, transforming his human body into a feather-light shape on a trapeze. I don't know that I could ever be so acrobatic. But then, you never know. I remember climbing up one of the impossible towers in the Sagrada Familia in Barcelona, spiralling up and up the narrow spire, and it was like climbing up through a stalagmite, a fragile delicate structure, step by step, further up into something quite foolish, and I suddenly lost faith in it. I panicked and started running back down the tower, thinking that nothing so strange and fine could hold me up. But I stopped at one of the sharp corners, a tiny landing, and looked out through one of the portals and saw how far down to the ground it was. It was very far and I was held up by something imagined in Gaudi's mind. It suddenly seemed necessary that I trust in it, in what he had imagined, or else abandon all faith in what might be imagined. I stood there for a few minutes looking out at the other towers and letting my heart slow again. Mani appeared at one of the other tower's portals and waved out to me, happily, his ten-year-old adventurer's smile on his face. I turned, still afraid, and began climbing back up the tower.

On the practice tape I sighed heavily. It was impossible. High or low is okay, but a mixture of the two? It was so much easier to deal with clear distinctions, with things that are unmixed, purely one thing or the other. Black or white? Male or female? Good or bad? But of course, nothing is unmixed – even the polarities contain the seed of their opposite. A voice with only high or low notes has a gaping hole in the centre of it.

I walked up the hill Theo and I used to trudge to child-care, practising high high, low low. I began to lose my breath and had to stop halfway to give my lungs a break. I turned on the hill to rest my calf muscles as well and looked out over the mountains towards the brown haze of the city covering the plains all the way to the coast. The skyscrapers of the CBD glowed in the distance like mythic towers as the sun hit them. Suddenly, and without a sequence of thoughts leading up to it, I was aware of being in a precise moment. This moment had never been known before. It was a physical sensation like something was being poured into me, as if someone was blowing gusts of airy light into my body. Ribs expanded, mind floated; I was obscurely grateful to something for my existence. It was ordinary, utterly commonplace, but at the same time irreplaceable and unrepeatable. In all eternity this was never before and never again. 'So, here I am in the world', was the nearest my mind could come to naming it, like the embarrassed just-married characters in the Dorothy Parker story who kept saying, 'Well, here we are then'. I turned and continued on up the hill, humming a bit.

Something in the heat of the day reminded me of days at school when it was too hot but it didn't matter because I was running as fast as I could, fighting as loud as I wanted, absorbed in the moment and the heat. I started singing notes again, this time with attention but no anxiety – no-one could hear me. Suddenly, I felt a note in my mouth as full and curvy as a mango, golden and round. I didn't know a note could fill the mouth like that. It felt as if it had shape and texture, filling out my cheeks, surprising my mouth. It was only one note – I tried to repeat it but it didn't happen again – still I couldn't stop smiling. I wanted to tell someone. Hey, you, I sang a plump, full note. Of course, I wouldn't be able to do it in front of anyone else.

Eighteen

Reflection

The water in the lagoon is bright and reflects light back up into the house. A Pandora vine casts shadows on the kitchen wall. I wonder for the hundredth time at the botanist who named the vine – there's no symbolic link between this scrawny vine, at least, and the setting free of all evil. Its shadow is cool and calm but outside in the sun its leaves droop with heat.

I forget to give it water and because its twining roots are restrained in an earthenware pot, it cannot search for water itself. Its leaves are sparse and the pink trumpet flowers wrinkle and fall off, but it doesn't die because it is an Australian native and used to an environment even more cruel than the one I offer. It is thirsty but it manages to live by cutting the supply of water to its flowers, and then its foliage, to keep its roots and stem alive. The odd thing is that when I do remember to water it, the water always runs off the surface of the soil. It dries to a strange dust which acts like a kind of oilskin, repelling moisture. Holes have to be pierced into the earth with a stick and water poured down the holes for there to be any chance of the moisture soaking in.

The shadow on the kitchen wall is leafy and when the vine outside shifts in the breeze, the shadow moves in a way that can't help looking poetic. I look at the Pandora in reality – it is as ragged and unremarkable as ever, then back to the shadow, delicate and mysteriously moving. Why do the shadows of plants on walls touch the soul in that way?

Why do reflections astonish more than the thing itself?

As a child I was fascinated by the reflection of bright blue sky and drifting white clouds in the half-circle of one of the dams on the farm. I gazed into the hemisphere of the world-through-the-water, the inverted blue dome, amazed that it was so much more beautiful than the actual world and wondered whether it was possible to exist in the reflected world if I truly believed it was real. I wanted to have enough faith to fling myself into the muddy water. Years later, when I was travelling with my family, we came upon a similarly perfect reflection; there was a lake in a yellow field with a rocky mountain rising almost vertically from the further edge. We all gazed, enchanted, not at the actual field and mountain, but at the field and mountain reflected in the pond. There was the stunning yellow field and the sheer mountain stretching downwards in the shining water-world, drawing us as if a spell had been cast. It was glassy still, polished, perfected.

The Pandora-on-the-wall moves; the stems and the leaves are imprinted on one plane, simplifying the messy confusion in the actual vine. As I gaze at the shadow, the tracery of light and blocked light, I feel foolish tear-stinging recognition.

Nineteen

Books

It was about a month after the haemorrhage when Theo first made a move towards me. It was in the evening, Mani was already in bed – it was a bit later than usual, although we were never very regular about bedtime – and it was time for Theo to go too. I picked him up to carry him to the spare bed in Mani's room and, as usual, he held his body slightly away, an uncomfortable posture when you're being carried. It was the same when he sat on my lap, his plump, stocky body unnaturally straight. I jigged him on my hip, carried him out across the hall and into the bedroom, then did the 'one, two, three, toss you on the bed'. He bounced and giggled and said, 'Again.'

'Once more. Just one.' I picked him up and let him bounce back onto the bed. Then he was wriggled out of clothes and slipped into pyjamas and tucked in, blankets and sheets up to his chin, Mani's discarded furry platypus in one arm and a rag doll in the other. He lay peeping at me.

'Want a book.'

Mani turned over in his bed and grumbled.

'It's a bit late tonight. Mani is already in bed. He needs the light off,' I said.

'Want a book.' A faint quaver in his voice this time.

'All right, all right. But you will have to come back out to the lounge-room. Mani does have to have the light off. He has school in the morning.'

He picked a book, I can't remember which, although when he was older it was often the gory Aboriginal stories where scary, blood-thirsty things happened as a matter of course. There was one with lots of spearing and blood flowing everywhere and half-men/half-kangaroo and half-men/half-snakes transmogrifying on the page, which I found horrifying and which he wanted for nights in a row.

We sat back on the lounge, me sighing a bit, Theo on my lap opening the book. I curved my arms around him to hold the book but not holding him so that he could still sit up straight. I started to read. Theo gradually leaned back and then rested his head in that perfect place on the neck under the chin – the Madonna and child place. He had never done that before. His cheek had barely touched my skin when he lifted his head, quickly, awkwardly, banging my chin, and held himself upright. I kept reading. I saw Theo take a quick glance at me. He sat upright for another minute, but he was sleepy and his back slumped, his head fell again and his cheek lay in the hollow of my throat. He snuggled his head, finding the exact fit of skull, cheek, chin with my neck, chin, breast. I kept reading. In a few minutes his breathing changed to a slow, regular rhythm. I closed the book and let the peacefulness flood through my body as he lay asleep on me.

The Book

It was a month since the haemorrhage. I arrived at the hospital and looked at The Book on the bedside cabinet first. It was made of recycled paper and had a hand-crafted pink and cream cover created by Bridget, an old friend of Dina's from Adelaide, using a 'twelfth century Japanese seaweed marbling technique', it said on the label. I don't remember anyone remarking on it at the time, but looking at it now, the bubbling pattern resembles nothing more exactly than cells and veins floating, separating and reforming like an enlarged cross-section of human flesh.

In the beginning of the book someone had written: 'This book is for all of us to share our observations, insights, suggestions with one another. We cannot expect the hospital staff to offer that kind of sustenance. We must bring Dina back with our love. Let's be fierce and unselfconscious about that. It is after all what binds us to her and above all what will make her well again.'

Then I read some of the entries:

> Friday
>
> Today I saw Dina smile, something I thought I would never see again . . . Last weekend she seemed an exhausted bundle and made me think of a newborn baby, too tired to take up the task of living.
>
> Rosie

Saturday
Today I brought Dina in the cassette I promised her, kd lang, cos I know she likes country music. And a scarf sprayed with Chanel No 5. And she looked and seemed to nod and smile a little and squeezed my hand. The change in her since I was here two days ago is clear.

Miriam

I looked up at Dina and she looked back. Should I read out what people said about her, or were the entries for us, her visitors? I closed the book.

'People are saying you are doing all right,' I said.

She eyeballed me and I grinned, embarrassed. She had pillows all around her, behind her head, under her arms, between her legs. She had the green scarf tied over her head and a bit of lippy on. Chrissie must have been visiting.

Often visits would overlap and I'd talk to Cathy or Chrissie or Michele, but today there was no-one to talk to. Or at least no-one to talk back. I chatted on for a while about my week. I was writing and the workshops on the stories of people's lives had just begun again and my boys were doing well at school. It was freezing cold in the Mountains and it had snowed last week in Katoomba. What else?

The antiseptic smell of hospitals; the squeak of rubber shoes as nurses hurried past; the photos Blu-Tacked to the pale walls; not so many flowers now, only one vase in fact, yellow roses, brought by Dina's sister over from New Zealand; the trach tube and the catheter tube and the food tube; the profound misery in Dina's eyes. What was there to say? I wanted to be somewhere else.

'Theo's good,' I said. 'He stayed over last night and we read a book together.'

I held Dina's long bony right hand, the fingers curled. She squeezed my fingers. I didn't even know her very well.

Then Theo kissed me on the cheek for the first time. He had let me kiss him for a couple of weeks already, just quick accidental kisses as I picked him up that we could both pretend didn't mean a thing. Then, one evening when he was sitting on my lap in front of the television, his back curved into my breasts, my head leaned sideways over his, he suddenly turned his head and gave me a kiss. Then he quickly said, 'My mummy is sick'. The implication was clear; I may have kissed you but don't go getting any ideas. You are not my mother. Remember your place.

The next time he kissed me it was the same: 'My mummy is in bed', and the next, and the next. For weeks, each kiss was followed by a statement about his mother. He was only a chubby toddler, but he understood loyalty and knew exactly the correct rhythm and pace for forming a new attachment. I was impressed with the delicacy of his awareness, and relieved; I didn't have to make any decisions, just follow his careful lead.

Soon, he curled up in my lap in the evening, climbed along the back of the lounge and sat on my shoulders, let me kiss his tummy, came running to me crying when he was frightened by the dog outside, 'walked' around the kitchen on my feet with an arm wrapped around each of my legs, played with the necklace at my throat.

Twenty

I have The Book open in front of me now. I've brought it with me to this place on the water's edge where I am trying to tell her story. Every morning I practise singing and then I sit with The Book, remembering. It was all so long ago now that it seems like history, something that doesn't matter any more, but as I read it brings back the hospital smells, the clutter of get well cards on the bedside table, the thinness of Dina's face. It's dislocating reading the entries, the conversations we had on the page with ourselves. What I remember from those first weeks after the coma is the desperation of near-annihilation imprinted in Dina's eyes, her immobility, her silence, the stagnation of hope, our helplessness, as if that is all there was. But I find I'm wrong about that.

Monday
Dina did this:

1. Followed me with her eyes and opened her mouth.
2. Followed me and closed her eyes 5 times. I counted with her.
3. Held my hands and lifted her thumb on instruction, 'Thumb', and pressed fingers on separate instructions.

She is doing bloody great.

A Morgan

PS Also gave me a beautiful smile.

Sunday
Dina is awake and totally with me although very depressed – I asked her if she was and she nodded yes. (She can nod yes and no.) Today she understood a lot of things – she knew who I was but couldn't remember my name. She appears to understand everything that has happened.

We practised opening and closing fingers ie spreading the fingers and bringing them together, and clenching and unclenching fists. With help, Dina practised handing a marigold from one hand to the other – she could hold the marigold between her thumb and forefinger on her left hand and I guided and supported her arms and she got her right-hand thumb and forefinger onto the flower and released the left. She managed this three times with a lot of patience – it was very exciting.

Then I asked Dina to move her mouth to make vowel sounds. It was difficult but the shape of 'e' and 'o' were coming. We also did arm exercises, Dina practised pulling on my arms and I moved them in all directions, carefully.

I'm not leaving until they throw me out tonight because she's awake and I know she is feeling blue. This has been an amazing visit. Dina is back in a big way – how much is coming back I'm not sure but a hell of a lot has happened since Wednesday.

The nurse just came in and said they are going to close the trach tube soon. Then she'll be able to work on speech.

I love this woman.

I just looked up and Dina looked into my eyes and smiled.

Chrissie K

Tuesday

Well, firstly, it's really good to see so many people writing in The Book. It's important that Dina be able to read this later on when she's better and wondering what went on.

But it's also important that you <u>talk</u> to <u>her</u>. What day it is, what time, is it sunny, what it's like outside, what you've been doing. It's not a test of you or her, just talk to her . . .

The good news is that I've spoken to the neurosurgical registrar today and Dina will definitely start the rehab she needs here and then go onto a good rehab hospital. There's no more talk of dismissing her into a nursing home!!! Obviously, we all have to be patient and persistent and see her all the way through. It's very good to see everyone's love and support coming through. It restores my faith in humanity.

Kit

Wednesday
This time we get the pleasure of playing handsies with you. We played piano with your left hand and sang songs. How wonderful to feel you recovering so quickly. Most important was the gorgeous eye contact we all had going, and even may I say 'a smile' (maybe confused, maybe frustrated, understandably pissed off even). The nurse told us you were tired because this morning the physios put you in the 'The Chair'.

We've chatted until we're empty of information. We'll be back again soon

love Tyler and Stephen

Thursday
Chrissie was here when I arrived and had done physio with Dina. Dina seemed very knowing but sleepy after her exercise. She woke for a while and I soaked her hands – she liked that, a kind of pseudo bubble bath . . . Several times she moved her mouth as though she was about to break into conversation (Oh for the day!).

Cathy

Friday
DINA IS EATING FOOD!!! (WELL, CUSTARD ANYWAY.) AND THE TRACHEOTOMY TUBE CAN COME OUT REAL SOON!!! HOO-FUCKING-RAY!!!

Kit

Saturday
Theo kissed Dina on the mouth today. The first time in six weeks!

Kit

Friday
I bought Dina some yellow roses today. I chose yellow because they mean happiness and harmony. That's her.

Noela

Wednesday
Today when I came in I made a kiss-kiss gesture to Dina with my lips and she reciprocated with the same gesture. What a delight!

Cathy

I'd forgotten her daily struggle towards life, her painstaking finger wriggling and mouth stretching. I'd forgotten the time her hands were bound and her legs cased in plaster in an attempt at straightening them. I'd forgotten the excitement of the move to the wheelchair, the thrill of her once holding a cup of tea, the scarves tied gypsy-fashion over her bald head and her intense gazes and sardonic smiles. And that we really were trying to believe that she would get better.

Or is the record scribbled there in so many different handwritings only the selected, artfully shaped version? Each one of us was aware of our readers, the stream of other visitors, some of whom I never met. There was always the need to protect ourselves and each other. Writing is so full of places to hide, a labyrinth, sometimes I think its whole purpose is to obscure. It is too easy not to tell the truth.

Perhaps the diary wasn't really to provide a record of the past, but to inspire faith in a future. It is curious that Kit was the one who wrote: 'It's important that Dina be able to read this later on when she's better and wondering what went on'. I don't think he really believed that. Of any of us he was the most realistic. He was the one who sat with her every day, who gazed at the face he had kissed a thousand times and stroked the hands that had touched him on every part of his body. He probably knew all along that there wasn't any hope. Maybe we all did. We should have known, it was blindingly obvious.

Sunday

Dina, when you come out, we'll all be around. Can't wait.

Michele

I suppose we wrote to protect ourselves, to make a spell, to make it all go away, to tie it up in ribbons, to convince ourselves that we were stronger than fate, to trick fate into not picking us.

Twenty-One

Theo was gone, playing in a back yard I'd never seen. The summer had turned and evenings were not quite as long. Days were quieter now. Theo didn't tell me in our telephone exchanges what his new house or back yard was like, except that it was excellent. I didn't ring him very often. Most of our conversations had been Theo elaborating in detail about how this space pod here detached from this spaceship and then connected onto that space station – and me nodding uh-huh. It didn't translate to the telephone – his was a voice-over narration that needed the accompanying action, not a description of events. I don't know that children ever describe things, locations or people – such things simply exist and do not need to be translated.

When I eventually visited him in his new place, I saw that his back yard had once been a pretty English cottage garden but was now overgrown, salvias and foxgloves and hyacinths and daisies spilling over brick paths, a perfect combination of safety and adventure, and I felt a twinge of jealousy because I'd thought our back yard was perfect for him. While I was wandering around it, trying to find secret fault, I came upon a missing plank along the back fence that led into the park behind the house. It was behind a tangle of lilac bush and quite hidden from the back of the house. I showed Theo, saying, 'I've found your secret escape route to the park,' but he had not noticed it before. He was full of admiration for my discovery, saying I was like a magician (he had become a reader of fantasy books by this time), and my jealousy dissipated under such praise.

This was later, though. Now, as the summer drifted by, I was trying to get on with things. I read manuscripts, went to writing classes, forced myself to singing lessons. I started to keep a record of the singing lessons, telling myself it would be encouraging later to see my progress, jotting notes and bits of our conversation straight after arriving home from the lesson or the next day, writing longhand in a book Anthony gave me. I didn't notice for several weeks that the cheap hardcover notebook, imported from India, was made by Nightingale Products. The gods of coincidence have an overly obvious sense of humour.

Lesson Five

When I arrived at the teacher's house he was already downstairs in his studio. I wore a black sleeveless top and short skirt which had been okay for writing class half an hour earlier but, now that I was student, seemed attention-seeking. He didn't appear to notice my skimpiness, so I sat down and kept my hands over the ends of my knees.

Remembering the mango note I'd sung on the hill, I was filled with renewed determination.

I told him I'd been practising and he said, 'Good.'

'Ma, ma, ma, ma, ma, ma ma,' I sang. It sounded worse than ever.

'I can do it when no-one is listening.'

The teacher nodded but I could see he didn't believe me and felt a childish desire to hit him.

He made a reverberating sound in his chest and told me to try it.

'Zooooooaaaaaaaarrrrrr,' I repeated. It sounded masculine and swaggering. 'I sound like a bloke.'

'Maybe there's something unconscious in that. You don't want to sound like a bloke. You want to be small and sweet, just a little person.' He put on a high sweet thin voice as he said this.

I couldn't really see myself as a woman who made herself sweet and small. I remembered a Dutch woman in a life stories class a couple of years ago who had a doctorate from Jakarta University, who had spoken and acted like a little girl trying to please. Every day she brought cakes to give to the class, she was self-deprecating, she used a sweet high voice. She had her reasons; she was the one who had heard both her parents being tortured to death by the Japanese army.

'Yeah, maybe,' I said and shrugged.

'Have we tried "Row Your Boat"?'

Doesn't he remember what we do in class, I thought irritably.

'Row, Row, row your boat, gently down the stream.'

The teacher gave a weak smile and said I could not expect to sing unless I opened my mouth. He told me to turn my chair a little and look at my mouth in the mirror.

I turned and saw a large mirror on top of what looked like a dressing table in one corner of the room. I hadn't noticed it there before. There was a tense-faced stiff-bodied woman staring back at me. She was casually dressed in a short skirt and top but she looked panic-stricken, her mouth thin, her eyes small and flat, her shoulders hunched. She looked sour. I hated her. Suddenly I had the absurd thought that if I was beautiful I would be able to sing. My eyes shifted furtively away.

'I look so frightened,' I muttered.

'What are you afraid of?'

'Of doing it wrong.'

'What will happen to you if you do?'

'I won't be good at it.' I was speaking in circles. Should I say I just wanted to be good at everything, it's the way I was made? There was no beating the infinite labyrinthine cunning of ego.

'What happens if you're not good?'

'I won't be praised,' I said suddenly. I laughed. I'd spoken the exact truth at last. *I won't be praised.* The adult woman disappeared. I am a child who depends on praise. I live off it. It's all I eat. I stuff it in by the handful. I will shrivel up and die if I don't get enough of it but the addiction is poisoning me. I'm one of many. Not a good girl, not neat or gentle or kind or pretty. I have short red hair, badly cut by my father who cuts all our hair, chop-chop, straight around, and I'm oddly dressed in hand-me-downs, but I can read before anyone else, do sums easily, get 100 per cent in spelling. I will always be the best at Everything. There are only twenty children in the whole of the little bush school I attend; it's not difficult to be the best, but even when I go to high school it's still easy. I can still be first in Everything.

Except for music. There's music lessons, a school orchestra and choir. Everyone in the school has to be in the choir, the Music Nun insists although the Maths Nun objects. The Maths Nun dances around in a rage when we file out of her class to attend choir practice for the Centennial of the Cathedral celebrations. She is passionately in love with mathematics and cannot bear the fact that the other nuns do not comprehend that it's much more important than mere singing. For her, mathematics is the underpinning of the universe. She grins conspiratorially when I return to her class after being thrown out of choir for laughing.

I was still standing at the mirror with the narrow-lipped woman who wouldn't meet my eyes. It was two o'clock. I walked out, red-faced and queasy.

Twenty-Two

I dreamed Anthony was digging at the farm and uncovered an octopus-like sea creature. It was covered in dirt and at first looked dead, but it moved a little when he poked it with his shovel and it became clear it was still alive. It was oval, dark bluish-white and had waving but fairly short tentacles all the way around it. We were astonished to find a sea creature under the ground and decided to ring the zoo to find out what it was. But when we looked in the telephone book for the zoo number, the Z page had been torn out.

I walked up the hill to the post office and back again, trying to practise notes, softly, but it was too hot and life was foolish. It wasn't so much sex (we tried – lots of poking with the shovel), but desire I missed. So much for desire being the cause of all suffering. Life without desire felt like dead flowers in an old vase, leaves crackling, petals fallen off, dusty pollen on the table. I fell to recalling the time on a beach in New Zealand, and on the balcony three floors above a street in Barcelona, and in the writer's flat in Paris with the noisy bed, and in the garden outside the bungalow in Indonesia; sex in exotic locales – a private collection. And then there was the domestic sex collection: in the shower, standing in the study against the bookcase, up against the wall in an empty flat, on the lounge during the ads (fast). Memories didn't help and left a dreary anger.

Anthony put his arms around me. 'You don't seem any different to me.'

'It's like knowing there was such a thing as language but not being able to remember words. Or knowing there was such a thing as music but not being able to remember the sound of it.'

The next night I dreamt I was sitting on the front steps at the farm writing in a notebook. The steps were painted dark blue – in life and in the dream – and were on the shady side of the house, so it was cool to sit there on a summer evening. In winter it was cold and frosty on that side of the house and moss grew beside the steps. It was the only place on the farm where there was any sense of shadowiness.

In the dream my head is dizzy and I feel a little nauseous. I try to concentrate on the writing but when I've finished a sentence and try to read it, it becomes incoherent. There are letters from the strange end of the alphabet scattered throughout all the words *Thxye chixyzld isz wayxiting foryz theqr magzqypie tox blinxqzk.* Then all the letters jump about and jumble completely; I feel an explosion in my head and am aware of sinking down into unconsciousness. As I disappear, terrified, into blackness, I tell myself I must remember to keep breathing.

I woke with my heart beating hard. It was just another reworking of Dina's story, wasn't it? It was seven years since she died and still my mind wouldn't leave it alone. Somewhere in the dark, on nights when the dream symbolist can't be bothered, the dream historian keeps retelling the days, months, years, in its own stubborn way. It uses straightforward fictional techniques – changing times, places, adding a few characters – which don't go far towards hiding the autobiography. I suppose it's doggedly trying to remind me that the past is always present. But why was I dreaming death? The mind dreaming its own annihilation has to be some kind of spell – a ritual theatre enactment to stave off the actual.

Or was it a portent? No, I must not even think it. I must quickly undo it. *?tnetrop a ti saw* rO.

'Like frogs with holes in them and worms coming out the holes,' my father said one day out of the blue. My heart thumped madly. It has always scared the wits out of me when language and perceptual reality start floating apart. I know they are both human constructions and that there's no law of nature binding them together, but that's no comfort when your father is saying weird things under the jacaranda tree outside the psychiatric ward.

I used to visit him every week straight after the narrative class I was teaching at the time, and my mother and I would sit there pretending that we hadn't heard anything about frogs or worms. I wrote a story about it a while later – my father having a nervous breakdown, his sentences fragmenting and me teaching narrative at the university. It seemed a dissonant enough juxtaposition of events.

I don't know why I was the one teaching narrative as I've always found story line tricky. For me, writing is a lacy simulacrum of life and the shapes of lives seem to wander intricately in all directions or stop suddenly without any narrative preparation. But it was a mainly theoretical class with discussions on discontinuous narrative and the unified subject, that sort of thing, so it was okay.

My father's narrative had become a bit discontinuous over the last few months despite my mother's best efforts to help him sew it together. She had even taken him on a holiday to Manly in an effort to connect him to the story of our family holidays when we played on the beach and he was our lifeguard and life was joyful necessary work, but it only made things worse. She rang me from Manly and said it was impossible. They couldn't leave the house because every time they walked out the door, he would have to go back in to check everything was turned off – again and again. He had lost all faith in the possibility of continuity – nothing might last more than the moment. Anthony drove down and brought them both home to our place in the Mountains to think about what to do next.

A couple of days later we lost my father in the bush surrounding our house. We hurried through the bush past cliffs and caves, yelling 'Dad, Dad' in loud angry voices. When we found him he was crawling on all fours under an overhanging rock, sobbing fragmented phrases from sermons about Satan and angels and God into the porous sandy soil.

I don't know the whole story. I don't know why a man who loved his family, was proud of being a farmer, loved the earth beneath his feet, why he fell into the abyss of meaninglessness where everything is terrifying, but I know it was something to do with God. He had always longed to know God. He was honest and just and generous in all his dealings to please God, he gave ten per cent of his own small income to The Poor, he prayed with his family every day. I suppose at the psych ward they were used to dealing with the longing for God – they gave him the shock treatment, his sentences misfired for a while, and then he was allowed to go home.

I visited him at home a while later and we sat at the formica table. I'd told him I was giving writing classes for older people.

"It would be a good thing to be able to write,' he said.

'It's never too late,' I said, a bit disconcerted by the sound of longing in his voice.

'Yes, that's true,' he said tiredly. I could see he didn't believe a word of it. He already knew things didn't go on forever.

The Book

What's the matter?'
I am just feeling blah.
Is there anything I can do? Anything you want?'
I just want to wake up feeling normal.

This last sentence, written in The Book in Dina's new tiny handwriting, was almost illegible. At the time we thought she'd written 'I just want to wake up fucking normal' and everyone cheered her feistiness, but looking at it again, it's definitely 'feeling'.

It was difficult for her to hold a pen at all. By August, nearly two months after the Event (as doctors referred to it), some movement and control had been restored to her right arm. She could curl her fingers loosely around a writing implement if it was placed correctly, but the sweeping forward movement of handwriting was beyond her, so the words were tiny, cramped, falling down the page. Kit wrote questions for her in his large blocky script – I don't really know why he wrote them at all as Dina could hear. He had even found that she could speak a word or two if he asked her a direct question and then pulled her jaw down to initiate the physical act of speech – upper glottic space and tongue and soft palate shaping the sound from the vocal folds. I tried to do it once myself, seizing the sides of her jaw with both hands and forcing it open with my middle fingers in the jaw sockets and thumbs pushing downwards on her chin, but it felt too intimate, too invasive. What if she hadn't wanted to answer me anyway?

Nicole, the speech pathologist, had been working with Dina for several weeks. There was a set of exercises that all her visitors were supposed to help her with, designed so she could practise making the shape of vowels and consonants. Nicole wrote in a green Victory brand exercise book:

> Using small amounts of sherbet or jam (to increase the amount of oral stimulation) as targets, encourage her to:

1. Lick her top lip with tongue tip
2. Lick bottom lip with tongue tip
3. Lick around teeth
4. Reach the tongue depressor held just outside her mouth with her tongue
5. Reach up behind front teeth with tongue tip – if possible.

I have also tried the lollipop (Chup-a-chup) with good results. She curls and waves her tongue around the lollipop. This is good as internal tongue movements are also important for moving food to the throat.

Also practise some consonants to encourage alternating tongue movements:

1. t-t-t-t-t-t
2. p-p-p-p-p
3. k-k-k-k-k-k
4. p-t-p-t-p-t-p-t
5. t-k-t-k-t-k-t-k

It was the painstaking work of recreating the neural pathways between brain and vocal folds, brain and tongue. She made the shape of a 't' first and then other letters, but no real sound came out until Kit tried the jaw-forcing.

Twenty-Three

The Gift of Losing Memory

It was still the summer of Theo leaving and the stormy tropical weather had passed leaving a searing heat, deadening inside the house and blinding outside. In the house-yard azaleas burned brown and the rhododendron leaves folded down like collapsed parasols. At writing class there was a community of endurance, a kind of pleasure that we were all sharing the intensity. We sweated even though we sat still and even though we wore clothes we normally only unpacked at the beach, tiny singlet tops and dresses. One of the storytellers opened the doors and windows, and another one sighed in delight at the little draught of air on the back of her neck.

But even with the grace of summer breezes, there was one storyteller who irritated. Sue had already arrived wherever she was going, was never foolish or fragmented, was pleased with herself and her own goodness.

'Of course, I always greeted the poor old men who were down and out. Even when I was with my fancy friends.' She sat with her kind expression, her hands in her lap. I nodded tersely.

Belle, a nuggety sharp-eyed Londoner, saved her from my irritability by beginning to read. Belle was white-haired and small like anyone's grandmother, and looked as if she'd always worked hard; the sort of person who'd pick the pieces up after the bomb had dropped and then find bread to put on the table with a smart remark to go with it. She read her story with a distinctively English working-class accent.

Belle had loved school and was a gifted student but she had had to leave when she was fourteen to care for her invalid mother. It wasn't fair but that's the way things were. After a time her father stayed home and she went to work in the public service to support the family. She discovered she was also a gifted athlete and began to train before and after work and was soon selected in a team for the upcoming Olympic Games. But it was 1939 and the world was getting ready to contort itself for war rather than sport. Belle's chance to run in the Olympics never came.

Just as war broke out she became engaged to a young soldier who went off to the Far East. She didn't see him again for four years. When he did return she barely recognised his skeletal frame and haunted face; he'd been a prisoner-of-war in brutal Changi. Their next fifty-two years together were shaped and coloured by the nightmare years he had endured there. Belle didn't go into details. 'I was always loyal to him,' she said, and her edgy smile did the rest.

Then he developed Alzheimer's and although he no longer knew whom she was, Belle took care of his every need. She said it was like looking after a very large, ill-tempered two-year-old. 'The thing is,' she read, 'after all these years, he's just this week forgotten Changi and for the first time in our life together, he is peaceful.' Belle was tough, but her mouth quivered and we all looked carefully away. She didn't ever expect life to be just, but she wouldn't have wanted anyone to see that she minded.

A Birthday Gift

Theo gave me a necklace for my birthday. He had just become aware of the importance of birthdays – he was two-and-a-half himself, and counting – so he was proud of having such a fine present to give. He and Kit had been invited to our place for my birthday. Nearly bursting with delight, Theo held out a small tissue-wrapped parcel, his face showing he thought this was the best present ever. I unwrapped the tissue and found a small wooden box inlaid with ivory.

'It's lovely,' I exclaimed.

'No. Open it! Open it!' cried Theo, almost dancing about with impatience and glee.

I opened it and inside lay an antique-looking necklace made of curiously coloured glass beads joined by flat gold chain. The beads were oval and creamy like moonstones but glittered with other colours like white opals. When I studied the beads it looked as if some of them contained gold leaf or gold paper as they had a strange sheen that could not have come from just glass. I exclaimed and put them on, then scooped Theo up onto one hip and kissed him.

Kit stood back at the door watching.

'They're beautiful,' I said to him. 'I love them. Where did you find them?'

'It was an antique shop near Canberra. Years ago. I was on my motorbike on the way to Melbourne and I just happened to stop in this little town to get something to eat.'

Years ago. They were Dina's. He's given me Dina's necklace.

'They're lovely,' I said.

Theo patted the oval beads at my throat.

For a long time afterwards, whenever he was sitting on my lap, Theo played with the beads. Sometimes he asked me to take them off – I wore them all the time – and he held them in his hands and poured them from one hand to the other, or every now and then put them on over his own head.

'You be careful with them. They're my favourite beads,' I would say sternly, and he would look pleased.

I knew there was something in all this, more than his pride in giving me a present that I really did like, something more to do with it representing a bond, a contract. It took a few years, but he did make it clear. It was one evening and I was scolding him for something; I can't remember what, but I was annoyed.

'You can't be angry with me,' he said accusingly. He meant, by his tone, that I had no right to be angry with him ever.

'And why not?' I snapped.

'Because I gave you that necklace.'

It stopped me in my bad-tempered tracks. I wasn't even wearing the necklace at the time – it had broken and I was waiting to take it to the jeweller's.

The Gift of Song

To carry the key to unlocking joy and grief in one's voice seems the greatest gift to me. Most of all, grief. What an honour to be given the task of releasing sorrow. When Picasso (in the play) said what he really wanted was to be a singer of love songs, I knew he meant he wanted to be the one whose voice would pierce through the facade of control to release anguish and joy and dread, whose voice kept singing until it had even quickened the soul. No-one can say exactly what happens when we hear a song that moves us in the centre of our being. Why does a particular pitch, a particular pattern of notes, inspire or soothe us? The waves of sound from the human voice-folds in one body vibrating in the cells of another, pulling at the bonds on the soul – that tugging under the breast – that must be what it is, the unlocking of fetters.

And perhaps a human voice cannot then carry anyone all the way up to heaven – maybe only the nightingale can do that – but to be able to lift someone far enough above the waves to be in sight of a fellow amateur sailor, that would be something. I realise now that it was the desire to be a vessel that I heard in Einstein's voice; the longing to be capable of carrying the spirit across the dark seas between souls.

(Not quite a vessel – rather to be clear and empty like a transparent funnel, or a silver flute; to have both ends open so that nothing will get stuck, sides polished, straight and simple. To be a conduit, without impediment; which also supposes there is something to flow through it.)

It's perverse to long for what is not possible, and pitiable. Like Salieri, I want what has not and will not be given. Whenever I listen to a singer who undoes my tight soul – ah, see, there it is, it's quite all right really, now that it's untied, and perhaps even capable of flight – there is a pang, a shard, of envy. The singer holds me in the palm of her hand and I love her – but still I'm greedy. I can learn to sing more or less in tune – I will; with long practice it must come – but I can never be the one to untie grief. That is the gift of temperamental and unreasonable angels who drop it where they please without regard for longing.

Twenty-Four

Art

It was at my father's funeral that I first noticed the words. I had been at my grandmother's funeral several years before but I was too occupied with the reality of seeing someone lowered into a hole in the ground for the first time to hear what was being said. At my father's funeral I stood there with my mother and brothers and sisters in the old cemetery at Curra Creek and remembered that his father's family used to own this land. It was his land; he was returning to it; his bones would become part of the soil he loved. It was a bright winter's day, blue sky, freshly turned red earth.

Then I heard the words.

May flights of angels sing thee to thy rest.

A door opened through the sky. That's what happens on the other side: flights of angels singing – hear them singing – beyond the sky, through the universe, banishing all fear as they take him back to the beginning of time. My father with his flat gravel road voice, his single song, his stocky peasant body longing for transcendence, being sung at last to his home. *May flights of angels sing thee to thy rest.* Not just one angel, but flights of them, all singing for him, their extraordinary cream feathered wings beating upwards through the blue and on and out through the blackness. All around him, angels filling his vision and filling his ears. They were singing their angelic songs for him continuously, not needing to draw breath (being angels), so that he would not be afraid to leave behind the red earth of his home.

I'm not sure about heaven or angels, but I understood for the first time how words could bless. May flights/May flights of angels/sing thee/sing thee to thy rest/May flights/sing thee. The spell of the words woven between heaven and earth. The bell-like sounds, the wing-beating cadence of the sentence, the shape of the benediction, repeated in my mind. The pattern of vowels and rhythm and images was one silken cloth drawn out of the mystery under everyone's days and nights. The lovely sentence felt like a silvery blue cloak thrown over the shoulders, a traveller's cloak for journeying through the night.

And Nature

I didn't want to go back to singing class, or to practise. Why did I think transformation was possible? I knew lots of people who could sing and they were as full of shit as I was; it was some sort of arrogance to think singing would change anything. It was a battle that I didn't have before, that was all. Why bother making such a fuss about it? Compared to what Dina had dealt with every day, it was nothing. A child wailing over a present it could not have.

I made myself practise – old-fashioned willpower – then went outside to sit on the back step. Willpower hadn't brought any joy. I looked at the uncultivated bush at the bottom of the yard. Wattles, grevilleas, boronia, apricot- and lilac-skinned angophoras, creeping hardenbergia with its purple-pea flowers, ti-tree, spiky hakea, a gnarled banksia, feathery bottlebrush, bush orchids and irises nearer the creek, white flannel flowers where you least expect them, all growing where meagre efforts at cultivation ended. No human mind had applied any principles or order or design to it; there was no desire to impress in any of it. Some of the angophoras were fine specimens, tall and elegant, some thin with oddly placed limbs – one with flying limbs looked like a goanna diving into its hole; ribbon gums leaned at unlikely angles in a circle; tree ferns gathered along the creek; a scraggly stand of wattles soaked up the sunlight in a clearing. Crimson rosellas, unconscious of their brilliant colour, flashed through the bush in search of food; a bellbird sang to establish its territory, unaware of its own pure sound.

What Dina Had to Deal with

I happened to visit Dina at the same time as Kit one day. We talked to each other and to Dina although she had her eyes closed much of the time. It was hard to tell if she was asleep or just not interested in the world out there. When her eyes were open she looked at Kit mostly. Her face was thin, making her eyes look larger and her hair had grown into a nicely shaped cap, but she still didn't look like herself. The immobility of her facial muscles robbed her of the liveliness of expression that had been her beauty. We asked her questions and she blinked or nodded but didn't attempt to gain our attention otherwise. Kit and I left together and he talked about Dina's speech therapy and the fact that she could respond to conversation but not initiate it.

'Didn't you notice? She never has tried to begin anything, never tries even to get our attention. She only responds if we say something directly to her.'

'I guess it's too hard to begin something on her own. I mean, it's just too much effort.' I felt as if I were defending her in some way.

'I reckon . . .' Kit stopped, looked away somewhere. 'Well, I reckon her thought processes have to be initiated as well. I don't think she can initiate a thought.'

'What do you mean?'

'Just what I said. She can't initiate a thought.' He spoke with the flat, severe tone that he'd begun using when he made statements about Dina.

'You mean she's not thinking anything unless we say something to her. Like she's not there?'

'Yes.'

'I don't believe that.'

'You don't want to. I don't want to, but I want to be realistic. She's in a sort of fog in her mind most of the time and things only gain clarity and focus when something stimulates her mind. The thought has to be initiated from outside.'

'How can you know that?' *Shut up, Kit, just shut up.*

'I look at her. I know she's not there a lot of the time. She's not.'

The image came to my mind of a thick sea fog of nothingness with occasional islands of clear distinct thought surfacing through it. And a feeling of panic. Drowning. What if she knew when she was on an island that she had come from the soupy fog and was going to descend back into it any minute?

'I still don't think that could be right,' I said. 'She's there, she watches intelligently.'

'When we are talking, yes, but not otherwise.'

We'd reached the car-park by now and I definitely didn't want to continue the conversation. He had more authority to argue; he had been in love with her for fourteen years. I muttered excuses for having to hurry and drove away.

Maybe he was right. Maybe falling in and out of being was the only way Dina could handle it. Sometimes her written conversation was very strange, as if her mind was on another track at least.

There is one exchange scribbled in The Book that I don't remember seeing at the time:

> Did you feel you ate enough lunch? [She was being fed teaspoonful by teaspoonful at this stage].
> *Yes, I did.*
> How do you feel about what you are getting to eat?
> *OK, I guess. Logging is all starting again. Logging gets it by virtue of its whole nature.*
> That's a very interesting concept. Do you mean logging as in cutting down trees?
> *Yes. Deforestation.*

It was off on a tangent, although perhaps she was speaking metaphorically. You could easily imagine she felt deforested, a moonscape of broken stumps and stripped soil.

But memory was there. Memory was still there. I found this exchange inside the front cover of The Book:

> How do you feel today?
> *OK I guess.*
> Do you know that I love you?
> *Yes, I do.*

Then one day when Kit was with her, out of the blue she wrote a line of a Vera Lynne song:

'We'll meet again, Don't know where, don't know when.'

Twenty-Five

Days at the beach-house have become monastic. It's not just the sleeping alone or the plain eating (steamed vegetables every evening) or even the solitude, but the rhythm of work. The work isn't easy, it's a daily struggle, but it is daily and there is no longer any need to think about why. It has to be done and that is all there is to it. There is some relief in work that is without question.

Second-last Lesson

I arrived at the studio and the teacher wasn't there. I waited down the back, pacing a little, and when I heard his van arrive, composed my face and body.

'You're late today.'

'So how are you?' he asked carefully.

'I'm okay. I'm not getting any better at singing. That's all.'

'You are learning. Feeling dreadful about it is part of it. It can bring up such feelings of inadequacy that some people can't cope and don't come back. You have to have the desire.'

I felt like defending myself but there didn't seem to be anything useful to say.

'Well anyway, I'm keeping a record of it.' I hadn't meant to say that. There were enough levels of selfconsciousness already.

'Really? You are writing about it?'

'Yeah. Just notes.'

'Really? Well, I'd best get on with it then,' he said.

We began. I sang as badly as usual, missing the pitch each time. A sensation like pieces of a jigsaw coming apart, the pieces falling into shadow, flooded through me.

'I'm just noticing something,' the teacher suddenly said. 'I think you sing what you think you ought to, not what feels right. Your mind is in charge of selecting what note to sing. You have to let go.'

And you're meant to show me how, I thought tiredly. That's what you're here for.

I stood there saying nothing.

'High, low, high,' he sang.

'High, low, high.' I sang the low note too high and the high notes too low.

Pieces of the jigsaw floating wide apart.

I suddenly thought, I really can't do this. I will just give up and walk out the door.

There was a feeling of lightness as I imagined striding away.

'How did that sound?' The teacher asked.

'No good,' I said. 'I just want to . . .'

'You just want to . . .? What were you going to say?'

'Walk out,' I said, shamefacedly.

'Are you afraid of doing it badly?'

My God! Hasn't he been listening?

'Yeah,' I said in a teenage 'what do you bloody think?' tone of voice.

'Well, sing badly – deliberately. Don't even try to get the notes. Just open your mouth and sing.'

'Not even try?'

'Yep. You don't give a toss.'

He sang through different patterns of notes and I headed off into them like the girl at school in the short tight skirt and too much make-up. She was going to get into trouble, so she might as well do it anyway. Who cares? I'm bad at singing; everyone knows it and I don't care. Something loosened a little. I was getting some notes, missing as many others, but there was energy in the sound. I suddenly remembered the first time I heard Janis Joplin singing 'Mercedes Benz', how it vibrated in my guts. The yearning sound, a kind of screeching wail, divided the dry air like a sword slicing through viscera, making me want to grab hold of someone and scream and yell with desire for everything. In the mirror, my hair was untidy, cheeks red and mouth open wide. For a few seconds, the raucous sound didn't shrivel me. The desire to impress, to be thought well of, was stemmed just a little and I sang a few more raw notes.

'That note was too high.'

'I don't care,' I said.

The teacher grinned and we kept going.

Twenty-Six

Via Dolorosa (i)

In August, Dina was moved to Parramatta Hospital to begin rehabilitation in earnest. The physiotherapists were booked to work with her from three to six hours every day, depending on how tired she was. Their aim was to retrain the undamaged parts of her brain to move her limbs as well as to exercise her muscles so that they regained their strength and elasticity. Two ward assistants lifted her into a wheelchair and brought her down to the therapy room morning and afternoon. They were wheeling her down there one afternoon when I arrived.

The therapy room was huge with a polished linoleum floor and sun streaming through wide windows, a weird gymnasium full of bars and stretching pulleys and machines with springs and pedals and ropes attached. There were dozens of patients working at the exercise equipment, mostly wearing tracksuits although some were in pyjamas and dressing-gowns. They sported bandages and newly unwrapped stitches and bruised, discoloured skin, but they had the focused air of people training at a gym.

Dina was lifted out of the chair and onto a sloping board where nurses and therapists rubbed her legs and arms and urged her to move them herself. I sat down on the floor near her chair, out of the way but in Dina's line of sight.

Sandra, one of the therapists, a dark-haired woman about the same age as Dina, placed what looked like small sandbags between Dina's legs at the knees, gently forcing them apart. She then eased Dina's arms above her head and put sandbags over each of her wrists. 'So your body doesn't set like a curled-up statue,' she said.

'Wriggle your fingers and toes. There's a girl.'

Dina moved the fingers on her right hand in a stiff way as if she was air-practising the piano.

'Left hand too. And your toes. Pretend you're being tickled.'

Dina's right toes moved a little. She stared straight ahead, not acknowledging anyone's gaze or words.

'Nothing's happening on the left. Have another go.'

There was no movement. The therapists exchanged a glance.

They bent Dina's slightly splayed legs up and down, bringing her knees up towards her chest. Dina groaned a little.

'What is it, Dina? Is it your leg?'

Dina moved her head sideways once. She had learned how to do this in the last few days. It was easier to read than eye blinks.

'No? Your arms? Getting sore?'

Dina nodded her head once. Sandra took the sandbags off and rubbed the upper arm muscles, then bent the arm back and forth from the elbow. She put the sandbags back on, this time keeping Dina's arms at right angles to her body, as if she was on a crucifix.

She went back to rubbing Dina's legs and moving them gently, up and down, up and down. After twenty minutes of this Sandra and the nurse stood on either side of Dina and lifted her up between parallel bars. Still supporting her, they put her hands on the bars. One of the nurses had put Dina's Doc Martens on her – apparently they helped straighten and support her feet – so she looked like she was ready to step out, except that her legs were thin and the muscles soft as blancmange under her white skin. Sandra tapped the right foot with her hand.

'Take a step with this foot. Come on, Dina, you can do it. There's a good girl!'

The muscles tightened slightly in Dina's arms but nothing happened.

'Come on. You can do it!' Sandra and the nurse cried in unison.

The muscles around Dina's mouth moved a little and her forehead creased. Her face was sweating. She slid her right foot a few centimetres.

'Good girl. That's great. Now your left foot.'

Her right foot slid another few centimetres.

'No, the left foot. The left. There's a good girl. You can do it.'

Her right arm flexed a little. Beads of sweat appeared on her upper lip. All her weight was being taken by Sandra and the nurse but the strain on her face was excruciating.

'Come on. Try. You can do it. The left leg. Feel my hand on it.'

Dina's legs quivered but didn't move forward.

Sandra looked at the nurse, who pushed Dina's left foot forward a few centimetres.

Dina groaned.

'Sorry, Dina. It's the only way. You do want us to make you, don't you?'

Dina suddenly slid her eyes towards me. It was the first time she had looked at me. I wanted to get up and run. It was bloody hopeless, anyone could see that. Sisyphus had a dream run compared to this.

'Go for it, Deen,' I said.

She looked away again.

'The left foot. Move the left foot. There's a girl.'

Outside it was nearly spring. I could see it through the windows, the glorious sunshine, blue sky, one or two white clouds painted on. There was a warm scent of blossoms out there and people walking about with a free and easy air. I wanted to be back outside in it, with them.

Via Dolorosa (ii)

From the green Victory exercise book:

Supine No 1 – ie lying on back

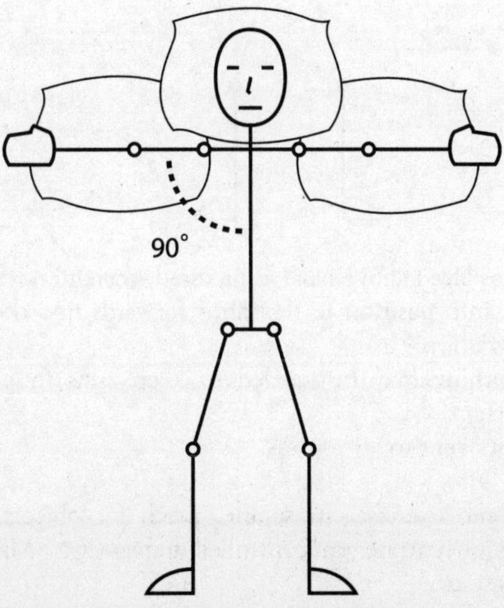

- Arms out to sides at 90°.
- It may be more comfortable to place pillows under arms.
- Something may be needed to keep arms in place eg sandbags.
- CHECK the elbow is straight.
- The arms need to be positioned in this way for at least 20 minutes every day to prevent arm muscles from becoming tighter.
- Remember to keep a pillow between legs to stop them becoming tight also, and keep legs as straight as possible.

Supine No 2

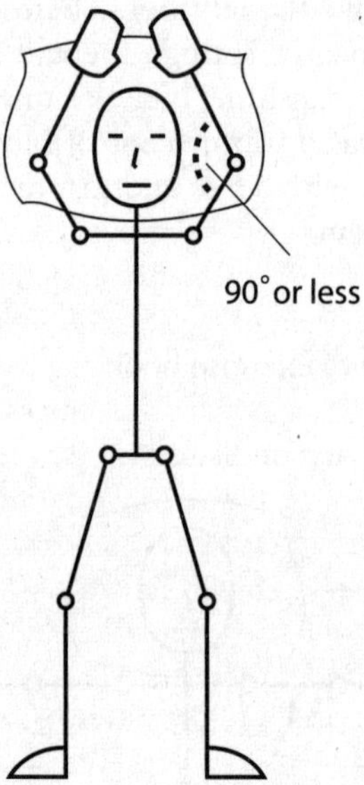

- Arms placed above head as pictured – careful not to force arms into position ie flex arms forwards first then take elbow down.
- Something may be needed to keep arms in place eg sandbag.
- Elbows bent to 90° or less.

Upper limb exercise: In supine, reach for objects, touch things. Concentrate on controlled movements. May need some assistance.

Prone No 1 ie lying on stomach

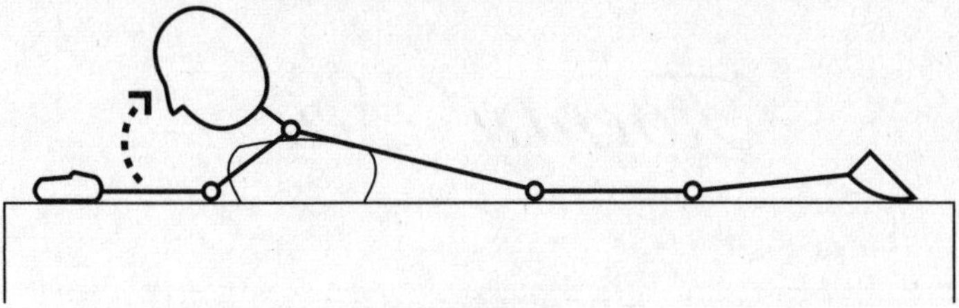

- Lying on stomach with pillow placed under chest.
- Arms forward.
- Lift head for the count of '5' five times.
- Lift each leg 5 times and slowly lower back, counting as you go.

Via Dolorosa (iii)

The eleventh Station of the Cross, part of the illustrated central story of Catholicism, is melodramatic: the dark blue of Our Lady's cloak around her sorrowful face; the dark red of the soldiers' capes and their muscular arms; His knee on the ground where He fell, the blood dripping down His face from the thorns; the miraculous cloth Veronica held. There is something about His body half-lying on the road, the cross skewed over Him, which worries more than fiercer images like the nails being driven into His hands or the Crown of Thorns being pressed into His forehead. That He fell once was bad enough, but that He fell three times was more than worrying. If He collapsed onto the ground over and over, what chance was there for anyone else? But Veronica had leaned forward, cloth in hand, to wipe His sweating face. His image appeared on the cloth like a kind of photograph and everyone looked on in amazement. She had that cloth to show as evidence that extraordinary transformation was possible and He staggered on to be crucified.

Twenty-Seven

Two kookaburras come to the railing of the verandah, demanding food. I would have thought there was enough for them in the lagoon. They look like bullies with their stocky bodies and fierce beaks, but I think of the swaggering kookaburra – hands in his pockets – in *The Magic Pudding*, and laugh at them. They still perch there, demanding with their unfeeling eyes. I hurry inside and cut two crusts of bread lengthways then put them out on the railing. The kookaburras snap them up and they both fly into a nearby jacaranda where they proceed to 'kill' the crusts, thwacking them repeatedly against the branch. One of them gives his mad-witch cackle and I feel reassured; despite discontinuities and irreversible change, kookaburras still break the silence irreverently.

In trying to chart the paths of change, the instantaneous transformation of Dina's life, the slow unfolding of my connection to Theo, the subterranean body shifts and painstaking efforts to sing, the need for something to stay the same begins to unsettle. I cling all the more to the patterns of memory, the sound of kookaburras laughing in the eucalypts on the farm. But the farm is long gone, and Dina and my father died and Theo left and other arrangements had to be made. Things have had to be put together in a different way.

The piecing together of that summer has become more about Dina than I had ever thought. I'm beginning to see that the cataclysm of her sudden loss and slow dying lay under everything that occurred later. It shook my faith in continuity, in life going on in the expected way; cracks appeared and once that happens it seems life never regains its smooth false wholeness. Katherine Mansfield wrote in her journal of a dream where she felt her life shattering like a glass mirror and after that she knew nothing was the same. She knew she was facing death.

Making Arrangements (i)

The singing teacher rang me at home. 'I meant to tell you before, but I'm moving away. Up the coast to Byron Bay.'

'No, you can't. How will I ever learn to sing?' Even as I said this there was a sense of relief; now I can give up. That was it, I gave it a go.

'We've got time for one more class. You'll be okay. '

'I won't be.'

'Yes you will. I'll ring around and see if I can arrange someone else for you.'

Making Arrangements (ii)

Despite my resistance to Theo leaving, I really only missed him – the hollow ache and repetitive mental images of missing someone's physical presence, slightly allayed by a voice on the telephone, on alternate weeks. By the time he left he had only been coming to stay every second week. Emotions had learned a timetable.

I rang Theo. He never rang me.

'How are you, my darlin'?'

'I'm good.'

'How's your karate?'

'Good. I'm going for my first grading soon.'

'Does that mean you get a belt, like a blue belt or something?'

'Yep. I'll get a yellow tip.'

'What's that mean?'

'First you get a tip. Then you get the whole colour.'

'That's good. Does your dad go with you?'

'Yep.'

We kept talking for a few minutes, the unnatural rhythms of telephone conversation, the lack of silences that occur in face-to-face exchanges making us both uncomfortable, and so we ran out of topics too fast. Tonight, though, I had a special arrangement to make.

'How long since I've seen you? Too long for me,' I said, fishing for a bit of encouragement.

'Yeah, I guess.'

'What about the holidays? How about you come and visit?'

'That'd be cool. How will I get there? Will Mani be there?'

'Yep, he'll be here. He'll be on holidays too. And I guess you will come by plane.'

'I'll have to ask my dad, but I think it will be okay.'

'We'll have to plan a few outings too. What about the Powerhouse Museum?'

'Okay.'

'And you can see some of your old friends.'

'Okay.'

'Well, all right, I'll see you then.'

'Okay.'

'Can't wait to see you. Can I speak with your dad now? I'll make the arrangements with him about what plane to get.'

'Okay. Bye.'

Making Arrangements (iii)

Kit had been halfway through a funded trainee directorship at a Sydney theatre that didn't pay much money, but After the Haemorrhage (it became a new calendar year zero), even that small income stopped. He was at the hospital every day, an hour's drive either way, and in the evenings there was Theo, so there was no chance of going to any kind of job, no matter how flexible the hours. Money had to be found. There was talk of needing to prepare the house for when Dina came home. The bathroom would have to be big enough for a wheelchair and a ramp would be necessary for the front or back door.

Michele decided to organise a fundraiser and the Brainstorm Variety Comedy Cabaret Benefit was born.

'Brainstorm?'

'Yep. What do you think?'

'It's a bit shocking. If Kit doesn't mind . . .'

'He thought of it.'

The Belvoir St Theatre was booked; a friend who was a producer offered his services; other singing, acting, dancing friends agreed to perform for free (Michele asked me to write a story for Dina); tickets were printed; a cartoonist, Phil, designed a poster.

I brought it in to show Dina when it was first printed. She was trying to do a crossword puzzle at the time, holding a biro and scrawling tiny illegible letters approximately in the squares. She stopped to look at the poster. She didn't always pay attention to her visitors; sometimes she lay there with her eyes shut or gazed at a magazine in front of her and didn't look up. She looked at the poster for a few seconds, her eyes moving sideways, taking in the panels of the picture and the names of the performers. I asked her if it was okay to put it up on the wall of her room and she nodded.

As well as a list of stars and fringe performers, the poster's six-panel cartoon illustration showed a bud or chrysalis unfolding. In the first panel the bud is tight, inert, with a background of sky and clouds; in the second there is a twist of movement as it starts to unfurl; in the third something brightly coloured is peeping through at the top of the bud; in the fourth enough is visible to suggest that some sort of creature rather than a flower is inside the bud; in the fifth the bud has opened out and a fairy-sized naked Dina with spotted wings is sitting there, eyes huge, as if amazed, besotted with the sky and light and fluffy clouds. The last panel shows the tiny-winged Dina with bright red lipstick and thick black hair, flying gorgeously, elegantly, free.

Twenty-Eight

Adoptions (i)

One day when I was a teenager my grandmother showed me a shoe-box of old photos and letters from my father. He had written the letters to her when he was in the army during the Second World War. His and other battalions had been posted to Geraldton on the West Australian coast when it was believed that the Japanese might try to invade from that side of the continent. They had travelled by ship from Sydney around to Melbourne and Adelaide, and across the Great Australian Bight to Perth. It seems absurd now to think how a few thousand men could have been expected to defend an almost limitless coastline, and as it turned out they sat between the sea and the desert for months and nothing happened while the war went on elsewhere, so I suppose there was a lot of time for letter-writing.

My grandmother gave me a letter my father had written from the ship. I unfolded the old notepaper. There was my father's handwriting in black ink – real pen and ink, not biro, firmer and clearer than I was used to, and with a young man's enthusiastic flourish. I read the letter and could hardly believe it. There on the forty-year-old pages was a poetic description of the journey, the moonlight on the waves, the glinting of light, the dolphins, the moving horizon, the cut of clouds against the sky. This was my obstinate, inflexible, conservative, tuneless father, short and stocky like a peasant, cleft palate twisting his nose and mouth. I read the letter again, seeing how the flowing hand complemented the romantic images. There was such a sensibility to beauty in his words and phrasing. My father had the soul of a poet! I was sixteen years old at the time, at the height of ungenerosity towards my father, and suddenly I was terribly proud of him. I remembered then the way he walked in from clear crisp mornings after the milking, a warm milk billy in his hand, singing his song, 'Where the deer and the antelope play.' And the way he walked around the farm in the evenings with my mother, the dusk enveloping them both, their closeness and the gentling of the light making it seem like they were weaving happiness for us in their quiet walking.

I don't know why my grandmother never showed me the letters before, or why she showed them to me that day, but I adopted a different attitude to my father after that. We still argued the case, but now I knew he wasn't just a dogmatic father. He was a young man on a ship watching the light play on the pattern of waves churning out from the stern, sitting with his steel-nibbed pen and ink, trying to express his singing soul on the page.

Adoptions (ii)

Theo asked me to stay at the child-care centre when I dropped him off there. We walked up the hill together – a long steep hill for a two-and-a-half-year-old – and up the steps through the back of the churchyard that brought us out near the centre. He started asking at the churchyard.

'Stay with me. Stay today. Just one minute,' he said. He had heard me say 'just a minute' enough times to mimic the inflection exactly.

For a couple of weeks I'd been saying I was busy and had to start work right away, until one day his pleading tone and eyes finally got to me.

'Just one minute, then.'

He held my hand as we walked in the door. I put his backpack in his locker in the foyer and then we went into the large playroom. There were five or six pre-schoolers milling about Sarah, a plump, pretty young woman, blue-eyed and blonde. She was putting balls of red and blue play dough on low tables, but the kids were more interested in her than the play dough.

Theo and I hung about. I didn't know what Theo wanted, what I was supposed to do, but it was clear we were hanging about to some purpose. His hand held three of my fingers firmly in case I had other ideas. After a minute or two he moved us closer to Sarah, who by now had sat at one of the low tables, and she looked up at us both. Theo planted himself in her gaze and held it for a few seconds.

'This is Patti,' he said.

'Hello,' said Sarah. She knew me already, but I felt as if I had been 'presented'. We exchanged pleasantries, but Theo pulled at my hand. There was no need for conversation.

'I might go now,' I said to him.

'No,' he said. 'Stay.'

He took me out the back door and down the stairs into the playground, where Mrs Baird stood near a jungle gym, watching two small boys as they stretched out for the bars just over their heads. We approached her and then stopped. It felt as if we were hanging about within a precise 'noticing distance'. When Mrs Baird looked at us Theo stepped forward, still holding my hand.

'This is Patti.'

'Hello,' she said. I had known her for years as she was already working at the centre when I used to bring Mani, but she was still *Mrs* Baird. Mrs Baird and I smiled at each other, neither of us exactly sure what we were involved in.

'How's Theo today?'

'Fine,' I said. 'He's good.'

Before we could engage in any further chat Theo tugged at my hand again and, with a bit of shouldering, turned me towards the jungle gym. Neither of the two boys looked at us. We waited. Theo took a step nearer, well into the 'I want to speak to you' zone. One of the boys, black-haired and almond-eyed, looked at him as he continued to clamber up the ladder on the side of the overhead bars. Theo eyeballed him. The boy stopped in mid-clamber.

'Patti,' Theo said.

The boy looked at me, a brief but comprehensive acknowledgment in his gaze, then went on clambering.

I knew by now what was going on. Theo wrapped his hand around my fingers and led me to a group of three girls sitting on the small terrace, looking pretty and knowing it. They each wore smocked dresses and would not have been more than four years old. This time Theo simply waited until they looked solemnly at the two of us standing hand-in-hand. They looked at me, not up and down but an overall gaze, reading a relationship in my stance, the line of my body. Nothing was said by Theo or the girls; the gaze was enough. Theo then gently tugged me by my hand away to the next group.

We spent a further twenty minutes moving slowly around the playground, hanging about near each teacher and each group of children until Theo had caught their attention. Sometimes words were said, greetings exchanged; other times it was the silent gaze. With the teachers there was always a word or two and a slightly bemused look, but each pre-schooler, whether silent or not, gave the required amount of recognition, accepting this ceremony as quite ordinary. It was a slow, formal, dignified procession involving all proper ceremonial elements: parade, presentation, acknowledgment. I seem to remember it was a sunny day: dappled light in the playground, a sense of the air parting gently for us. At a certain point Theo dropped my hand and it was time for me to leave. I kissed him on the cheek quickly, feeling the tears pricking by now, and left him in the playground.

I turned back at the gate and saw him sitting on the edge of the sandpit with another little boy sitting beside him. They were filling a bucket with sand, concentrating, absorbed. He didn't look up.

I walked home, going over and over the ceremony, remembering the purposeful moment of each presentation, the delicate but unmistakable declaration, as if a little boy could know the necessity of formal procedures. I kept breaking into a foolish smile as I walked down the hill.

'Today, I think, I was adopted,' I told Anthony when he arrived home from work that evening.

Adoptions (iii)

A more private adoption took place within a few weeks. It was early October, four months since Dina collapsed and still cold enough for a fire in the evenings. Anthony and I sat on the lounge. Theo was on my lap telling us of Jason's adventures. Jason, by this time, was an unquestioned reality. Anthony leaned over and tousled Theo's hair. Theo looked at him and tossed his head, as if Anthony might have overstepped the mark, and then was quiet for a while. He leaned in against my chest, his head under my chin. Suddenly he sat up straight.

'I know Jason's mother's name,' he declared.

'Do you now?'

'Yes, and her name is Dina.'

'Oh yes,' I said. 'That's a good name.' Over Theo's head I exchanged a knowing look with Anthony. This was the first overt acknowledgment that Jason was his perfected self, just like the psychology books said.

There was a moment's careful silence.

'Well, you see, Jason has two mothers,' he said.

'Does he now?' It was my turn to be careful, as I aimed for a perfectly nonchalant tone.

'Yes, and one is called Dina and one is called Patti.'

'That's good, I'm glad he has two mothers.' I kissed him on the cheek and he stared straight ahead and didn't say anything. It was all done.

One day a few weeks later, Theo was trying to get my attention and accidentally called me 'Mummy'. He didn't even notice.

Twenty-Nine

What is Forbidden

In early medieval Europe, the Church forbade the singing of certain intervals in Gregorian or any other kind of liturgical chants. The fourth and fifth were considered perfect, but the third and sixth were forbidden. It was ruled that these were not sacred intervals. I listened to the intervals on a tape another singing teacher had given me and couldn't imagine what wicked things might happen in those spaces. Plato, too, was suspicious of music because of the passions it could arouse. In his ideal Republic a calm, rational mind prevailed, the citizens unswayed by the beat of song, except, he said, for patriotic music to inspire loyalty. It would seem music and singing are most dangerous.

What is Inadmissible

Dina was in her wheelchair sitting in the garden in the grounds of the hospital at Parramatta. Kit was on a bench and had her chair turned towards him so they were facing each other. He leaned in towards her and seemed to be helping her with a sort of keyboard, and there was a book open beside him. Theo was there too, picking dandelions from the unmown edges of the grass. It was the first time in a long while that I had seen Dina in her own day clothes; silk trousers and olive-green shirt, straw sunhat and her Doc Martens. From a distance she looked like her old self, so that walking up the path towards the three of them a passer-by could be forgiven for thinking that everything was going to be just fine really soon.

It was the first day of spring, warm and still, so I had picked one of each kind of flower from Dina's garden to show her. Kit moved the little electric battery-powered typewriter that had been balanced on her knee. I sat down beside him and began putting the flowers on her lap one at a time.

'This is from that camellia up against the back of the house.'

She looked at it and nodded.

'This is from the dogwood down near that rock wall, where it steps down to the next terraced bit. It's early, the first one out. And this is from the big azalea near the front steps.' As I described where each flower had come from, she nodded. It was clear she could see her garden in her mind's eye. She touched the motley pile of flowers as if to pick one up, but didn't.

'That reminds me,' Kit said. 'Yesterday when she was being assessed for rehab by the resident and the registrar – they have to review rehab every couple of weeks – she picked up a sweet pea flower from her lap with both her hands and held it to her nose to smell it.'

'Wow. Both hands. So she can use her left hand now?'

'It's awkward and I've only seen her do it a few times. I think the messages just aren't there. But there must be a few cells still firing.'

'She really is coming on. It's so good.' There was silence for a moment and I heard the 'she' echoing.

'So, Dina, what else have you been up to while I've been raiding your garden?'

She looked at Kit then back at me. It seemed strange, because she had never been one to look to her partner for anything. She had been bold, upfront.

'She's been cheeky,' Kit said. 'She wrote "You've always been a deaf bastard," to me.'

'You're kidding. By hand?'

'No. On this typewriter. It's like a sort of laptop, really, but lighter. A couple of lines come up on this little screen here. It's much easier for her to just tap a letter than form it with her hand.'

'That's great. It must be a relief for her to be able to communicate.'

'I know. But she still does try to write things for the hand exercise. See, here, I asked her what she'd like to eat and she's just written "bread rolls, some camembert and some pork". Nothing wrong with her taste buds.'

'That's amazing.' I looked at the spidery scrawl, almost indecipherable. 'Yep, it's definitely camembert.'

'It'd have to be pretty runny. She still can't chew. But apparently she has said a few things. Without initiating.'

'She spoke? By herself? Without anyone pulling her jaw? '

'Well, I haven't heard her, but apparently she said "Hi" to Pia and Monica. They begged her to, they said, and she did. And Chrissie wrote in The Book that she said "My knees are sore",' but I don't know. Chrissie might have just meant she wrote it on the screen. I'll have to ask her. Anyway, it means she can move her mouth.'

'That's wonderful. Are you going to talk to me, Dina?'

She looked at me then closed her eyes.

'Come on, Dina, can you talk to us?' Kit said. She flicked her eyes open and looked at him then at me. Her mouth twisted a little.

'She's trying. Aren't you, Dina?' I shifted forward on the bench, shoulder to shoulder with Kit. Dina kept her eyes on him but didn't try to speak.

'Can you say "no" then?' Kit asked. A trick question.

She gazed at him for several seconds. Her mouth worked in the way old men's do when they are about to speak. Chewing over their words inside their mouth.

'Come on, I bet you can't say no.' Kit winked at her.

'No,' said Dina in a low frail voice.

'Omigod!'

'Fantastic!'

Kit and I laughed. Dina's mouth twisted in a grimace that could have been a smile. Theo came running, clutching a bunch of squashed dandelions in one hand.

'Mummy just talked,' said Kit.

'Mummy.' Theo leaned on her knee, his free hand holding the silk of her trousers, and gave her his flowers. Her right hand lay palm up and she curved her fingers over the dandelions.

'She said no! Trust her!' Kit was holding Dina's hand. His usual unreasonably calm tone was wobbly.

'Mummy's knee. Mummy's knee.' Theo pulled at Dina's trouser leg, trying to scramble up. I picked up the flowers from her lap and Kit lifted Theo and sat him facing her. Her arms were propped up with pillows on either side and she moved her right hand so that it was on Theo's chubby leg. It wasn't curved around his leg but lay on it, fingers curled, stiff like a claw.

Theo put his hand out and touched Dina's. He stroked it softly.

I sat back and picked up The Book lying open on the bench. The page was covered in large exuberant handwriting.

'I see Pia's been this morning too,' I said. 'Did you read this? She's complaining that she has been with five men in the last two months and she needs Dina to get better and tell her which one to fall in love with!'

'Dina was always the one for that. Dorothy Dix.' There were tears in his eyes. He put his had on Dina's knee. 'But how about that, Theo? She said no!'

Theo leaned forward and kissed his mother on her sallow cheek. Such a stiff, silent mother.

'We'd better go in now. It's time for more physio.' Kit stood up.

'I'd better go then,' I said.

'You can stay. You can sit on the floor and talk to her, if you like. It helps distract her from the torture.'

Theo played with the faux pearl buttons on his mother's shirt. His head and hers were nearly touching under her hat.

'I would, but I do have to be going. I was only calling in for a few minutes. Mani will be home from school. I don't want to leave him alone for too long.'

'That's all right. You right there, Theo?'

He pushed the wheelchair and I went ahead carrying the flowers. As we walked, Theo steadied himself for the ride with both his hands on his mother's arms and he kissed her rhythmically as the wheels of the chair rumbled over the regular joins in the cement path. I stopped and held the door open, and when Kit had pushed them through I gave Theo the flowers and said I had to go.

'See you all later,' I said.

Many Years Later

Before coming to the beach-house I visited Theo. We walked along the riverbank near where he lives now. Along the river we stopped and picked some eucalypt leaves and used them for leaf boats. We raced them for a while but mine keep sinking and Theo was gleeful and I got tired of losing and looked around for another game. Theo spied a clump of bullrushes and persuaded me to lean over the edge of the river and pull a couple out to use as swords. We played sword fights with them all the way to the bridge, thrusting and parrying and running until our swords had become daggers and then pocket knives. It looked like I was having a good time but I don't really like playing children's games.

We crossed the road to a cafe on the corner and sat at a table outside. There was a man at the next table with long grey hair tied back in a ponytail. He stared at us.

'What are you wearing that for, little girl?' he said suddenly.

I glanced up at him. Whom was he talking to? He was looking at Theo, who was wearing an unusually long T-shirt, and then he looked at me in a taunting way. I realised as I saw his eyes (I wanted to say glittering eyes, but who would believe me?) that he had his own private havoc reigning, so I said softly to Theo, 'Take no notice. He doesn't know what he's talking about.'

'Take no notice ! Take no notice! That's right, girlie! Take no notice of the world. Little girlie too, take no notice! ' He was chanting loudly and people walking past looked at him and at us.

'Nothing wrong with his hearing,' I said even more softly to Theo, smiling, but he looked frightened. His face, always creamy pale, had gone a bluish-white, like translucent marble. The man was still staring at us both.

'Girlies out wearing their dresses. Take no notice of the world. That's the way, that's the way, that's the way,' the man crooned angrily.

'Come on, Theo, let's sit inside. This isn't very relaxing.' I took his hand and he stood and walked close to me. The man flung his arms around wildly in a mockery of someone out of control, and then laughed. We ignored the taunts as we walked inside but I felt hot and discomfited.

'He's brain-damaged!' Theo accused as soon as we got in the door. His body trembled. The words were meant to be the most insulting thing he could think of. As soon as they came out he looked at me furtively. He knew what he had said.

Our eyes locked for a moment and then I looked away at the glassed display of deli food.

I squeezed his hand. 'It's okay,' I said. 'Forget about him. Let's see what they've got to eat here. You can have whatever you like. But something nourishing first.'

His eyes brightened. The cafe was bustling around him and he'd changed back in a moment to a little boy on an outing. He ordered soy and honey chicken wings and a slice of humming-bird cake and we sat at the window bench. An elderly woman sat on the stool next to us and smiled a greeting. She was wearing a black silk beret on her dark hair and she had large dark brown eyes.

'Hello, my dear,' she said gravely to Theo.

'We came in to get away from him.' I gestured towards the man outside, whose back was now to us.

'Yes, he's often here.' She smiled in a way that allowed him to be in the world as well, and I was embarrassed. I wanted to explain that it would have been all right if it hadn't been for Theo, but that would mean telling her the whole story of Dina, so I said nothing. I wanted her to say something else. I liked her but was a little daunted by her beauty. She must have been seventy or so but she looked so elegant and bohemian. She was wearing a jade-green and black Mao suit, which looked exactly right on her dainty figure.

'I've just been to my Egyptian hieroglyph class at the community college,' she offered.

'Like Robert Dessaix,' I said. 'Except he taught himself.'

She nodded. I knew she would know what I was talking about.

She included Theo in the conversation, saying how lucky he was to have a day off school. He told her that we had been exploring along the river and that we'd had a sword fight with bulrushes. She told him that she knew where Orion, the sword fighter in the sky, was. 'I studied astronomy,' she said. 'Do you know what that is?'

'Of course,' said Theo, disgusted that anyone could think he didn't know the obvious. He spoke to her in an easy, familiar way, as if he already knew her.

I explained that I wasn't Theo's mother and she smiled and said, 'Yes, I know.'

I was impressed with her attentiveness. When we were out together people always thought that I was Theo's mother, but I knew if they had watched and listened carefully they would realise I wasn't.

She told me her son was a professor of literature at a New South Wales university and I told her I used to teach literature. We talked about books for a while but she kept including Theo, so the conversation spiralled and crisscrossed and jumped in the way it does when two conversations are happening at once on two different levels. She said she was eighty-two and I told her I'd thought she was at least fifteen years younger than that. I was comfortable with her, as if I had known her for years but still with that thrilling feel of having just met a kindred spirit. Theo offered her a piece of his cake which she accepted, matter-of-factly taking the broken-off bit from his fingers. We were all excited and happy at having found each other, but I didn't ask her name and she didn't offer it. I gave her my address and phone number, although I knew I would never hear from her.

It wasn't until after we'd said goodbye and we were on our way home that I realised she looked exactly like Dina would have one day if she had lived to be old.

Theo trotted along in silence for a while.

'She was really nice,' he said.

Confession

There is something fundamentally unsettling about the sound of 'usurper'. It has a snake-cold feel to it, like a steel coronet pressing into the temples, a cool-hearted word that most often wriggles its way into the company of kings and rulers, ministers and courtiers, but not always. It is a cunning theft, to spirit away the position and power that rightfully belong to another, and one that I am impressed there is a word for at all. It's the sort of thing you could almost pretend wasn't even happening.

Thirty

Some Photographs of Theo

1. Round-faced, solemn, wearing a brown-checked flannelette shirt. It's the official pre-school portrait. He looks shell-shocked. Around this time he told lots of stories about a witch who came down from the sky and tried to destroy his house and steal all his toys. He described in detail the trapping, smashing, punching, kicking, stabbing, blowing-up, shooting he would do to her the next time she came.

2. Solemn again, but safe-looking, with the arms of my chubby little niece, Grace, around his shoulders and my arms around them both. The sun is shining and there are blossoms out. I am sitting on a cane chair in our back yard with both of them leaning against the chair. He is about four years old. I think Jason was still around then.

3. Theo and Mani in the back yard. Mani is tickling Theo and he is giggling wildly. He always had the best laugh, even when things had become very bad at school. One evening I watched comedians Flacco and the Sandman on the television with him at my mother's place and he kept falling off the lounge he was laughing so much. My mother and I laughed just watching him.

4. Halfway through primary school, wearing a neat blue uniform. His face has started to lengthen, his smile is uncertain, his eyes shifty. He is picked on most days at school. He is different, sensitive, he doesn't have a mother, the world is a dangerous place. His tears bring further insults. Cornered, he hits out with sticks and fists. It is easier to play computer games inside.

5. He is framed by the kitchen window looking out at the courtyard of the old stucco holiday house at Wamberal. He comes with us and other families every year for a week at the sea. He sleeps in the room leading out onto the verandah and is tucked in under the mosquito net every night. His face is smooth, utterly absorbed as he stands at the kitchen bench sketching. The sunny courtyard is in front of him; he is in shadow, but his face glows.

6. Theo and Jake stand side-by-side dressed in their white karate suits with blue belts. Their bare feet are apart and their elbows bent out and down in the 'ready to fight' pose. Jake is Egyptian brown, Theo is creamy pale as always. They both look as if they are concentrating, and seem serious, proud. You can see that they are friends although they are not looking at each other.

There are lots more photographs. Looking on the kitchen noticeboard or through the photo drawer, anyone would think he was my child. Except I don't have any photographs of him as a baby. My photos start when he is about two-and-a-half years old.

One of Kit's photos

Theo is a fifteen-month-old baby walking unsteadily up the beach, both hands up and out for balance. His plump belly is covered in sand and his face is sunlit, eager, eyes squinting a bit against the light. Dina is standing behind and to one side of him, her shoulders straight and back in that erect posture that always made her look ready for the world. She is wearing a stylish dark red swimming costume and her hair is tied up on the back of her head. She is gazing proudly down at Theo. It's just an ordinary family day at the beach; there are thongs and a red and green T-shirt on the sand and in the background are four unknown kids, one of them on her knees building a sandcastle. Behind her is the ocean stretching out to the horizon, bobbing with swimmers.

Home Video

Theo is sitting on my knee. It's a year since his mother died.

'I'll kiss you on . . . the knee,' I threaten.

'No, no.' He wriggles away. I hold him and force his leg straight and manage a quick kiss on the knee. He laughs delightedly.

'Now where else shall I kiss you?'

'On the tummy. You can't get me on the tummy.'

'Oh yes I can.'

'No, no.' This time he slips off the lounge and runs for it. I catch him easily, swing him upside down and carry him that way back to the lounge. I bounce him onto the cushions then hold him and use my elbows to force down his flailing arms and hold his legs down with my knee. He tries to hold his shirt down but I tickle him and he lets go. He is wholly dissolved into laughter by now. I whip his shirt up and plant a kiss on his belly button.

'How can I watch this program with you two making all that racket?' Anthony says. He's watching us comfortably and we can tell he doesn't mind. Theo has the kind of laugh that makes other people laugh as well.

I tire of the game after a few kicks and elbowings on the chin and nose, but Theo is insistent.

'Chase me again. Chase me.'

I wrestle with him a few more times, planting ever noisier kisses, and then we eventually settle down in front of the television. He sits on my lap and plays with the necklace he has given me, touching and twirling the beads. He asks me to take it off and when I do he pours it from hand to hand, over and over. He sits with his head resting on my shoulder and my arm is around his middle. Anthony smiles at the picture we make and I reach out my hand to him. Theo takes my hand and puts it back around himself.

'Just about bedtime for you,' I say. It's way past his bedtime, but I'm still undisciplined about bedtimes. Mani is already in bed, but I know he's reading.

'You come and sleep at my place.' He's said this a few times lately.

'That would be good.' I've been saying this each time in reply.

'You say that, but you haven't. You come and sleep at my place.'

'But there's no room for me. There's no bed.'

'You can sleep in my dad's bed. It's a big bed.'

I look at Anthony. 'I don't think so. I don't think your dad would like that.'

'Neither would I,' says Anthony.

'Why?' asks Theo.

Anthony just winks at him.

Afterwards, when Theo is finally asleep in Mani's room, Anthony and I watch the late night movie. He is lying with his head in my lap.

'You're well in there with Theo. He wants you to move in,' Anthony says.

'It scares me sometimes. It can't last. Someone will come into Kit's life and then it will be over for Theo and me.'

'Not over, just different.'

'Yes, but we'll both have to let go.'

'All is change, they say. Deal with it when it happens.'

'I know, I know.'

It was obvious things would change whether I wanted them to or not. Theo would grow up and his loss would always be there, a scar inside him, and one day he would realise that his loss has been my gain. I wouldn't have had Theo all these years if his mother hadn't died.

Thirty-One

The summer of the singing lessons was almost over. The formal end of season had not yet come and there was one more lesson to go, but autumn had arrived on a particular day the way it always does, stirring memory and desire. On the walk up to the post office the air was chilled and clear and the oaks at the top of the hill were pink ochre, the colour of Italian villages on postcards, although the leaves underfoot were a disappointing brown. The maples along the road across the ridge were astonishing maroon and cerise flames against the blue sky. The trees leaned over the road forming a fiery tunnel of dark red and pink which, when the light was shining on it, looked like a glowing invitation to step along the road to who knows where. One day when we drove past them, Mani said that this was the first year of his life that he had really seen the autumn. 'Is it always like this?' he asked.

The Chinese herbs had begun to work. The black brew had flowed through my bloodstream, darkening the body, making it more yin, dark, wet, receptive. My vagina felt like a cone piercing up into the body, almost stinging with longing to be filled, then the blood started to flow, heavily, thickly. Back aching as if I was having contractions, stomach rounded, labia plump and open, letting the blood fall. I walked around the house weighted to the ground, almost swaying. It was difficult to concentrate or make decisions, words mispronounced thickly in my mouth. I wanted to curl up in the sun somewhere and dream of life unfolding easily and beautifully in front of me.

At the writing group there was an air of longing and restlessness as we tried to settle into the rhythm of stories. It was still not cool enough for a fire and the empty grate was dusty. Someone had burnt some papers in it, a few unburnt scraps lying against the firescreen.

The only person left to read her story was Wendy, a big-boned blonde woman who had something of Ursula about her – a similar acceptance of grief. She read her story of bringing her mother violets just before she died. Her mother was a severe woman who had never kissed or cuddled her daughter even as she maintained strict control over all her movements and decisions. Unless she obeyed her mother in every little thing, she was unlovable. A small moment of defiance when Wendy was sixteen – she wanted to wipe up rather than wash up – and she was thrown out of home.

She looked up briefly and smiled at our gaping amazement, then read on. Of course the violets were inadequate. Even if total obedience had been possible, it would not have been enough to satisfy a woman with such a craving for perfection and control. Her mother didn't have to say anything; she couldn't, she was dying, her eyes closed, her mouth open and dry. As she gazed at her mother's papery yellow skin and bloodless lips, Wendy suddenly realised that she would never know what it was like to feel a mother's arms around her. Some things can never be changed, never be helped.

She took the white washer from the bedside table and dipped it in the jug of water and placed the tip of the washer in her mother's mouth. Her mother sucked greedily on it. Wendy felt an unfamiliar surge of childlike pride and satisfaction. She wet the washer again, and again placed it in her mother's mouth. Her mother sucked again, this time feebly.

It was something to satisfy my mother's last thirst, she wrote.

This is what I think of here in the evenings as the water becomes silvery and the reflections of the she-oaks a mysterious black script on its surface: how Wendy, Ursula, Michel, all the rest of us, translate experience into memory and then into words where the experience can be felt in other hearts, considered in other minds. It is ordinary and has been done since the invention of language, but it still seems the most strange magic to me, a spell. It's not transubstantiation – the substance it is made of changes, with only the illusion of time and space remaining of the original experience – but a change of medium. And as the experience becomes symbolic, is lifted out of the body and into the mind and emotions by the spell of words, there is somehow a kind of relief or reassurance. Hard knots of horror and fear dissolve. I don't know its exact purpose in terms of our survival, the translating or transmuting of experience, but I don't think we could bear life without it.

When my father was born, his maxillary bones had not fused. His palate, and consequently his top lip, was unjoined, as if the two halves of the baby mould had come unstuck. Instead of a dainty rosebud baby mouth, there was a fleshy inside-out split. The doctor said they would have to wait several months until the bones had fused before he could sew the lip together, so my grandmother took him home and looked after him carefully. Because of the cleft he could not suck, so she soaked the corner of a linen hankie in the milk that she had expressed into a bowl, and dripped the milk, drop by drop, into his mouth.

It must have been painstaking feeding a hungry baby this way, soaking the hankie with not too much milk, not too little, so that it dripped at just the right pace for a newborn to swallow. My grandmother's breasts would have swollen and grown hard as she struggled to express enough milk with the glass and rubber pump, and the unfinished baby would have wailed with an unshaped sound coming straight from the voice box and up through the open palate. He was a baby who could neither feed nor cry properly, and what else can a baby be expected to do? But he was her baby and she was his mother and that was that.

When my father was old and soon to die, he had Parkinson's Disease and sometimes his hand trembled too much for him to be able to feed himself. My mother saw him every day in the nursing home and helped him eat, but one day when I was visiting, my mother stayed home to get a few things done around the house. It was lunch time when I called in to see my father and there was a plate of purééd vegetables on the tray. Baby food. My father picked up the spoon with steady effort but had a sudden tremor as he put it in the sloppy pumpkin and potato and the spoon flicked upwards, splattering orangey food on the sheets.

'You'd better let me, Dad.'

He put the spoon down with a clatter and looked at me tiredly. Life had come to this. He could speak but most of the time didn't bother. I guess making conversation no longer seemed a reasonable thing to do. Often when he did speak he was in another time frame – when we were all kids and the paddock needed ploughing after the rain and life was as good as it ever could be.

I picked up his spoon and dipped it in the vegetables, automatically blowing on them and wiping the bottom of the spoon on the edge of the plate. I'd had two babies, I could do this without thinking. I brought it towards my father's still misshapen mouth (the doctor had sewn it roughly those seventy-five years ago – the valley that normally sits neatly under the nose had been pulled under the left nostril, causing his top lip to be lopsided and squashing down the side of his nose). His pale blue eyes watched the spoon and his mouth opened a little, the lips soft and a bit dry. In that moment it suddenly seemed all wrong and horribly right. It all turns over in a moment, in a lifetime, the universe folds back and everything is reversed, just as the Scriptures have said, and everything transforms into its opposite, life giving way to death giving way to life and it goes on forever. But I still didn't like the feeling of spooning mush into my father's mouth. I wanted him to be my father forever.

The Last Singing Class

'I want to try something different seeing it's our last day,' the teacher said. His hair cascaded around his face and down onto his shoulders instead of being tied back into the usual ponytail. The effect was quite beautiful but it seemed excessive and made me feel as if I was being taught by a guardian angel. I gave him my lesson tape and he put it in the cassette player and switched it on.

'All I want you to do is not worry about getting it right; be bad if you like, like last week, and as well, close your eyes. And the other thing is we'll sing a song, not just notes. I think you are happier with words. What's an easy song you know the words of already?'

'About the only thing I know is "Kumbayah". I used to sing it to my sons before they told me to stop.'

'That will do. "Kumbayah". Okay, close your eyes.'

They were the words for the beginning of a spell. *Close your eyes and hold out your hand.* In dropped a treasure – a galah feather or a little green frog or, if you were unlucky, an empty lolly wrapper or a tea-towel. *Close your eyes and open your mouth.* Nothing would be given, nothing could be received, until the eyes were closed.

I shut my eyes and, oddly, there was an immediate sensation of relief. It was dark inside my head. I was still nervous but it was a feather of nerves rather than the fully beating, panicked wings.

Something was changing. Even as I opened my mouth, I knew. In the darkness my voice sounded light but on pitch.

'Someone's prayin', Lord.'

'Good!'

There was a moment of the pleasure of praise, but without the confidence that I would be able to do it again.

'Someone's prayin', Lord.' Flat and full of strain.

'Sink into the dark. That's all there is.'

It was red-black inside my head, red from the bright autumn light flooding into the studio. I was conscious of the lines of veins in my eyelids.

'Someone's crying, Lord, Kumbayah.' The vibration of the voice box seemed to go up the back of the throat, up through the nasal passages and into the skull. I'd done this before, I'd sung this song to my babies and they didn't care about the tune. I sang the line again, breathing in more deeply this time and having more faith in the sound. It resonated in my head. In the darkness I felt it, not just heard it. A subtle shift was happening and words were having a difficult time trying to name it. Some gap was closing, a separation.

I sang another line, true and stronger, and then another. Something *was* happening. I was holding the note inside my head, immersed in the sound of it. I wasn't outside the note, the note was in me and I was in the note. Being with voice. My skull felt like the inside of an instrument. I started to smile.

We sang through a whole verse. The notes in my mouth were tangible, like a mouthful of ripe blood-plum. The sound wasn't soaring or spine-tingling, but it was mine. A bit sweet, brave enough, a sense of longing for more, an uneven mix of small joys and sorrows. I opened my mouth wider in the middle of a note and was surprised at the way it filled my mouth, swirling around in it and pouring out into the room. The teacher smiled at my surprise. I laughed, reconstituted in that moment. I am a body, a mouth, a voice.

'Fantastic!' cried the teacher.

I laughed at his relief.

'Listen to it on the tape and hear for yourself.' He turned to look at the tape recorder and we both suddenly realised it wasn't going. He hadn't plugged it in at the wall.

'Damn!' The teacher stood up. 'But never mind, you know you did it, don't you?'

'Yes,' I said. But I felt furious. For Christ's sake, why didn't he bloody well check? I do it right for once and there's no evidence of it!

He untangled cords and plugs and connected the tape recorder.

'Someone's cryin', Lord.' I was thinned with disappointment. The split had opened up, gaping enough to fall into, flat on my face.

'Shut your eyes. Go back into the dark.' He moved quickly, asking me to sing line after line, eyes still shut, no time to think.

'With your mouth open wide.'

I shut my eyes and an image came: my mouth as I was giving birth, not screaming but smiling as I pushed my younger son out into the world. My lips were stretched but still loose and joyous, vagina wide. I realised it was the only time I could remember such a mouth on me.

'Someone's dancin', Lord.' I was smiling, eyes squeezed shut. It was the warm voice again, not powerful, but strong enough for what it had to deal with. It was almost easy. It felt too astonishing. I burst out laughing and opened my eyes.

'Why are you laughing?'

I tried to explain that it was because I was singing, but he didn't know what I meant. How could he?

'Someone's leaving, Lord,' I sang, changing the words for him.

He smiled, then there was awkwardness. How do we finish this? He had seen me more undressed than anyone and now he was leaving.

He gave me the name and phone number of a new singing teacher. Chella. She had a choir but he thought she taught people individually as well.

'I can't sing with other people,' I said. 'They'll hear me.'

'Well, anyway,' he said, 'give her a ring.'

Thirty-Two

Dina had walked from the physiotherapy ward back to her room! She had her wheeled frame and a nurse on either side holding her up and it took nearly half an hour, but she did it. The last time I'd seen Dina in the physio ward she had been struggling to take a few sliding steps, not even lifting her feet. None of us saw it, not even Kit. One of the nurses told Kit about it.

There she had been, in the wide hall down from the ward, her feet sliding along the pale, polished lino, her hands clenching the aluminium frame, probably beads of sweat on her lip and forehead and a look of all-excluding determination on her face. The nurses held her under each elbow so she didn't have to hold up her own weight, as just moving her legs would have taken all her attention. The irregular firing of messages from the damaged motor region, struggling to obey the will's impossible requirements, pushed the muscles of her legs and feet along that corridor as if it were the entrance to the Promised Land. Her bluish-white skin was damp with effort, her new wiry hair sweaty on her broken skull.

I saw in The Book an entry from Noela, Dina's older sister: 'She was always a very determined and gutsy child.' I showed Kit and he grinned and said, 'It sounds like code for she was always a pain in the bum.'

In that same week, late November, Dina was allowed out of hospital for the afternoon for the first time. It was too far to go home to the Mountains so Kit and Theo had loaded Dina and her wheelchair and catheter and food drip into the car and driven to Chrissie's place at Pymble. Dina had been particular about the way she was dressed for the outing. Kit said he'd wanted to put her pink mohair jumper on her – he thought it might be a bit cool out – and she looked down at her green shirt and at him in disgust and shook her head.

In Chrissie's house they parked her chair in the lounge-room and sat around her. She had asked, on the keyboard, to listen to some music, 'nothing too woeful' she wrote, and Chrissie put on some Joni Mitchell. Kit served up the mashed avocado, which she could move about in her mouth and swallow, very slowly. Dina watched Theo climbing on and off the lounge and along the back of it as if it were a high ridge. Chrissie talked with her about the performance project she was designing and Kit put his hand on Dina's knee and winked at her. And then she sang. Kit told me, she sang with him. It was her old school song that she had taught him for fun in their early days together. He had started singing, looking at her and trying to remember the black-haired laughing woman in leotards in the dance studio, her eyes mischievous, and she had looked back at him and then opened her mouth of her own volition and joined in. Her voice was low and soft, not her usual style, he said with a grin. It was a silly, rousing song like all school songs and Dina's mouth had twisted into a grimace-smile. That afternoon was the first step back to the way things used to be.

It was only a few weeks before Christmas and the talk was that she'd be at home at Terrace Falls Road for Christmas and New Year for a couple of weeks, then she would go back to hospital for more intensive therapy, then home again to live. While she was back in hospital, the house would be modified for a wheelchair with the money from the Brainstorm Benefit. A verandah would be built on the back, a ramp installed, the bathroom door widened and the shower redesigned so the chair could be pushed in and out. It would cost several thousand dollars, and of course she wouldn't need them for long, all these modifications, but still they had to be done.

If you say things often enough maybe they will happen. Close your eyes and say it over and over. Things are on the mend. Things are on the mend. Soon everything will be the way it was. Soon.

Thirty-Three

The Book

> A journey of a thousand miles starts with one step. You've taken that step, Deen. You will get there.
>
> John

It was odd that John had written the 'thousand mile' cliché. He visited only the once as far as I can tell from entries in The Book. I didn't know him but others told me he had been a beautiful young man, long red curls, always dainty and ironic, and famous for knowing famous people. I guess the depth of Dina's horror brought out the banal in all of us; the soft fluffy surface protected us, or seemed to. I read in the paper recently that John had died of cancer and, although I had not met him, I felt the tug of another thread in my life being removed.

The Brainstorm Benefit

The bar was hidden behind a surge of bodies and arms passing drinks back. The foyer of Belvoir St Theatre was crowded with Dina's friends, all talking and laughing like extras in a film. There seemed to be an undercurrent of anxiety beneath the speedy gaiety, as if we weren't quite sure how good a time we should be having. The pre-concert auction was about to start and the raffle was ready to be drawn so people milled around the poster listing the goods for auction and prizes to be won: two tickets to the next Belvoir St production; a dinner for two at someone's cafe; a Thai massage; a landscape by an actor turned painter.

I didn't bid for any of the items or buy any raffle tickets. I was busy alternating between quick trips to the toilet to check whether the peacock-blue cocktail dress with sequined straps was over-the-top and trying to look nonchalant against the back wall. I was going to read a story I'd written, not sing, but apart from reciting 'My Country' at the school concert in sixth class, I hadn't performed on stage and certainly not with real actors. All the others were professional performers – a few years later one of the actors was in the play where Picasso declared he really wanted to be a singer. The synchronicities of life can't help but make you wonder if there isn't some sort of narrative unfolding at times.

I did get a prize, though. A friend of Kit's gave me the tickets he had won in the raffle, to the new play *Cosi*. 'It's a Louis Nowra piece about some inmates of a mental hospital putting on a musical,' he said. He was an actor and had been cast in the role of Henry, the chronic depressive.

'Never won anything in my life,' he joked, 'and now I win tickets to the only play I'm in all year.'

Later, I sat on a stool in a spotlight, the sequin straps scratching. The stool was high and my feet wouldn't reach the ground so I curled them under the rung like a sixties folk singer. The background music – violins, bellbirds and magpies – faded down. My cue to start reading.

A SYMBOLIC DINA

Dina is up to her neck in symbols. In fact, some days I can hardly see her for the thick layers stuck all over her. It's my own fault, I've been bringing them in. By the box load. (I see other people scurrying past with cartons too.) Often I try to leave them at home but somehow they always turn up at the hospital as if magnetically stuck to me.

I can't be sure what is in other people's boxes, but in mine there are a variety of symbols of differing colours and sizes. I take them out and stick them on right under Dina's nose.

First there is Dina as symbol of the imprisoned human spirit, a mirror-person, trapped as if under glass, a mute bearer of Fate staring back from her mirror-prison. This symbol is a dramatic silvery-grey and has a timeless quality to it. It is a most elegant symbol.

Then there is Dina as symbol of human hope. This is a huge symbol and, I must admit, my favourite. It is stretchy and rainbow-coloured and suits Dina extremely well except that it almost covers her face as well as her body. In fact, it practically obscures her with its glowing folds.

But then there is the one I try to hide. I stuff it down to the bottom every visit, but it keeps spilling out of the carton. It is red, slashed with black and glitters horribly with scratchy half-sewn seams and dangling threads that threaten to catch on everything. I know Dina sees its shiny reflection in my eyes every time I visit. It is Dina as a symbolic offering to the gods to keep me safe.

The Finale

All the performers and all the children from the audience were on stage holding candles and singing Christmas carols. 'Come All Ye Faithful', 'Silent Night', 'We Three Kings', and the Australian version of 'The Twelve Days of Christmas' – soap on a rope instead of a partridge in a pear tree. Then slides of Dina began flashing up on the wall behind the stage. The images were so magnified that Dina's face, laughing, pouting, smiling, considering, covered the whole high brick wall of the theatre. Mane of hair, laughing mouth, sparkling eyes, all metres wide. Everyone on stage began to sing 'Amazing Grace' and almost immediately the audience joined in. The voices swelled and the theatre rang with fervour, although I don't suppose many of us believed in a God who would intervene. The ocean-wave beat of the song and the rousing faith of the words washed through the theatre until most of the audience was in tears. It really seemed as if the Fates could not resist, such voices, such images. Dina had walked, she had sung, she had eaten food. One day soon, soon, she would be striding, laughing, kissing, one day soon everything would be all right. Love would save her. Hundreds of singing voices couldn't be wrong.

The Book

Amelia, Cathy's six-year-old daughter, drew a picture of Dina lying in her bed. It was an 'x-ray' picture with Dina lying flat on her back and the blanket drawn over her body. The blanket had a striped pattern, which, with the body showing through, made it look like a long narrow cage. Dina's head was squashed up against the bedstead, which leaned backwards as if from the force of her skull pressed against it. Above, in a thought bubble that went right outside the 'hospital' (a child's peak-roofed house), was a drawing of herself – more than twice as big as Dina – floating in the sky with her hands thrown joyfully upwards.

Out of her mouth in a long sausage shape came the words,

'Yippee. I'm Amelia.'

Out of Dina's mouth came, 'Not Yippee. I'm Dina.'

There's a long gap after this picture. The next entry in The Book is not for another two months.

II

Thirty-Four

Dina was transferred to Coorabel Hospital in the north-western suburb of Ryde at the end of September. Parramatta Hospital was closing down, part of a restructure of medical services in the western suburbs, but it was also a move downwards on the priority list for rehabilitation. In fact, despite Coorabel being a rehabilitation hospital, there was going to be much less 'rehab' for Dina. She'd been having the three to six hours as scheduled every day at Parramatta, depending on how tired or alert she was, but it was considered a waste of resources now. She had been taking up the time and expertise of at least three highly trained staff for most of the day, seven days a week. The young man whose spine had been damaged in a motorbike accident could use them better, or the cheeky red-haired girl who had fallen off the climbing equipment at school. He was already walking along the parallel bars, she was racing down the hall in her wheelchair, clipping heels.

The problem was things had changed again; there had been another haemorrhage. Or that was what the doctors thought. They didn't do another CAT scan. There really wasn't any point.

It wasn't as if there hadn't been any progress. She had walked along that shiny hall, she had said 'No', she had passed a marigold from one hand to the other, she had wriggled her right fingers and toes, she had flipped through a *Vogue* magazine, she had sung a silly school song, she had even put on eye gel one morning. Now it was the New Year, six months after the Event, and she could only move her right arm and hand.

No-one noticed when exactly it had happened. Her progress was never consistent. It seems it's an illusion that life goes in straight lines forward or backward. Isn't everything actually always in flux, a constant vibration to and fro, and at certain points we simply fix a time of judgment and decide things are better or worse? The next moment it all might be different.

Dina had pulsed ahead on some days, done all her exercises and said several phrases, and then other days she had done nothing but stare or sleep. Reading through The Book, I see time and again the thrills of her small achievements recorded:

> 'It was great to hear you speak last weekend. The glow lasted me a couple of days.' Bobby (He was an actor friend of Kit's.)

> 'Dina remarked quite spontaneously in response to my flowers 'they're beautiful'. Every day it gets better.' Chrissie (She was always the most regular of visitors.)

> 'Dina decided she wanted a manicure so we involved ourselves with that.' Mish

And every now and then an occasional recording of the steps back:

> 'She's watching telly at the moment but she is very depressed.' Chrissie

> 'Lying so still with a desperate look in your eye and beads of sweat like diamonds all over your face.' Rosie (I never met Rosie.)

> 'Not much to say. I chat, Dina listens.' Chrissie

One day she must have stopped going backwards and forwards and slid inexorably backwards, bit by bit, our mindless hope obscuring the micrometer edging apart. Perhaps it wasn't another haemorrhage but the functioning part of her brain wearying of the extreme effort necessary in learning to direct voluntary skills – speech and the movement of limbs. Her brain may have decided it needed to keep all cells available for maintaining autonomic body systems: heart beating, lungs breathing, glands secreting, guts digesting. There was enough to do already.

She was still having some physiotherapy at Ryde, an hour every morning and night, but that was to encourage circulation and muscle tone, not to develop any further skills. I don't think I was aware of the change in approach at the time. I hadn't been to see Dina for three weeks. A few things had changed; it was nearly twice as far to drive to Ryde from the Mountains; then the car was at the mechanic with a shot gear-box; then there was Christmas and a week of holidays at the rented beach-house. They didn't seem like good reasons even at the time, but after a few weeks had passed without seeing her, it began to feel as if she had disappeared.

Kit said not so many of her friends were coming to see her any more. 'It's too much like hard work,' he said. 'So much for all those hours she listened to them and all their problems.' His bitterness burnt like acid on flesh. I wouldn't have gone either. In those weeks she had become an idea, a damaged woman in another place, another dimension. She was easier to think about that way. She could have just faded away in my mind like the souls in the existential play I saw once who stop moving gradually as people in the world stop thinking about them. If it wasn't for my irrational bargaining with Fate, I would have stayed away and let her fade.

Dina did come home for Christmas. It wasn't quite the way everyone imagined, not the salvation all those singing voices had promised.

I didn't see her then either. We had Christmas that year with my parents at their place. My father was in the nursing home by then and could only come out for the day. He could walk in the slow, interrupted Parkinson's shuffle, but couldn't initiate standing up and my mother wasn't able to lift him or support him on her own so, although there was nothing in the world she wanted more, it wasn't possible for her to look after him any more.

It was one of those stinking hot Christmases out west. In all the photos of unwrapping presents, everyone is shiny and flushed – even the kids are lying about looking dazed and red-faced amongst the tinsel and discarded paper. My father sat in his reclining chair, mostly with his eyes shut, or if they were open, with a bemused, slightly hurt expression in them. His presents, socks and hankies, the sad presents you get when no-one knows what you want or need any more, were piled in a tidy heap on the traymobile. My mother sat with him on a footstool all day while we made Christmas lunch: tabouli, rocket salad, ricotta pie, yoghurt and beetroot salad – unfamiliar food for him, but so late and so tired in his life, he ate it anyway without complaint.

Things were much the same for Dina's Christmas at home.

The naso-gastric tube had been taken out, which meant she could taste food – as well as feeling more comfortable and looking less strange – but she couldn't chew, so Kit had to put everything through a blender. He had been passionate about food; so had Dina, but he was the real devotee and loved to make elaborate food for other people. He would make his own pasta from scratch, mixing up the flours, leaving the pastry to cool in the fridge, rolling it flat, feeding the sheets through the pasta mill, hanging the strips over the back of a kitchen chair, all the while talking, pouring wine, going out into the garden to pick fresh herbs for the sauce. Whatever he made for Christmas dinner that year, he would have had to spoon it all into the blender and mash it softer than baby food before Dina could have any of it.

They had a Christmas tree, the three of them. It was still up when I visited Kit a few weeks later. We'd given them some presents; for Theo, the 'castle' Lego that Mani no longer wanted; for Kit I'd bought Kundera's *The Unbearable Lightness of Being* or *The Book of Laughter and Forgetting*, I can't remember which, and a book for Dina too, but I have no idea what it was now. Some things are starting to fade.

The last time I was out west visiting my mother, I walked to the cemetery with her to visit my father's grave. It's out over the bridge and past the showground, alongside Curra Creek on the road that used to lead to our farm. My mother remarked that she used to walk out along here with her father when she was a little girl and I felt the faint imprint of the cycle of time moving over me. I felt reassured somehow by the repetition of ordinary things.

I am at home in this graveyard; twice in the last century it was part of a property owned by both sides of our family. My mother's family possessed it first – it was named 'Sarsfield', after an Irish revolutionary – and they donated the land for the cemetery, then my father's grandfather bought the property. What was their house is now on the showground near where the carnival people set up sideshow alley and transform the dry paddock into a transient street of magic each year. I never thought of it before, but it's curious that the carnival and the cemetery are right next to each other there.

The grass was long in the cemetery, a good season. In drought the cemetery is as dry and spiky as any other paddock. I remembered again how blue the sky was and how red the earth, the day my father was buried. Now the grass has grown over the red and there is a neat marble headstone. My mother stayed beside Dad's grave, missing him horribly, but I didn't like seeing the blank space next to his name on the double headstone, so I wandered down the back to the old part of the cemetery. There are lots of my ancestors in this cemetery, all the Irish side, and the oldest headstones have shamrocks and Celtic crosses carved on them. 'Pray for a son of Limerick' one of them says and I wonder, did he always miss his wet green homeland and curse that he had been cast up in this raw, bony place?

I came upon a child-sized grave with two names engraved on the marble. Joan and Irene. 'In Death together as in Life' was carved underneath. I wandered back and told my mother about it and she said, 'Oh yes, I was on duty at the hospital when their bodies were brought in. The little girls – best friends – only six years old, they had been at a church picnic on the Macquarie River and fell in and were swept downstream and drowned. They were found in one another's arms – holding tightly to each other – and so they were buried in the one grave.'

I felt that nihilistic pang of envy again. To have died so poetically that you transcend the demands put on ordinary lives, to never have to be good, beautiful, successful. They will always be the children who died in one another's arms, a pure union. The rest of us have to carry on after the transcendental moment, after the clear mango note filling the mouth, the almighty walk down the polished hall. There's still another bloody step to take. And sometimes, no matter how many songs you faithfully sing, how many offerings you make, it really is not going to happen, ever. Fate never has been one to bargain.

Theo and Fate

'What I really want is to see my mother just one more time.'

Theo sat next to me as we drove up the Mountains. He was seven years old by then, over halfway through my time with him; four years since his mother had died and, although I didn't know it, three years until he was to leave.

We had been talking in our usual comfortable way, sounding like any mother and son; making plans, occasionally ignoring or manipulating each other, exchanging news, teasing. We started talking about Dina, which wasn't that unusual – we both mentioned her every so often.

I can't remember what either of us said before or after, but I remember this particular sentence exactly; I even remember exactly where we were on the road: it was just after the primary school and before the turn-off to the railway station. He had gone quiet, falling into himself in that intense way he had, and then he said it.

I turned my head to look at him even though I was driving, and he repeated, 'I just want to see her one more time.' I can see his face framed by the car window and the yellow calliopsis on the railway embankment behind. He wasn't performing, although he knew by now how to play the 'poor motherless child' when he felt like it. This was coming from the furnace of his being. His eyes, his skin, his voice, pleaded. It was shivery, the longing in him. I can't say I've ever known such longing, or even heard it in anyone else's voice before or since. I know my mother longed for my father's return, but not with the same extraordinary need. She missed him, wanted him, would always miss him and want him; Theo needed. He fully understood the impossibility of it, he was old enough to know that nothing and no-one could give him what he asked for, and yet still he begged. I remember seeing a small installation in an art gallery once, a glass box viewed from above that had a mechanised toy man standing in a greyish street throwing himself repeatedly against a huge solid steel gate trying to open it. It would not budge and he couldn't see over or around it, yet he kept trying again and again. From above, the viewer could see that there was a Garden of Paradise on the other side, beautifully made tiny trees and flowers and fountains. Theo was throwing himself headlong against the steel walls and he too knew they'd never yield.

What do you do with things impossible to change?

Thirty-Five

Visiting (i)

Ryde is a pretty, leafy suburb. It has a river and a national park in the middle of it and most of the houses have large gardens. Coorabel has its own gardens and lawns with native and deciduous trees and is a light, airy hospital. It's not as if Dina was locked in a dungeon.

It was the height of summer, a searing blue-sky day. I seem to remember the dryness of ribbons of bark on the ground, the overpowering heat that can make a pleasant suburb feel desolate, as if the forces of nature are about to dissolve human order. The air-conditioned coolness hit like a chilly breeze as I walked in and found my way through yet another labyrinth to Dina.

She was in her room, propped up in her chair. Her hair was a thick crop by now, and she had make-up on. Chrissie or Cathy or Mish must have been visiting. Kit was being too hard on people – they were doing what they could. On her lap there was a magazine open at a crossword but she wasn't looking at it.

'Hi, Dina. How's things?'

She looked at me briefly and then out the window. Blinding light. This was the first time I'd seen her in at least three weeks. She did look different, thinner, more dried out, despite the make-up.

I sat down and looked around. The floor-to-ceiling window let too much summer light pour in. There were several other beds in the room; it was a ward really. There was a young woman in one of the beds who did not register my entry. The bush garden outside the window was in need of a water. There were a few red roses in a vase, probably from the garden at Terrace Falls Road. The Book was still there, and a few cards and the photographs of Dina. It seemed pared down, a long-term sick room rather than the gift-laden room of sudden catastrophe.

I didn't want to be there.

'Theo's good.'

She looked back at me.

'He stayed over on Saturday and Sunday. Kit probably told you. It gave him a bit of a rest. And Mani has been trying to teach Theo to whistle. He looks so cute. He can't quite work out if he has to blow or suck.'

I rattled on.

Dina kept watching me. I waited and spaced the sentences out. Was that too much about Theo, or not enough? Did she want to hear about him from me?

What else was there to say?

'Is it okay here? Are they treating you all right?'

She looked down at her crossword.

I remembered the books in my bag.

'I brought a couple of books. Do you want to be read to? I've brought some poems. Gwen Harwood. And some Isabel Allende stories. Or do you want to do the crossword?'

She flicked her eyes back to me. Eyes are expressive but without any other muscles around the eyes or mouth moving, it is actually quite difficult to read what the pupils and irises alone are saying. I couldn't tell if she was saying help me, or piss off, or I want to die.

'Sorry, I forgot about not asking like that. Do you want me to read?'

Dina blinked once. I waited. That was it. She wasn't bothering to nod today.

'Okay then?'

Her lips twisted a little and she blinked once.

'Allende?'

She blinked again, tiredly.

I started. It was the story called 'Tosca', which I hadn't read before. I hadn't read a lot of the South Americans – their fantastical worlds made me feel pale and plodding. Tosca is the tale of a woman who lives in illusion about love. In the last paragraph she makes a decision, but I couldn't work out whether she had decided to live on in illusion or reality: 'She hesitated for an infinite moment, on the borderline between reality and dream, then stepped back, left the tavern, opened her black umbrella, and walked home with the macaw flying above her head like a bizarre archangel from a calendar.'

I put the book down on the bed. Its gaudy cover looked like a cutout from another world on the pastel bed cover. The story discomfited me.

'What do you reckon, Dina? Does she decide on illusion or reality?'

She looked at the cover of the book.

'Do you want to hold it?' I handed it to her.

She held it in her left hand, seeming to study the picture of bright tropical foliage.

'Did you like the story?'

She didn't look up but continued to study the cover as if it held some answer for her.

There was silence. I'd run out of things to say. A nurse came in once and checked Dina's posture, rearranged the pillows a bit. The woman in the next bed had not moved. It was quiet in this hospital; there wasn't the same air of life and busyness as Parramatta. It felt more like the nursing home my father had lived in.

I sat for a while longer, read the entries in The Book – it was Chrissie who had been visiting that morning – and made a few suggestions for the crossword. Dina could still hold a pen, just. There were a couple of spidery words almost impossible to read. After an hour and a quarter I left. I always tried to stay for more than an hour and tried not to look at my watch.

Visiting (ii)

Kit visited Dina at Coorabel and stayed late discussing her prognosis with the doctor. She had been there three months and nothing had changed. That's what the doctor said. Things did change every day – a little movement, a word from Dina, suddenly, out of the blue – but it was nothing. The situation needed to be faced. Kit rang and asked me to collect Theo from childcare and bring him home. It had become a matter of course by now, as if I were the other parent. I dropped Theo off at Terrace Falls Road in the evening after dinner and stayed for a while. Kit made us coffee.

We talked books, as usual. As if everything was normal. Sitting forward, sparring, laughing. As if Dina would come in any minute, after tucking Theo into bed, and put her hand on Kit's leg and I'd know it was time for me to leave. Kit had just read the Allende book I'd lent him after saying I didn't know what the ending of one of the stories was about. The point was, he said, that the different levels of reality were given the same weight, that's all. I'd only just finished reading *The Satanic Verses*, and was full of interpretations that he couldn't contradict because he'd read it ages ago when it first came out. He said I should read *Perfume*, that it was one of his favourites. He found it on his bookshelf for me. We sat in the lounge-room, at either end of the fifties lounge that Dina hadn't had a chance to re-upholster. She wasn't here. She wasn't ever going to be here drinking coffee and talking about books. Or putting her hand on Kit's leg. There were too many unsayable things that she'd never do again. It was time to go home. It was too late at night.

I stood up, book in hand.

'Have a quick look at what we've done to the house before you go.' Kit jumped up and showed me down the hall. The builders had renovated the bathroom completely. The doorway was wide enough for a wheelchair and the shower, too, could have a wheelchair pushed right into it. It was spacious and uncluttered, with steel handles screwed into the wall around the shower and the toilet so that it looked like a hospital bathroom instead of someone's home. I remembered it from before, the aqua tiles and the pot plants and the maroon cabinet above the handbasin.

'It's pretty good, isn't it?'

He seemed proud of it. I nodded.

'And the deck and ramp are going to be started now.'

'Why a deck?'

'Dina is going to be living here, at home. Things are not going to be a lot of fun for her. I want it to be as comfortable as I can for . . . a nice place to sit in the sun.'

'When's all this happening, Dina coming home?'

'As soon as the house is ready.'

'Did the doctors say it would be all right? I mean, there's still not much she can do for herself.'

'I'll do it.'

'She needs a lot of care. And there's Theo too. Do you think you can do it? I mean, it takes a team of nurses to do it all for her.'

'I can't leave her in that place. I couldn't live with myself.'

'Don't you like it?'

'It's fine. It's a nursing home really. I'm not going to let her be left there until everyone forgets about her. Imagine having to spend the rest of your life there.'

'It'd be horrible.'

'It'll be horrible here too, but at least she'll be home. She hated me bringing her back to the hospital after Christmas. I can't leave her there. I have to bring her home. I know things aren't going to change. She's not going to get any better.'

'You can't say that. You can't know that.' I turned back from the door. The hall was dim and edgy, like a dark forties film, but less comforting than the bleak light in the bathroom.

'Someone has to face reality and it has to be me. Everyone else can dream their hippy-trippy "the universe will work it out" stuff, but I have to change the catheter bag.'

There was nothing to say for a minute. I didn't think he was talking about me. I had said things like that but not in front of him. I hadn't accepted Dina would never get better, I couldn't accept such finality, but at the same time, I couldn't see that she would ever recover. Not enough for life to be anything like recognisable, at least.

Then the silence seemed to shift like the space in one of those expressionist films, elongated and distorted, with verticals and horizontals all slipping.

'And you know what else? Dina doesn't have any feeling any more for me. Or Theo.'

'You can't say that! What do you mean?' My heart began thumping hard.

'She doesn't love us. She has no feelings.' His face was young, fair, in need of a shave. Blood-shot eyes as tired as a very old man's.

'You can't say that.'

'Yes I can. It's not a judgment. It's a reality. The feeling part of her brain is gone.'

'I don't believe that. How can you possibly know that?'

'How do you know that anyone cares for you?'

We were in the narrow hall, an uncomfortably small space for this conversation. Kit's hair glowed white-blond in the light from the bathroom; he had dyed it for a small part in a film – he still did small acting jobs when he could fit them in. There was an odd shadow across his face from the bathroom's sliding door, making a sharp dissection down his nose.

I folded my arms across my chest.

'Well, you know, you just know. You can feel it.'

'Exactly. And I can't feel anything from Dina.'

Silenced again. But not for too long.

'Well, I don't know about that, but she does care for Theo. Of course she does.'

'You want to think that. So do I. But I have to face it.'

'How can you think that?'

'I just see what's there. The other day, for example, Theo fell off the hospital chair onto his shoulder and cried, and Dina didn't register anything.'

'That's because she can't. She can't move her face even if she wants to. You know she can't. But she watches him all the time when he visits her. Every time I've ever been there, if Theo's there, she just watches him. She can't express feelings, but she keeps her eyes on him. I've seen her, he runs about and her eyes just follow him like she can't get enough of him.'

Kit's face softened a bit. His jaw had been hard and his voice needling, like he might unpick every notion of love and truth anyone ever had.

'It's true. Actually, it is true. I think you're right about that.'

'I am.'

'She does watch him all the time,' he repeated.

'She never takes her eyes off him. She loves him. Of course she does,' I said. I blinked fast a few times involuntarily, as if adjusting the lens. The hall stopped looking so film noir-ish. And Kit was reframing to the right shape and size, the right distance away.

'And you too; why would that be any different?'

'Yeah, well,' he said. 'I don't know.' The conversation was over. He sidled along the hall a few steps and looked in at Theo. He was fast asleep, curled, slightly foetal, his cheeks glowing softly in the light of his bedside lamp. A photo of Dina, smiling, was stuck on the wall where he could see it as he drifted off. I suppose she was always there in his dreaming. Kit and I stood at the door, watching him sleep.

Visiting (iii)

Mani and Theo were playing soccer in the back yard. At least, Mani was trying to teach Theo how to kick the ball. He had been coming to Mani's Sunday morning pre-season matches with us down in Gloria Park. He would watch Mani for a while, and what must have been the incomprehensible running up and down, then he would ask to be taken over to the swings and climbing 'equipment' as he had taken to calling it. I think he had heard

Mani call it that. He always kept a lookout for the state of play, though, and hung around Mani when he came off the field at half-time. Mani was a star in his team, much admired for his sudden and very fast runs, often the length of the field. Whenever he had the ball, a current of excitement ran through the team and spectators as his wild runs often ended in a goal. Theo stood near him to make his claim.

At home, the back yard was grassy but sloped away from the verandah, so the ball usually rolled away down the hill. Just below the verandah there was a semicircular bare patch where Mani kicked the ball at the steps for hours on end, practising his goal-shooting, so the surface was uneven and rough. The skinny almond trees, which only yielded nuts one summer and then gave up, were the goal posts at one end and at the other, Theo's goal, were two piles of bricks, twice as far apart as the almond trees. The 'field' between them was about ten metres long.

I watched Mani demonstrate how to kick the ball with the top edge of his foot and how to dribble the ball back and forth quickly between both feet. Then he scooped the ball up onto his ankle with a quick twist of the other foot and began bouncing the ball expertly up and down, one foot to the other.

'Give it to me. Give it to me,' Theo cried.

Mani let the ball roll away. I had reminded him often enough that Theo was seven years younger than him, and to allow him a few concessions. Theo ran after it and picked it up and held it against his chest with both hands.

'You're not allowed to touch the ball with your hands in soccer,' Mani said.

Theo's mouth trembled a bit.

'Don't be a crybaby. I'm just reminding you so you know.' He rolled his eyes.

Theo's face cleared. He put the ball down and kicked it awkwardly, almost tripping over on it. He was really too young for ball games, his motor coordination not developed enough, but he was desperate to do whatever Mani did. The ball rolled a short way. Mani danced towards it and stopped it with his toe, sliding it this way and that with elaborate grace. He dribbled it forward towards his goal. Theo couldn't get anywhere near it. His face started to tremble again. Mani saw it and feigned kicking the ball and missing, so that it rolled towards Theo. It stopped between his chubby legs. He kicked out and it rolled sideways.

'Good kick! Kick it again!' He ran towards it himself as if to capture it, but then pretended to trip and Theo laughed and kicked it wildly. It went into Mani's goal.

'Own goal!' cried Mani.

Theo's tears spilled over. Mani had already explained to him the enormity of the shame in an own goal. I stood up, preparing to intervene.

'Come on. Don't be a spoilsport. Everyone does that one time,' Mani said. He retrieved the ball from the flower garden behind the almond tree goal posts.

Theo held his tears and looked up at Mani.

'Except me,' added Mani with a grin. Theo grinned back, his face still tear-stained. Whatever Mani did or said came with the authority of the gods themselves. He was the fount of all knowledge and skill: the best soccer player, the best builder of spaceships, the best drawer of eagles and dragons and the best climber of trees. He put his hand on Theo's shoulder then walked over with him to sit down on the steps.

'Time for a break, anyway.'

Theo looked up towards where I was sitting on a cane chair on the verandah in the shade and then sat down on the step next to Mani. He sat with his knees apart, the same as Mani. I went inside to get some juice for them. It was still too hot for soccer.

Thirty-Six

Family and Friends

I thought I drove up to Ryde every week, I thought that was the deal I'd made, but when I look back through The Book, there aren't entries from me every week, and I'm sure I would have recorded it if I had visited. It was my evidence. Then again, there isn't the same frequency of entries from other friends as in the first couple of months after the haemorrhage either. Except for Chrissie and Cathy who came every couple of days, there was only a few, really, who came most weeks – getting on for nine months since it all happened. Ryde wasn't near where anyone lived or worked and everyone's life was so busy with shows, jobs, children.

Dina's sisters had come over from Christchurch – her father had come but only for a week as he was too old and ill, and her mother had died a few years earlier – but her sisters came and stayed at Kit's a couple of times. They and Kit didn't get on so well; Kit didn't have any energy for the niceties and they valued niceties. Neither of them seemed much like Dina – I imagine she was the one they shook their heads over at family gatherings. Noela was plump and pleasant and appeared to have most things sorted out and she tried to do her duty; Lizzy was taller and irritated Kit with her Christian understanding. They knew a different Dina to everyone else, even knew her by a different name. She had been plain Dianne at home and that's what they still called her. They knew her with plaits, practising the piano and giving cheek to their mother; they remembered her frightening everyone, especially their father, by running away for the weekend when she was fourteen. Their father adored Dianne, always had. This was breaking his heart – he probably wouldn't last long. Noela bought yellow roses for Dianne; she had always loved them, Noela said. Kit didn't remember Dina ever saying she liked yellow roses. It was clear from The Book entries, though, how much her sisters loved her.

Then there was Kit's family, his young-looking blonde mother and his two younger brothers, both of them built along the same 'builder's labourer' lines as Kit. His father had left the family when Kit was fourteen; he hadn't seen him since and didn't care if he ever did again. His mother lived on the north coast, too far away to do much, and she had a sick husband and her own failing mother to look after, but the brothers lived in Sydney and visited Dina, and more often Kit, keeping him company, playing with Theo, watching television, supplying a few beers or vodkas. When all three brothers were in the lounge-room at Terrace Falls Road, they took up most of the space.

The Dog

Jock waited near the front door most of the time. He was upset and confused and would seem to ask everyone who visited if they knew anything of Dina's whereabouts. A few times I saw him sidle up to visitors and sniff them, and you'd swear he was checking to see if they had found her. He was an old dog already, and a bit weepy-eyed.

With Kit at the hospital all day, he was locked in the house most of the time. Kit asked Mani and me to go over during the day to let him out for a run. Although he hardly knew us, he was thrilled when we arrived and gambolled like a puppy. Kit had told us he liked to play with a lump of four-by-two, which we first thought was a joke, but when Mani found a piece about a metre-and-a-half long and heaved it awkwardly for him, he bounded off after it, seized it in his scary jaws and bounded back. It looked so silly, a short squat dog with a length of four-by-two in his mouth as if it were a stick. He looked so pleased at our laughter. I don't much like Oxford bull terriers usually, their mean-looking eyes and snouts, but Jock was a sweet-natured old dog. We played in the front garden for a while, heaving the lump of wood and laughing every time he came back with it, and then let him sniff around the yard.

When it was time for us to leave he saw me look at my watch and so I pointed at the front door. He plodded back up the steps slowly, his head hanging down, so perfect an image of 'a hangdog expression' that we had to laugh again. He lifted his head then, thinking we would relent and invite him back to play, but I shook my head and his head went down again.

The house started to smell of dog and dog-food after a while. Jock was fed just inside the back door, which opened straight into the kitchen and the living area, so the smell hit as soon as you walked in. Old sad dog. And the place wasn't kept as fresh and welcoming as Dina used to have it. Corners weren't quite swept out, photos were dusty, the dog-food bowls weren't washed, the pile of old newspapers was too high. Not that Kit and Dina were a conventional couple with her doing the housework and him the garden, but she had a designer's eye for detail, for having things arranged so you didn't even notice how pleasing it all was, you just felt glad to be there.

The deck out the back had made a difference, though. You stepped straight out of the kitchen onto it through a double sliding glass door, which let quite a bit of light into the house. It was wide, big enough for a fair-sized party, and had a lattice fence around it as it was a few metres off the steeply sloping ground. It looked down over Theo's sandpit and the terraced dogwoods and rhododendrons and fruit trees, and beyond you could see the gums and banksias and grevilleas of the bush. There was a long ramp coming up to it instead of the usual steps.

When Kit was home, Jock liked to lie out on the deck in the autumn light and sun himself there. It was too chilly in the house by late afternoon.

Thirty-Seven

Autumn Slides (i)

Dina came home at the end of March. On the first morning, Kit put the wheelchair at the window so Dina could look out into their garden. She liked to see the change of seasons, he said. She had spent winter, spring and summer in hospital. The summer had been long and the season was just turning, the pang of nostalgia stirring like a weather ache. The fresher, cooler air in the morning and evening and the earthy scents brought sensory half-memories and a longing for something not quite distinct enough to name. The Chinese maple outside the picture window had turned a brilliant pink. It looked hallucinatory against the blue sky, too pink to be natural, Kit said.

Autumn Slides (ii)

On my first visit to Dina at home I brought Theo back from child-care with me. He wanted me to carry him up the front steps – they were too high and steep for his short chubby legs. I looked up and seeing Dina looking at us through the front window, I felt immediately guilty. I put him down at the top and knocked on the door. Kit opened it and Theo ran in and straight to his toy-box, which was kept in the lounge-room. Dina followed his movements with her eyes.

'Say hello to your mum,' Kit said, but Theo was leaning into the toy-box and took no notice.

'It's good to see you home at last,' I said. I sat down on the end of the lounge.

She looked at me then back to Theo. Kit offered to make a cup of coffee and I said yes, thanks. Theo picked something out of the box and dropped it then picked something else up and, satisfied, closed the lid. He walked solemnly over to Dina and put a red matchbox bus in her lap, careful not to bump into her legs. She put her hand over the bus. Her fingernails had been painted the same fiery red colour.

Theo patted her hand gently. His hand was plump and white, hers bony and white. After a few seconds he trotted back to his toy-box, opened it, then came back with two large blocks. He placed these on her lap and Dina moved her hand to cover the blocks and the bus. Again he went back to the toy-box and this time found a small teddy and came back with it. He continued trotting back and forth, gradually filling his mother's lap with toys.

'I think they're for you to play with,' I said.

Autumn Slides (iii)

It was a cloudy Saturday afternoon, the wind starting to get chilly. Kit had put the heater on in the lounge-room so I stood near it, folding the washing. There were mountains of it – Dina went through heaps of clothes; shirts had to be changed after spoon-feeding and her incontinence and inability to control her bowels made a lot of changes of sheets and towels necessary. And then there were Theo's and Kit's clothes as well.

Dina sat by the window as usual. She was dressed in a long-sleeved T-shirt and trackpants. It's hard to dress a body that can't move of its own volition – you need loose, stretchy clothes – so Kit used Dina's own T-shirts and bought a few trackpants at Kmart. My mother did the same thing with my father. He wasn't fashion conscious but the sight of him in trackpants made me sad. He used to only wear heavy work pants or his Sunday suit pants – the same for sixty or more years. He wouldn't even have thought of changing the way he dressed.

I folded, selfconsciously. Dina watched. As I worked her body slipped gradually forward into a curled position and her head was at an awkward angle. I called out to Kit, who was working on his computer in the bedroom. He came in and pushed Dina's shoulders back and adjusted the pillows behind her and on either side, stuffing them in beside her shoulders and under her elbows to keep her sitting upright.

'Do you think she's comfortable?'

'Are you comfortable, Deen?' Kit asked. She nodded. 'You curl up like a possum, don't you?' Then to me: 'You know, you can do this sort of thing for her. Just ask her directly and then take her firmly by the shoulders and uncurl her. It has to be done. Otherwise her muscles shorten and she won't be able to sit up or straighten out at all. And it compresses her lungs when she's curled up. It's hard for her to breathe.'

'Sorry. I wasn't sure what I should do.'

'It's okay. You can just ask Dina what she wants. Can't she, Deen?'

I continued with the folding. Kit sat down by Dina, holding her hand.

'This is nice,' I said, holding up a silk shirt. It was a curious greenish colour, a sort of olive-green. She nodded.

'What colour would you call it?'

'Dina has a lot of clothes that colour,' Kit said. 'What's it called, Deen?' He put his hands around her jaw, placed his thumb and middle finger in the socket and pressed. With the pressure of his palm on her chin, her mouth opened. He'd become expert at doing this.

'Chartreuse,' she said.

I'd not known what colour chartreuse was before.

There was saliva dribbling from her mouth a little. Kit wiped it away.

Autumn Slides (iv)

The fifties lounge was re-covered. Kit pointed it out to everyone who came. Each time he said, 'Dina chose the fabric.'

He said he'd been thinking about how bored Dina must be sitting in her chair all day and had remembered her wanting to do the lounge. 'She was doing an upholstery course last year.' So, he asked her if she still wanted it done and she had nodded. He asked Mish to sit with Dina and went down to the city and brought home a book of fabric swatches from a home design shop. Mish said he looked pleased with himself as he walked in with the large bulky book and placed it on Dina's lap. She looked at it and tried to lift the heavy cover, but she couldn't open it far enough. Her hand wouldn't lift that high. Kit opened it for her and she studied the printed fabric at the front of the book. She touched the swatch, stroking it for texture.

'Is that the one you want?'

She shook her head and looked at him. Kit turned the swatches and both Kit and Mish remarked on how she studied each one. It was as if she was clearly visualising how each one would look. She looked up at the lounge then back down at a particular aqua swatch several times.

'That one?'

She didn't answer but kept looking, touching other pieces of fabric and occasionally looking up at the lounge. Kit kept turning the pages. She stopped again at a peacock-blue piece and put her hand on it.

'That one?'

She ignored him and left her hand on it a while longer. When she lifted her hand, Kit turned to the next swatch. They reached the end of the book. It still wasn't clear what she wanted.

'So, which one? Or none?'

Dina looked at him.

'Sorry. I'll turn the pieces slowly and when I get to one you like, nod like mad.'

He turned back through the book. He stopped at the peacock-blue piece but Dina just looked at it. He slowed again at the aqua and this time Dina nodded.

'This one?'

She nodded again.

'I asked you that before. You could have told me then. Making me stand about all day while you shop.' He put his arm around her shoulder and kissed her on the cheek.

He had the lounge sent to a local upholsterer and it came back in two weeks looking magnificent. It had appeared oversized for the space before, but now it was in proportion and brought the whole room together. The aqua fabric suited it perfectly; made you feel as if you needed a ponytail and swing skirt to sit on it and rock'n'roll playing on the transistor in the kitchen.

Autumn Slides (v)

Dina lay propped up in the bedroom in their four-poster, wearing one of her old T-shirts. She was too tired to be got up and dressed, Kit said. He was red-eyed himself, but he had offered to help me out with some layout work on his computer. My software was old and didn't have the layout choices or even the fonts that his did.

I greeted Dina and briefly sat on the bed. She didn't take up much space but because her limbs didn't have the fluidity of movement, it felt as if you were sitting next to a brittle doll, one that would break easily.

'You can watch me work. A big thrill.'

She didn't bother nodding at the poor sarcasm, but turned her head slightly so that she could see Kit, who was already sitting at his desk just inside the bedroom door.

'Okay. Kit's ready. I'd better get to it.'

He began at the keyboard and I stood behind him, pen and paper in hand, reading out my notes about how the pages should be arranged. The writing itself was finished; it was students' work that I was putting together as an anthology for them, and it had been edited, but it was still in folio form. Deciding on layout took some concentration and we both became involved, discussing options, trying different arrangements. I don't think Kit knew much about layout but he was always willing to give anything a go. It was a new area for me, a new relationship to the words, thinking about the look of them, the shapes and spaces. I recalled how, as a child, I had loved the mouse's 'tail' in *Alice in Wonderland* as it wriggled down the page; the childish delight in recognising the pun on 'tale' and then the correspondence of the visual shape. And 'Easter Wings' too, the George Herbert poem, shaped like the wings of the Holy Spirit.

'Don't know that one. Don't know "The Mouse's Tale", for that matter.'

'Yeah, you do. Everyone does.'

Kit and I talked and laughed as we worked and I could feel that pleasure in a shared task, the warmth and reassurance of it. We spent half an hour arranging the anthology's contents page to our satisfaction, all the story titles and authors neatly lined up. I have to say I practically forgot Dina was there until she groaned.

'What's up?' Kit said. We both turned. Dina gave another groan. It was more like a whimper really, soft and pained. Her upper body had slipped until it leaned sideways at an uncomfortable-looking angle.

'You feeling sore?' He got up and crossed to the bed.

'She often gets sore sitting or lying in the same place. Even without slipping. You don't realise how much shifting and adjusting we do automatically until you have to do it for someone else. I turn her all the time but she's still got a pressure sore on her hip.' This to me as he leaned over and, slipping his arms under her, shifted her to a more upright position.

The warmth of our working together was still in my body. I sat down at the desk but facing away from it, towards Dina. She didn't look at me but at Kit as he talked to her softly, rearranging the pillows and smoothing her hair back from her forehead. He ran his finger gently along her cheekbone.

This was private, this was their bedroom, I shouldn't be here, not even just sitting at the computer.

I looked around the room. The tiger skin rug still covered most of the wall on the other side of the bed and above Dina, behind the bed, the framed mirror that had saved her the summer before last.

Autumn Slides (vi)

Kit asked me to feed Dina while he went out to do a bit of shopping. Mish hadn't been able to make it as she had the flu – we had a bit of a roster and it had been her turn. Kit had already made Dina a spicy spinach-and-potato purée that was keeping warm on the stove. On the bench was the calorie-counter book that he used religiously to make sure she was getting enough nourishment every day. Dina sat in her wheelchair in the lounge-room in front of the cream calico curtains she'd made.

'Do you trust me to feed you?' I asked.

Dina looked at me without expression.

'First, I have to show you the Heimlich manoeuvre,' Kit said.

'The what?'

'You have to know it if Dina starts to choke.'

I stared at him and he raised his eyebrows. 'Yeah, I know, it's weird, but it's like that every day for me. Her gag reflex isn't spontaneous so it could easily happen. Turn around and I'll show you how to do it.'

I stood there, not understanding what he meant. He took me by the elbows and before I could be too startled he turned me around so that I was facing away from him.

'This is how you do it. Be warned, it's a bit fierce.' He put his arms around my body without touching me then linked his arms together and brought them in and up suddenly and shockingly against my diaphragm. My breath was expelled sharply, but I was more conscious of Kit standing so close behind me and Dina hunched in her chair.

'Whew! That was a bit rough.'

Kit let go and moved away. 'It's what you have to do. Have you got it?'

'I don't know. It's a bit scary.'

'It's all right. You do it if you have to. That's one thing I've found out – you can do anything if you have to. I won't be gone long anyway. About an hour.'

He left and I turned, bright and cheery, to Dina.

'Feel like some purée, Deen?'

I sat down with the bowl and spoon and gave her a mouthful. Her mouth was not open very wide and I dropped a bit on her lips and chin and had to scrape it off like you do with babies. She held the food in her mouth for a while as if considering what to do with it, then she started to work it around her mouth. She had been doing the tongue and lip exercises for a couple of months to redevelop her ability to move food around her mouth so, despite how things had been going, that bit wasn't too hard. When it came to swallowing, though, nothing much happened. I watched her throat anxiously. Kit had said to see that she swallowed little by little rather than continuing to put food in her mouth, which could cause her to gulp and maybe choke.

'Swallow it, Dina.' Her throat moved a little. 'That's the way.' Had it gone down? Her breathing was rattly, as if there was a lot of phlegm in her throat or chest. Was there something I ought to do?

A few more mouthfuls seemed to go down, no more than four teaspoonfuls, and that was it. Dina pressed her lips shut and wouldn't open them. I remembered 'aeroplanes' of food with babies, zooming spoons through the air to coax mouths open, and wanted to giggle. I looked away out of the window to the view across the mountains and when I looked back, there was a puddle of food on Dina's chin and she was working the rest of it out with her tongue. She'd swallowed practically none of it. I wiped it away with a tissue and waited for Kit to return. At least I hadn't choked her.

Autumn Slides (vii)

Kit woke up four or five times every night to turn Dina over. She had to be moved from side to side every two hours, day and night, to minimise the risk of thrombosis and nerve damage and to avoid developing pressure sores. She couldn't roll herself over in those near to waking moments like the rest of us do every night. Even though she was small and lightweight, it was awkward with the catheter. Sometimes the tube came out or apart and there was urine spilt and Kit had to change the sheets. Sometimes Dina's body expelled the catheter of its own accord, which would have caused her great discomfort because the balloon full of air, about the size of a large marble, which held the catheter in place, would have been passed down her urethra. Not to mention the discomfort of both of them lying in urine. He didn't get more than ninety minutes of sleep at a time. He set the alarm clock each time in case he didn't wake.

The community nurses came to help wash Dina in the mornings at first. The chair was wheeled right into the shower recess and the hand-held nozzle with the thermostatic valve to prevent accidental scalding made things easier, but everyone still ended up getting wet. The bathroom and three or four towels were sodden by the time they finished each morning. Dina was soaped and rinsed and dried and moisturised and dressed every day. Incontinence pads were inserted between her legs like nappies. Her hair was washed twice a week. Her nails were cut every week. They didn't shave her legs, although she always used to.

I don't know if Dina found it undignified and mortifying, a stranger and Kit together washing her twisted body. Perhaps she was beyond mortification by this stage, wanting only to be comfortable, not in pain. Her unused leg muscles would have stung agonisingly when they were moved by the nurse, her back and neck would have ached as she leaned into awkward positions. None of her internal organs were working very efficiently either, so she would have felt heavy, sluggish.

Kit did physiotherapy with Dina twice a day for about an hour each time. The tendency of her body to curl up meant the muscles shortened; there was rigidity and arthritis in the joints. Kit stretched and massaged her limbs and weighed them down with the sandbags the hospital had given him to hold them extended. She groaned often while they were doing the physio.

The naso-gastric tube was reinserted after Christmas as Dina was losing too much weight. The tube was sometimes accidentally pulled out of position – coughing would move it too – and it sometimes ended up dangling into the lungs. Before Kit attached the plastic sheath of food to the frame that stood behind Dina's chair, he had to do a litmus-paper test each time to check where the tube was. He used a syringe to extract some fluid, put it in a small dish and used the litmus paper to check if the fluid was acid – if it was, the tube was in its right place in the stomach. The feeding equipment, the tubes and bags and connections, had to be cleaned and sterilised every day. Kit tried to feed her orally as well.

Then there was shit. The incontinence pads were really for shitting. Kit cleaned Dina up each time as if she were a baby, simply changing her nappy. Every now and then, because of her lack of physical movement, the faeces would become compacted in her bowel and Kit would give her a Microlax enema. On some occasions she was so badly compacted the Microlax didn't work at all and Kit had to put on rubber gloves and extract the faeces with a finger. Sometimes it worked too well and there was shit everywhere: up her back, on her clothes, on the sheets.

Autumn Slides (viii)

Mish invited Kit and Dina and Theo to visit. Dina didn't get out much. Taking her down the ramp to the garden gave her as much change of scenery as could be managed most days. Going out meant the community-access van had to be booked because she couldn't sit safely in a car. She needed the support of her wheelchair to sit upright at all. The van had to be booked well ahead of time as there were other people who needed it.

On the day, Kit dressed her in her tan jersey pants (they were stretchy enough to get on her) and her dark red cardigan (cardigans were much easier to manage than pullovers). She had always looked striking, with her pale skin and black hair, in that dark red. He put some make-up on her, which wasn't difficult for him as he always used to put on his own make-up as an actor. When he'd finished he showed Dina her reflection in the mirror and she looked at it without expression.

And then he had to dress Theo as well. Theo had a plentiful supply of overalls and jumpers and boots from friends and aunties. It was easy to buy clothes for a little boy.

The ramp made it straightforward to wheel Dina down to the van – Theo ran ahead – but care had to be taken with the catheter and the naso-gastric tube. The chair with Dina still in it was wheeled directly into the van and strapped with specially fitted seat-belts. It was only a short drive to Mish's place a few streets away, but the whole performance had taken half a day to organise. Mish had asked me to come as well and we were waiting for them together out the front. When they arrived Mish hugged them both and cried. I undid Theo's seat-belt and lifted him out of the van.

'You look great, Dina,' I said.

'A bit late, you guys, but you finally made it,' Mish said. She was still crying. The three of them had been on their way to Mish's for lunch the day the aneurysm burst a year ago.

Autumn Slides (ix)

It was luck, really. I was at the dentist and I picked up an old *Readers' Digest* that happened to contain an article about a businessman somewhere in the US who'd had a brain tumour, but I don't remember the details because what mattered was the alphabet board. It seemed such a simple and obvious thing that I wondered none of us had thought of it already. It gave me an idea.

I made an alphabet board when I got home, then went over to Terrace Falls Road and showed it to Kit and Dina. All it consisted of was a sheet of A5 paper with the alphabet written in large upper-case letters in bunches of three or four in a semicircle across the top half and a 'Yes' and 'No' written on either side at the bottom. The letters were bunched to make it easier to anticipate what letter she would select.

Dina was over by the kitchen bench near the telephone, her hands resting on her wheelchair tray. Kit said Chrissie had just rung and chatted to her. She was looking fresher, more clear-eyed than usual. I put the alphabet page on the tray and explained what it was for and that I had this idea about what we could do with it.

'Let's see if it works. Let me ask you something. How are you feeling today?' I grabbed a biro and an old envelope from my bag and sat myself on a kitchen chair beside her.

Dina studied the sheet of paper in front of her for long moments. I was just beginning to think she did not comprehend what it was for when she started moving her right hand – the left hand had become unusable over the last few months. The movement of her hand and its precise indication felt like a slow-motion sequence in a film, the moment of breakthrough, the moment sound pierces the everlasting silence. I felt as if I was holding my breath. Her hand moved slowly but purposefully towards the left until it stopped in front of the 'EFGH' bunch and her finger touched under the 'F'.

'F?'

She didn't say anything but started sliding her hand a little to the right and pointed to 'I'.

Okay, so I just had to write it down. It would use up too much of her energy if she had to confirm it every time as well. I wrote down 'FI'.

She moved further to the right and waved a finger at 'N', then back to the left to 'E'.

'FINE. You're feeling fine?'

But her hand was still moving. Back to 'I' again. She stopped for a few seconds then slid towards 'G', then a wide slide towards 'U'. The paper bunched up under her hand and she stopped, unable to lift her hand high enough to smooth it out. I put down the biro and envelope and smoothed it for her then held the top and bottom of the paper to keep it flat. She looked across the board then slid back towards 'E' and then, without looking, slid right back across the paper to 'S'. She tapped her finger lightly.

'IGUES? Ah, I get it: I GUESS. You're saying "Fine, I guess". You feel fine, you guess. Fair enough.' I grinned at her and Kit, feeling ridiculously pleased with the whole conversation. It was as if the plaster had been ripped off my own mouth. Dina was talking back to me of her own volition, she could talk, we could talk!

'Shit, Dina, this is great. Do you want to try my idea? Writing your story?'

She looked at me then moved her right hand across the page and put her finger right on 'YES'.

'Yes! Fantastic! Do you want to start on it right now?'

Without moving her hand she lifted her finger and put it down again on 'Yes'.

Kit had been sitting on the end of the lounge watching. 'I've got another one of those notebooks like The Book, if you want. Bridget made them. She sent them from Adelaide. Better than the back of that envelope.' He got up and went into their bedroom and came back with a notebook with a seaweed printed cover. The pattern on it was long and fluid and swirling, like oil in water, quite different from the cell pattern of The Book.

'Okay, then. Let's get started on it.'

Kit picked up a pile of mail from the bench. 'Good. This is good,' he said. 'I'll leave you to it. I want to catch up with some bills.' He gave Dina a kiss then went down the hall to the bedroom and his computer. He seemed pleased in a reserved sort of way. Maybe he thought it would stir things up too much.

We sat there together, she at the hastily scribbled alphabet page, me with blank notebook and biro in hand.

'So, where do you want to start?'

Dina sat there looking at me.

'Wherever you like. It's your story.'

There was a sort of nonplussed blankness about her, as if she wanted to say something but couldn't think what.

'An early memory? Your family?'

She looked at me and then back at the page. Maybe Kit was right about her not being able to initiate thought. Not being able to begin your own thoughts sounded hellish, like living in a worse than usual mental soup. Perhaps it was like the undifferentiated thoughts and sensations that sometimes occur in the middle of the night when you come near to waking but the distinguishing or organising part of your brain stays asleep. It's distressing because none of it is distinct enough to be encompassed by language – you try to grasp the weird agglomerations like 'jealous Chinese verb waterfalls' or 'steep-sided hills of Aboriginal descent', the making-sense part of your brain anxiously looking for articulation and meaning, but it all slips just out of reach. There is a cloudiness to the sensation, not clear-edged enough to be named anything. It's the stage before thought finds a shape, before language drops down over it and makes it safe with a nicely fitting word net. You try to wake because part of you remembers it's not always like this.

'Do you want to start with your parents? With your mum?'

Dina looked down at the page and moved her hand to 'Yes'.

'Okay. That's good. Mothers are always a good place to start. Whatever way you look at it, they're there at the beginning. What do you want to say about her?'

The blankness again. This is not going to work. I can't put words in her mouth. Dina looked down at the board as if thinking, but nothing happened. In the silence and with her head bent, her hands like curled-up paws on the page, she looked weary and unutterably sad. The enormity of her loss seemed to cling around her like a miasma from some dank and oily swamp.

There had to be something. Find a key, quickly. Find a distinction. Ask a question precise enough to begin a thought.

'What was your mother's name?'

She glanced at me. Then her hand began moving. 'M'. And then without stopping she swung back to 'A'.

It's working! It's working! Thank Christ.

'R'. Her hand fairly glided across the page, as if on a polished surface, although with the edges held down by me, which was a bit awkward. We were going to have to do something about the design features.

'M.A.R. Mary?' I guessed.

She ignored me and kept going. 'G'.

'M.A.R.G. Was it Margaret?'

Dina ignored me again and kept on spelling. 'A.R.E.T'.

'Margaret. It was Margaret.'

She looked at me. Her breath came out in a puffing sigh. There seemed to be huge relief in her eyes. She had spelled out her mother's name. Kit told me how much she had missed her when she died. The painful grief of losing a mother in another country. She hadn't even seen her that often since she'd moved to Australia in her twenties.

'Okay. That's great. What would you like to say about her?'

She looked at me.

Too vague, too big a question. The question had to be precise, like a code, to set off a response.

'What was her character, her personality? What was she like as a person?'

She looked down at the page, studied it for a moment, then the slow slide started again.

'L.I.K.E'.

Okay, this is looking okay.

'M.E. I. T.H.I.N.K'.

'Like me, I think?' I showed her what I'd written in the notebook and she nodded. 'This is interesting. Your mother, who lived all her life in quiet old Christchurch – like you?'

She looked at me again and I thought I could see the sadness of missing someone in her eyes.

'In what way? How was she like you?'

'S.T.U.B.B.O.R.N. A.N.D. O.P.I.N.I.O.N.A.T.E.D'.

I laughed and she grimaced a little. We kept going. She spelled out each word letter by letter. I wrote down each letter, sometimes not getting where one word ended and another began. When she didn't move her hand very far it was difficult to see what letter she was indicating and a few times it took minutes to establish just one letter. As we got going and I lost my anxiety about putting words in her mouth, I would predict the word or even the phrase and I'd say it out loud to check and she'd point to 'Yes' or 'No' and we'd speed along. But then she tired and could barely drag her hand for the last couple of words. It took about an hour to write a paragraph. By the end of the first session I was elated.

'I'll write it all up for you. Join it up into sentences a bit more, if you like.'

She waved towards 'Yes'.

'This is so great! Now we can talk about life, the universe and everything!' I said. I was bubbling with the thrill of it. It is not often one thinks of the right thing to do at the right time.

Dina gave me one of her grimace-grins and then she started spelling something out. I waited.

'T.H.A.N.K.Y.O.U'.

She looked back up at me and uncurled her fingers a little. I took her hand. I could feel the blood pulsing through her thumb, see the blue veins in her fine white skin. She sighed one of her puffing sighs again and I felt my breath expanding my lungs. Rarely, and just for a moment, the universe and I get along. Distances melt, tangles resolve into a pattern, and the breath and heartbeat make sense of things.

> The First Paragraph:
> My mother's name was Margaret. She didn't work outside of the home but I think she would have liked to have done something – music – she played the piano. I think she was like me in her personalitiy and her abilities. She could be very stubborn and opinionated – about everything.

Autumn Slides (x)

The naso-gastric tube was replaced with a tube going directly into her stomach. Kit had tried, and wanted to keep on trying, to feed her orally, backed up by the nose tube, but she was weighed and assessed by her doctor and he said the tube inserted in her stomach was the safe and reliable option. She was taken down to Westmead Hospital to have it surgically inserted. When Kit told me, he looked defeated. I'd thought it would be a relief not to have to struggle for an hour or so to get her to swallow a few mouthfuls, not to have to worry about her choking, but he said, 'She ought to at least have the pleasure of food; it was the only pleasure she had.' He'd been run over by a truck once and he had kept going, but now his large body sagged as if he couldn't go any further.

Smiling, cuddling, kissing, licking, tasting, sipping, sucking, swallowing, stroking, rubbing, fondling, whispering, murmuring, teasing, joking, laughing, wriggling, stretching, striding, running, dancing, humming, strumming, singing. She couldn't do any of them.

Autumn Slides (xi)

It was Theo's and Kit's birthdays within a few days of each other, so Kit organised a combined birthday party. Theo was three, Kit thirty-three, both of them late April Taureans, but the party wasn't arranged until late May. It took a while to organise things. The week before I'd asked Dina if she'd like me to buy a present for Kit on her behalf. She indicated 'Yes' and when I asked her what, she spelled out 'book'. I asked her which book, but she looked at me mutely, tiredly, and didn't even attempt to spell anything out.

'It's okay, I think I know what Kit likes.'

She flashed me a look – as much as a paralysed woman can flash, anyway – and I felt discomfited. I had thought I was trying to be helpful but now I'm not so sure. The line between being helpful and usurping is easy to leap over without blushing or anyone even noticing. On the day of the party, I arrived with Primo Levi's collection of stories, *The Periodic Table*, and slipped it onto the alphabet board. Kit had made a proper board with neatly drawn letters after the first time. Dina touched the cover of the book and tried to take it between her thumb and forefinger.

'Do you want to see the blurb?'

I turned it over for her and she put her hand on the back cover and read. The party swirled noisily around us. Dina's friends from Sydney had come up; there was Chrissie, dramatic in a flamboyant skirt, and Cathy in a suit of her own design, and Roger in boots made of the same flowery leather as Dina's, from Rocco's in Melbourne. Theo's new friends from child-care were there too, with their mothers standing together near the kitchen. Loretta Young sang over the laughter and talk and the smell of Kit's cooking drifted: Indian korma, Malayan satay, soy and ginger chicken wings, crumbed eggplant and the sweet scent of his fabled 'cake of a thousand nuts' cooling on the bench. He was out on the new deck, pouring vodka and laughing boisterously with an old acting friend, the one who'd given me the *Cosi* tickets. Dina had been dressed up for the party in the chartreuse top and a sarong; lipstick had been carefully applied. She was hunched as usual, pillows stuffed in beside her, and amongst all the standing, talking people, she looked small and separate, caught in a tiny world of her own. You could almost see the membrane separating her from the rest of us.

'Do you want to write in it?'

She pointed to 'Yes'.

She held the pen in a slippery fashion and tried to write. A spidery squiggle appeared, a barely decipherable 'H'. She must want to write 'Happy Birthday'. Then another thin letter appeared, an 'e' it looked like.

'Is that an "a" or an "e"? Don't you want an "a"?'

Dina ignored me and kept on with the next letter. An 'r' this time. What was she saying?

The pen looked as if it were made of cooked spaghetti, between her fingers, slithering about, making little feathery marks all around the letters. There was a kind of rhythm to the marks as she tried again and again to make the shape of the letter she wanted. A skinny capital 'E' emerged. 'Here'? Why is she writing 'here'? She must mean 'Happy', surely? Maybe the neural labyrinth to the right words has finally got too much for what is left of her functioning brain. The message has got lost, jumping walls in the labyrinth and ending up in the wrong place altogether.

'Don't you want to write "Happy"?'

She ignored me again. Her head was bent over, her forehead almost touching the pen. I took her shoulders and pushed her up a little. She kept hold of the pen and didn't look at me. The feathery marks of another letter resolved into a cursive 's'. Her head sank forward and she let the pen go.

'Do you want to write anything else?'

Without moving her hand she indicated with one finger towards the 'Yes'.

'Are you too tired? Would you like me to write it now?' This was so slow.

'Yes' again.

'What do you want me to say? Show me on the board.'

She began indicating the letters, slowly, so slowly, her arm dragging across the board. Noise and laughter surrounded us, although no-one joined in our strange peeved conversation. 'L', or was it an 'M'? Her finger was still a few centimetres from the actual letter.

'L?' I asked.

Her finger waved towards 'Yes'. Her hand moved slightly and she waved again.

'O?'

Another wave to 'Yes'. Okay, so this is working.

Her hand stayed where it was. Her head was bent very low and I thought she may even have gone to sleep. She would often go to sleep just like that, just close her eyes and be unconscious. Easy sleep was probably her only blessing.

'What letter's next, Dina?'

She lifted her finger ever so slightly, almost just a pulse, but left it in the same place.

'Come on, Deen, you can do it.' This was taking forever. The party would be over before we got this written. A sudden burst of insight: 'Do you want "v", do you want to write "love", "here's love"?'

A tired wave towards 'No'. She lifted her finger again, and again just a pulse.

'Another "o". You mean another"o"!'

She turned her head a little and looked at me. Yes, at last, another 'o', you stupid woman. Then, still looking at me, she moved her finger slightly back towards the left of the 'KLMN' sequence.

'K?'

She blinked at me.

'Here's look?'

Dina turned her head away and slowly dragged her hand further to the left.

'Do you mean "I"?

'Yes'.

'New word?'

'No'.

Another drag back to the right. A wave in the middle of the 'KLMN' sequence.

'N? Okay. So G as well. "Here's looking?" Oh, I get it! I get it! You want to say, "Here's looking at you, kid!"'

Dina turned her head and gave me a sardonic look and the mouth-twist I'd learned was a smile.

'Whew, what a relief. I'm sorry I was so thick about it.'

Her eyebrows lifted a little and then she yawned hugely. It was the most her face ever moved, when she yawned, and it was always tight, as if she was trying to keep her mouth shut because she couldn't move her hand to cover it. She seemed put out by the gracelessness of the wide open-mouthed yawn and turned her head away from me. I wrote the rest of the message in the front of the book.

'And do you want me to say "Love, Dina"?'

She turned her head back and looked at me, then lifted her finger faintly towards 'Yes'. Her gaze stayed on me as I wrote.

'Should I get Kit now?'

She ignored the question.

'Okay. Well, I'll go and get him. I'll leave the book here with you.'

I got away out onto the verandah and after telling Kit that Dina had something for him, I stayed there, trying the chicken wings and making conversation with people I'd only met before at the hospital. It was warm for May in the Mountains, so we were able to stay outside most of the afternoon. Dina was parked outside for a while as well. Once I went to her and asked if there was anything she wanted. She spelled out 'G.O.', and I felt a sting of humiliation, especially when the next letter was 'A'. She was going to tell me to 'go away'! Silently, in front of everyone. The relief was a long time coming but the sentence finally resolved itself into 'G.O. A.N.D. C.H.A.N.G.E. T.H.E. M.U.S.I.C'.

Later on the birthday cake was cut by Theo and Kit and everyone except Dina sang 'Happy Birthday'. I saw Kit gazing at Dina at one stage. She was included in the circle of people but no-one was talking to her. With her thin body hunched in the wheelchair and her slightly dribbling mouth, she looked like something misplaced from another film amongst the well-dressed, bright, upright people.

Autumn Slides (xii)

I leaned on the arms of Dina's chair, chin on folded arms; Kit sat back on the lounge on the other side, Theo asleep beside him. Anthony was on the floor leaning against the lounge with a cup of coffee in his hand. It was a Sunday afternoon in winter and the three of us had finished pasta and red wine and were sitting around in the lounge-room with Dina. Of course, she had not eaten anything as her food tube was inserted directly into her stomach. She had sat through the meal, her wheelchair near the table, sometimes watching but mostly with her head bent down.

Anthony had been reading *Far Tortuga* by Peter Mathiesson and was saying how brilliant he was at dialogue. Kit said he liked *The Snow Leopard* and Anthony said, 'Yes, but this is a novel, and he uses a very different style.'

'Almost entirely dialogue – and in Jamaican dialect as well. It takes a few pages to get used to the dialect, but after that, you're just in that mind-set and it's not difficult.'

'He's not Jamaican, is he?'

'American. I used to think he was English. I always think there's something very English, a kind of preciseness about the way he writes.'

'Well, he's a biologist or something too, isn't he? *The Tree Where Man Was Born*, that was a kind of natural history book, I thought.'

They continued on but I didn't say anything – I hadn't read any Mathiesson. I waited for a chance to get a word in sideways so I could change the topic. I took a sip of my coffee and let the steam dampen my face a little. There were piles of washing up on the sink, from our meals and a few meals before, it looked like.

I glanced at Dina. Her torso was curling over and there was saliva dribbling from the corner of her mouth. Her breathing was loud, like someone with a cold, as if her air passages were blocked with mucus. Her breathing was often loud these days. I could see my reflection in the window behind her, my smooth face. I put my hand on her arm.

'How's it going?'

She lifted her eyes briefly. They were glazed and distant. Then she let her head drop.

It wasn't even as if she looked at me.

Autumn Slides (xiii)

Kit's eyes were red with tiredness. It was midday and there was washing-up all over the sink and bench and a pile of sheets in the corner of the kitchen near the door where he'd dropped them in the night. He'd had to change the bedclothes twice last night and hadn't gotten around to bringing the second lot down to the laundry under the house. There was a faint smell of urine in the house. Something in the intensity of his fatigue emanated that middle-of-the-night feeling, the space-out that comes when you're tired past tiredness, an acid weirdness that lets anything happen. I stood there feeling as if I shouldn't sit down. Kit had already told me Dina was worn out and asleep in the bedroom.

'You look like you could do with a sleep,' I said.

'Yeah, well.' He was sitting on the lounge, leaning forward as if he couldn't sit up straight. He looked up at me. The blue of his irises looked startling against the redness around them.

'So, not so good last night?'

'I had two hours sleep last night. Three the night before. And the night before. That's eight out of seventy-two.'

'What happened last night?'

'I have to wake every hour and a half anyway, to turn Dina. She's supposed to be turned every two hours and I'm always up for at least half an hour, changing her pads and whatever. And then I got mess on the sheets.' He stopped for a few seconds. His voice had got wavery. 'Twice last night.'

'Like having a baby,' I said.

'No, not like having a baby. Like having your wife totally fucking blown to bits.'

The middle-of-the-night air stretched and fingernails scratched on hard surfaces. My limbs felt unjointed, like a cheap doll.

'No-one knows,' he said. 'Nobody at all. It's the same every day and night.' His voice wavered again, ready to shred into sobs. I hadn't seen him like this before. I stood stiffly, not able to sit down or move forward or rearrange my body at all. Kit was looking straight at me, his gaze like pins through an insect. 'I bought the first lot of sheets down to the laundry last night. Two o'clock in the morning. One of the enemas I gave Dina in the afternoon decided to work at last. Shit went everywhere. Doona too. I had to find some old blankets in the wardrobe. I was standing in the yard, freezing cold, stinking of urine and shit, and I thought – this is my life. This is Dina's life. It's horrible. It's fucking horrible. There's not one thing about it that's any good.' His voice was stretching, thinning, twisting upwards.

What do I do? What do I do? My plastic arm reached out and touched his shoulder. It was shaking. His large frame felt as if it had reached the edge of what it could hold in one shape.

'I was going to rip the sheets and hang myself in the yard. Dina first.' His voice broke and he stopped for a second, the sobs heaving through him. 'And then me. Dina doesn't have a life. I don't have a life.'

Then there was only sobbing. It wasn't violent, but despairing. Frightening. All those trees in the back yard. Dina's tiny frame.

'Kit. You wouldn't. Not really.' And other helpless words. I said them. More words. More helpless. A stiff claw hand on his shoulder.

'I would. I nearly did. It was only that I thought of Theo. I wouldn't do it to him. I'd never do it to him. How could he live?' It wasn't a question but a simple statement of fact.

'Thank Christ for that.'

'I'd never do anything to hurt Theo. He's all I have. The rest is fucking hell. Hell for Dina and for me. Nobody knows.'

I suddenly thought of something. All those pretty decorative trees with their slender trunks and limbs. Kit's large builder's labourer body.

'You wouldn't have found a branch strong enough for you.'

He grinned, sort of. Wet-eyed. Red-eyed.

'And I'm glad I didn't have to find the lot of you on my next visit.'

He shrugged. I took my hand away from his shoulder. It was only an encumbrance to both of us. The stretching middle of the night was starting to sag back in and a greyish light was coming in the picture window. It was an ordinary cloudy day, just before lunch. Tuesday 16 June, a year since the haemorrhage.

'Anyway, I went back to bed and then I was up ninety minutes later doing the same thing. Wet, shitty sheets again. I dropped them at the back door. That's the way it is.'

Autumn Slides (xiv)

It took Dina about an hour and a half to spell out each of these paragraphs.

> As a child I lived in a yellow house made of wood. There were shrubs in the garden. The house had four bedrooms, one of which I shared with my sister, Lizzy. Our bedroom had flowery curtains and red and beige flowery carpet.
>
> I went to Amberly Primary School where my favourite teacher was Miss Dawkins. I had a particularly close friend called Susan Shier. My best subject was art.
>
> A favourite dress I had as a child was a pink one with a square collar of bright pink and buttons down the back. I wore white

slip-on shoes with it. I was seven years old then and my hair was short and curly.

When I was six I had my first boyfriend. His name was Geordie Hadler. He had blond hair. We never kissed. He had no brothers or sisters. He called me Dianne and he lived in Bank Street.

As a child I went to Leith Field Beach which was a black sand beach. There were pipis and cockles and mussels. And there were rocks with rockpools where I found starfish and crabs. My favourite thing to do was playing on the beach.

I went to Rangiruru High School and sat School Certificate in 1968. My mark was 276 out of 400. My best subject by then was English, my other subjects were art, maths and science. The next year I was accredited with university entrance. I went to Canterbury University but did not finish my degree. I left university in the early 1970s.

My mother looked like me. She was a smart dresser, very forthright and very honest. I think about her and miss her. She could be very stubborn and opinionated – about everything. I love her.

This time I said, 'Your mother died a couple of years ago, didn't she? Shouldn't I change the tense for you? Don't you mean "loved her"?'

But Dina pointed to 'No', and I suddenly thought, she means to join her mother.

Autumn Slides (xv)

On 7 July a choking, rattling sound woke Kit in the early morning. The light was dim in their bedroom but he could see Dina's mouth was open and her head was flailing wildly. She couldn't breathe. She was already a purply-blue colour. He hauled her up immediately, and as well as he could kneeling in bed, did a rough Heimlich manoeuvre, jerking his arms fiercely under her ribs. Her breath sucked in suddenly, noisily. It sounded as if her lungs and throat were full of phlegm. She drew breath again, the same clogged sound. Then another breath, noisy and frightening.

It struggled and stopped halfway through, then broke free and continued. Kit grabbed the telephone beside the bed and rang the ambulance. He dressed quickly and washed his face, listening for Dina's breath as he ran into the bathroom. A bubbling, clagging sound. She was drowning in something.

The ambulance arrived and rushed Dina to Katoomba Hospital. Theo had stayed overnight with me, so Kit rang me from there mid-morning. Apparently what had happened, according to the doctor, was that Dina had vomited, and because she couldn't sit up or roll over or even cough properly, the vomit had run back down her throat and some of it had gone into her lungs. She had been drowning in vomit. They had suctioned her lungs but Dina was still struggling to breathe. They were trying to stabilise her.

'Just tell Theo that Dina's back in hospital. Don't do anything yet. Don't take him to child-care. I'll give you a ring in a while when they know what's happening.'

I told Anthony.

'It looks like this is it, doesn't it?' He was getting Theo's breakfast.

'It looks like it.'

'You can't wish for her to stay alive.'

'No.'

Theo and I had the morning together. I can remember the thumping of my heart and the cool sunny day and Theo on my hip. The bush wisteria that grew around one of the eucalypts was flowering, a purple slash of colour, and Theo and I pulled off a strand of flowers and put them in a vegemite jar to take up to his mother.

Kit rang again. The doctor had told Kit that Dina had pneumonia as well, and there was too much material in the lungs and they couldn't do anything more about it. It also looked like she had recently had one or more epileptic fits. Respiratory failure was likely within the day.

'Bring Theo up,' he said.

'Is she conscious?'

'Yes, she's sleeping now, but she's been conscious. She goes in and out of dozing. She hasn't opened her eyes, though, and her breathing is pretty rough.'

'I'll bring him up right away. Should I say anything?'

'No. I'll explain when he gets here.'

It was time to do it.

'We're going to see your mum.'

'She's sick.'

'Yes, that's right. But she wants to see you anyway.'

I picked him up and carried him out to the car. He was three but he still liked to be carried like a baby. I strapped him into the seat-belt. He held the wet bits of bush wisteria in his hands.

'Off we go then.'

It was such a bright day. Theo was unconcerned and chatted as I drove. It was only a fifteen-minute drive to the hospital, no time to think about life or death, and although I really have no memory of what we might have talked about, I know it was ordinary. It was out of visiting hours so there was plenty of room to park at the hospital. I carried Theo along the corridors of the hospital and then put him down as we neared the ward. He ran into the pastel quietness of the room where Dina lay in the neat hospital bed. Kit was sitting by the bed.

Dina's eyes flicked open at the sound of Theo's running footsteps.

'That's the first time she's opened her eyes,' Kit said.

Theo didn't look at his mother. He put the wisteria on the end of the bed. Kit picked him up and spoke softly to him. Theo shook his head back and forth then wriggled down. He ran towards the fire extinguisher on the far wall and started to pull on the hose. He didn't glance at his strange mother with her caved-in temple and stiffly held limbs.

'Shall I go and wait outside?' I asked.

'No. It's all right. Stay here.'

I sat on the opposite side of the bed and took Dina's hand.

'Hello, Dina.'

She didn't register that she'd heard my voice or felt my touch. Kit stood up for a stretch. She didn't look at him either. Theo ran across the room and slid unexpectedly on the polished linoleum and landed on his bottom. He giggled at the sensation and got up and deliberately tried to fall and slide. Dina watched his every move, not turning her head, but her eyes sliding to keep him in view.

'Come over and see your mum,' Kit said.

Theo took no notice.

Kit and I said little to each other. Today we had nothing to say. Theo kept running and sliding, sounding noisy in the silence. A nurse came in and checked Dina's pulse.

'Hello, sweetie,' she said to Theo. He didn't answer her. She went out and came back with a lolly which she gave him. He popped it in his mouth but he still didn't say anything to her. She shrugged and left.

Theo came and stood by my chair and put his hand on my shoulder, then he scrambled up onto my knee. Dina turned her head with great effort and looked directly at him. He reached out to stroke his mother's fingers. She gazed at him for the longest time, for a lifetime, and her eyes filled with tears. It was the first time I had seen her cry since any of this began.

Dina didn't die that day. Three days later the doctor told Kit that Dina had recovered remarkably and was no longer in danger of respiratory failure and could go home on Sunday morning. She was as well as she had been in months, breathing cleanly and easily. Kit organised a coming-home lunch for her and invited Anthony and me, but early on the morning of the homecoming, the hospital rang. Dina had died suddenly half an hour before. No-one was with her. She never saw Theo again after the day she cried.

A mopoke calls over the lagoon. Whenever I hear the sound of mopokes calling, there is a strange mixture of fear and comfort. Even as a child I had learned that the mopoke was the messenger of death in Aboriginal lore, and when I heard its cry in the evenings on the farm I would immediately begin magic-thinking: not me, not me, not me. Now, as the two low notes repeat in the shadowy evening, the chant has changed a little to 'not my children, not my children, not my children'. I go inside from the verandah, eager to put walls between me and the sound. But at the same time as being a harbinger of mortality there is something eternal about its sound, something that makes it fit with everything around it: the night, the trees, the moon, cool air. It's as if it reminds me that death is what I'm dodging every moment of life, but it's all right, it will come when it does, and there will be no discussion. It's the change I pretend won't happen, breath leaving the body and never coming back. There is nothing on earth more unarguable.

Now there is more than one mopoke, one nearby and one answering from the other side of the lagoon. They have called in the night for thousands of years before me and mine. I am glad I'm inside the beach-house. I won't go outside again tonight.

Autumn Slides (xvi)

Kit asked if I wanted to see Dina's body at the funeral parlour. He was taking Theo up to see her so that he would know that his mother was gone.

'Just so he comprehends what has happened to her. I know he will forget consciously, but he will understand deep down.'

He picked me up on the way and we drove up to Katoomba. It was a quiet drive, it was cold and sleeting and the road was getting slippery so Kit had to concentrate, but there wasn't a lot to talk about. Even Theo didn't say much.

The funeral parlour was opposite the railway line and next door to a nursing home, a plain building fronting directly onto the street. Inside, it was much like the funeral parlour where I later saw my father's body – the same sound-absorbing carpet and fake wood panelling, except there were vases of real flowers instead of plastic ones. There was also a yellow bubble-glass wall that was probably meant to create a golden glow in the room but made it look like the entrance to an RSL Club. To one side, at the end of the bubble-glass wall, was the door to the chapel. Kit carried Theo in and I followed.

Dina's body was lying in an open coffin at the front of the chapel. The coffin was a polished reddish wood lined with white satin and stood on a metal trolley, just the right height for an adult to look down. Theo was still in Kit's arms. I didn't look at him at all as Kit spoke to him softly. I'd never seen a dead human body before.

I looked at the waxy solidity of her flesh.

Dina?

It was a face and body that looked a bit like her, but it wasn't her. I wanted to touch the solid flesh to see what it felt like but not with Kit and Theo watching. The utter absence would not sink in. I stood with my hands behind my back. There was no feeling.

This is death? A vacuum? No wonder so much religion and ritual rushed in. How could any one tolerate such nothingness? There was a crucifix on the wall of the chapel, a silvered metal Christ on a wooden cross. The place was much too warm. I wanted to take my jumper off but it didn't seem the right thing to do.

My mind fixed on the details of Dina's appearance, note-taking to fill the absence. She was dressed in a flamboyant red and white dress, like the Spanish one I had dreamed her in once.

I never saw her wear it when she was alive, although I've seen a photograph of her in it, the Happy Family snapshot, her and Kit and Theo on a bench in their back garden, Dina straight-backed and stylish – she always had good posture, like a model – Theo perched on her knee and Kit's arm around them both. The red and white dress covered her stiff limbs now and the fabric itself looked somehow stiff. The immobility of her body had robbed the dress of the flamboyance it had in the photograph. I wondered if it was the outfit she would have chosen for getting buried in. It's not the sort of fashion decision featured in style magazines.

Her face was framed now by her curly dark hair. Even though it had kept on growing right through the year she stayed alive, it still didn't hide where her skull caved in. It had been brushed forward in an unflattering style she would never have worn, and the death-set of muscles made her fine face look thick and heavy under the wig-like hair. The mortician-beautician had made up her face – powder, lipstick, blue eyeshadow. It had been carefully but thickly applied, so that it looked like a mask. It was macabre – the solidness of her face, and the bright colours on her dead flesh. Dina always had pale skin but, rather than colour it in, she had always used it to dramatic advantage – red lips slashed across a creamy pale face. Now she was a painted corpse. I kept thinking of *The Loved One*. Perhaps Mr Lovejoy would have done a better job and we would be admiring his handiwork with awe. It must be an art like no other, painting a dead face for its last outing. A few years later when I saw my father's body in the funeral parlour, I was relieved to see he was unpainted. Perhaps only women are made-up, or perhaps it was a specialty of that funeral parlour.

'She looks nice, don't you think?' A brown-suited man – the mortician, I guessed – was standing at the door of the chapel.

'Yes,' lied Kit.

Encouraged, the mortican sidled in and gazed with us at Dina's face.

'She must have been beautiful,' he said. He was a plain, sweaty man who looked as if he spent his life saying what he thought people wanted to hear but nearly always saying the wrong thing. Theo turned in Kit's arms and burrowed his face into Kit's shoulder.

'She was,' said Kit, truthfully.

'Your wife?'

'Yes.'

'It was difficult, working with that cavity in her skull. I tried to brush her hair over it.'

'She had a piece of her skull removed,' Kit explained.

'Why was that?'

'She'd had a cerebral haemorrhage. The surgeon removed a piece of her skull to relieve pressure on her brain.'

'Ah yes. I had one like it a couple of weeks ago. It makes a tricky job. Didn't know what caused it before. Don't they usually put a plate in though?'

'If she had got well, they would have. It's a long operation.'

'Yes, but it needs something to support the flesh. Makes it easier, you know, to prepare the face.'

Kit and the mortician were facing each other, a couple of blokes discussing the ins and outs of the job at hand. It was a scene from an English comedy, the unctuous mortician and the solemn widower. I backed away and sat down on the front pew with my head down. I studied the criss-cross pattern on the carpet at my feet. Kit and the mortician exchanged a few more comments, both of them leaning back a little in that way men do when they are discussing something they don't want to appear too interested in, then the mortician excused himself and disappeared behind the yellow bubble-glass. I avoided Kit's eye as he sat down with Theo. I knelt down for a bit and tried not to laugh, tried to think about Dina.

She had a great laugh.

Autumn Slides (xviii)

The funeral was at a lawn cemetery, smooth and grassy, no stone angels or Celtic crosses or leaning tombstones. It was in the western suburbs of Sydney at the foot of the Blue Mountains. I didn't recognise the names of anybody else in that place. It was a bright, sunny winter's day and Dina's sisters and crowds of her friends and Kit's family came. They weren't all dressed in black, but they were all wearing their most beautiful clothes. It was the best-dressed funeral I had ever been to. Kit spoke about Dina, and so did his mother and Chrissie. I wanted to say something but didn't. Then the coffin slid away behind the curtains on smooth and certain rails. And that was that. I can't even remember what music was playing, or even if there was any. I wish I had known about flights of angels singing her to her rest.

III

Thirty-Eight

The first time I dream it, I am climbing a narrow path up a high mountain range. The path is fraught with danger, slippery and steep, and seems to be going on forever, higher and more frightening, but, when I finally reach the top and look out, I see the valley below glowing with unearthly beauty and hear a surge of voices singing joyously. It is conventional imagery but I've never even imagined in conscious life the dissolving joy the dream-singing arouses in me. I wake with my body still remembering the molten gold feel of it. It was the first week after Dina died.

I've dreamed the mountain range several times since, and always begin by striding out confidently, but soon the path is blocked by fences, or rock walls, or the path falls away in front of me. The thing is, when I turn to go back down, the path behind has also disappeared. I cannot retreat. I dreamed it again last night. It's the kind of dream that echoes all day and especially at twilight. I put a Joni Mitchell song in the CD player and sit. She always sits me down. 'A Free Man in Paris' floats out and concertinas time. It is always evening, a glass of wine, the song, no-one else about. The water is pale and still. The brush turkey scratches at his mound at the end of the yard, right on the edge of the water. I listen to the unfamiliar water-bird sounds that have begun to be reassuring, the hooting of pelicans and clacking and splashing of ibis and cranes and quacking and clicking of black ducks, and then the bellbird chimes from further up the valley, reminding me of home in the mountains. Then the birds of childhood call: peewees crying, crows cawing, magpies still warbling like happiness itself, just as they did across the dry stubbly paddocks. They are all here in this place where I'm telling the story of the summer, when and how things changed.

Telephone Calls (i)

It wasn't as difficult to pick up the telephone this time. I rang the number the teacher gave me and a friendly voice answered.

'No, I don't teach individual singing.'

So I can give up, gracefully.

'I have a singing group, though. A choir. You can come to the choir.'

'I couldn't. I can't sing. I have to learn to sing first.'

'Perhaps it will be easier to learn with others.'

See, here is the chasm, but it's full of air to fly in.

'I'm no good at singing at all. I can't hold a tune.'

'That's all right. You can come and just listen.'

The choir met at the next village up the Mountains, at Lawson Community Hall, on a Sunday afternoon all term. It was a few days away, long enough to change my mind.

Telephone Calls (ii)

I stood in the study, leaning against the bookshelves above the telephone.

'How's it going? Is it still hot down there?' I asked.

'No. It's cold and rainy. Melbourne's a lot nearer the South Pole, you know.' Theo's voice was cheeky, confident.

'I know where Melbourne is. Have you seen any icebergs?'

'Yep. I run across them to school.'

'Sure, sure. So how is school anyway?'

'It's good.'

'Is your teacher still good?'

'Yep, she's excellent.'

'How's Jake?'

'He's excellent too.'

'Good. Well, I've got your ticket for the holidays, so you can have a break from iceberg-running.'

'When?'

'Well, the Victorian school holidays are around the same time as here, so it's a couple of weeks.'

'Will Mani be there?'

'Yep.'

'Good.'

Starting Again (i)

Mani's room had to be cleared out a bit to make space for Theo. The spare bed was piled with school books, discarded T-shirts, towels, a guitar, loose essay pages, bits of chocolate wrapping, the detritus of Mani's school term. He was seventeen now, and although he didn't mind Theo sharing the room with him for a couple of weeks, he didn't see the need for more than pushing the pile to the end of the bed. I didn't touch his room without asking permission.

'He's only ten; he'll still fit in half the bed.'

'I want to make it nice for him. Welcoming.'

'You can if you want. But he won't notice.'

I began shifting things about anyway; books back onto bookshelves, dirty clothes into the cane basket, essay pages onto writing-desk, chocolate-bar wrappings in bin, relaxing as I moved about into the familiar rhythm of ordering that doesn't have to be created but simply restored. There on the shelf above the bed was Theo's little plastic Oxford bull terrier he'd placed there before he left. It was brown but otherwise looked just like Jock, who had disappeared a few months before Dina died. Kit had yelled at him one day when he was underfoot – told him to get the hell out of the way – and Jock had plodded outside and down the ramp into the garden and never came back. Theo missed him and Kit had searched in the bush behind the yard and up and down the street and asked all the neighbours, but there was never any sign of him. He was an old dog and probably went out to die somewhere.

There were other things of Theo's left about: two odd socks, a pair of underpants, a pair of summer pyjamas, a small globe of the world that slithered in a sideways fashion when you touched it, a plastic dinosaur, a tattered copy of *The Hobbit*. I had meant to post them all on, but new bits and pieces kept surfacing and the weeks slipped by into months and I couldn't find a post-bag to fit them all into, and then it seemed it was only a few weeks until he'd be back. I didn't really want to be without them.

Starting Again (ii)

The choir had already been meeting for a few weeks. As I walked towards the community hall I could see people through the glass doors, a shadowy stand of strangers. I slipped inside aware of being the new girl, conspicuous.

A woman around my age walked towards me. She had short

blonde hair escaping in wisps from beneath a pink tasselled cap, not exactly pretty, but sexy in the way of people who are at ease in their body. She had a slim figure and was wearing tight-fitting jeans and a loose jumper. I took in the detail of her clothes as if it were a kind of singer's outfit that must be emulated – first I must look like a singer. She smiled and held out her hand.

'You're here to listen. I'm Chella.' Her voice had the same lilt I'd heard on the telephone.

'Yes. I might join in.'

'That's all right. Whatever is comfortable.'

She smiled again and returned to the group which started forming itself into a circle. A tall Modigliani woman, slim and doe-eyed; a gnomish man in a bright jumper swinging his body about to an imaginary rhythm; an efficient-looking woman in skirt and jumper; a curvy woman in her thirties with short, dark hair; a broad, sturdy woman in jeans, and next to her, a tall man in a colourful waistcoat, not old but balding, with a little boy leaning against him as if he were a piece of furniture.

I realised I had to join in now or leave if I didn't want to draw attention to myself. I stepped up to the circle while it was still shuffling into shape.

'Warm up first,' Chella said over the babble of voices. She clicked her fingers and swayed her body a little. She flashed me a smile and I felt absurdly grateful. She knew I was the handicapped student, the one who needed special attention.

'Uu-uh uu-huu uu uu oooh.' She swayed back and forth to a slow sensuous rhythm as she sang. The notes were low and her voice was sweet and earthy at once. Her face became prettier. 'Uu-uh uu-huu uu uu oooh.' Her eyes were closed and she seemed to be finding the sounds in the dark of her body. Her feet moved, stamping lightly, accompanying her clicking fingers.

I felt as if I had been made wrongly, all my bones screwed tight at the joints so they clacked stiffly like an old toy. I needed oiling.

'Uu-uh uu-huuu uu uu oooh.' The group repeated the vaguely mournful chant.

'Yes, that's it, low and bluesy. Be sad, let's just relax into slow and sad. 'Ya ne naa ne naa ne naa-aah.'

I joined in softly, so softly I couldn't even hear my own voice. It was lost in the sounds of twenty other voices. Chella opened her eyes and looked straight at me.

I was startled. She couldn't hear me, could she?

The group sang again and this time I mouthed the words, no sound at all. Chella gave me a wry grin.

I tried singing softly again but I could hear my voice and it didn't blend in.

'Oo lala dada da dee.' The Modigliani woman next to Chella sang a line of notes on her own. Her voice was sweet and high and she looked up at the roof of the hall as she sang. The group repeated the sounds. Another tall woman with lovely creamy pale skin standing next to the Modigliani woman sang another pattern of notes and the group repeated again. I suddenly realised that this singing alone sequence was going around the circle and began to panic. *I'll slip out and not come back. I just won't do it.* My bowels loosened, my mind began ducking and weaving. *I can't leave. If I run now, I'd never be able to come back. Okay, so I'll leave. No. I know, I'll sing proper words.* The efficient woman sang with a clear strong voice, although it wavered a bit on the last note and in the midst of my self-absorbed terror I saw that I wasn't alone.

'No, no, no-no, no,' I sang. The group tittered and repeated my 'No'. I looked down at the floor to hide my blush. I'd sung a sound in front of a group of strangers. Relief buzzed through me. The rest of the circle must have sung their patterns of notes one after the other but I heard nothing.

'I feel like going on,' Chella sang and smiled at me. For a moment I thought she was making it up just for me, but then I realised it was a gospel song.

I feel like going on, I feel like going on, I feel like going on
though trials mount on every hand
I feel like going on.

The notes rose and rose, like someone struggling up the path, fighting the odds. It was melodramatic and everyone laughed but there was a kind of recognition in the laughter.

Without anything being said, the circle shuffled again and seemed to resolve itself into three or four groups. I didn't know what was happening so I stayed where I was.

'Are you alto or soprano?' the dark-haired woman next to me asked.

'I've no idea. I can't sing anything. I don't know.'

'Stay here then. This is the altos.'

Chella sang the soprano part again and the sopranos sang after her. It was so high they sounded like angels, like the choir in the promised land on the other side of the mountain, and they laughed when they finished.

It was the altos' turn. There were only five of us.

'I feel like going on.'

I sang in a whisper. I felt hot. Chella walked nearer to the altos and turned her head and I realised with horror that she was listening to me. She looked at me and mouthed silently, that's good, and smiled. Relief surged and I sang a little louder.

'Beautiful!' Chella exclaimed when we finished. She wriggled ecstatically and everyone laughed.

'It sounded great,' one of the sopranos said.

'Now the tenors.' Chella turned to the group of three men. There were only five men altogether, three tenors and two basses, and they looked defenceless in their own small groups amongst so many women. The tenors were shaky. And there was nowhere for them to hide. The tall one with his son still leaning on his leg was confident with the tune first and the other two joined in. Their voices blended sweetly, astonishingly on the high notes, and I thought of men-angels singing in the sky.

'The basses.' The two of them faced Chella, one a thick-set man and the other tall and gentle-looking with long wavy hair. Chella laughed as she tried to get the low notes. The rumbling notes of the men seemed to vibrate under my stomach, to form a curved shape, cupping my pelvis.

'Now, all together. 'Everyone straightened their bodies. Chella swayed and counted. I opened my mouth and started singing when I was sure the others had started. It sounded ragged and mournful. Chella shook her head and we stopped.

'Listen and watch me. You say you feel like going on but you sound like you'd rather lie down and forget about it. On the beat.'

On the beat I opened my mouth but I didn't let a sound emerge until I could hear the others begin the note.

Chella called a break for afternoon tea and I grabbed a cup and sat outside in the cool sunny air. Someone inside sang a line of 'Swing Low Sweet Chariot' half to herself, and four or five others joined in. A few people sitting outside started singing as well. Voices joined in here and there, warm cups of tea in hand, voices rising and swelling and dropping away and joining in again when they remembered the words. It sounded easy, the sort of thing anyone would do around the house, not trying to impress. It was no big deal, it was just singing.

I waited for Theo at the airport. It was Easter Thursday and quite cold. Anthony was away for a couple of weeks and Mani said it was boring to drive to the airport and back so I had driven down by myself. I left early in case I lost my way and now there was too much time. I had a cup of coffee and tried to read the newspaper but kept looking at my watch. Fifteen minutes before his flight was due I went and sat inside the arrival lounge as instructed.

It had been four months, our longest time apart in seven years.

There were a few other people waiting. Two businessmen in suits looked as if they had just rushed away from their offices and didn't have time to be there. They both took several mobile phone calls while they waited. I tried not to keep checking my watch.

His flight landed and the disembarkation corridor was attached to the plane. I stood where I could see passengers walking up the corridor. It seemed important that I was watching when he emerged.

There he was, the very first person out the door with an air hostess and two girls just behind him. He was wearing a new black and white shirt and black jacket and trousers and looking very smart. He looked taller, a little clearer in the eye, more confident. I saw him a second before he saw me, his eyes scanning quickly and a brief moment of anxiety until he caught sight of me.

I held my arms open wide, but he stood stiffly. The air hostess was watching, a faintly disapproving look on her face.

'You too big to hug now?'

He shrugged and gave me a quick awkward hug. His arms were stiff, his elbows out.

'Can I see your ID?' The air hostess had Theo's ticket in her hand.

Theo is my ID I wanted to say, but I looked in my bag and found my driver's licence and gave it to her. She looked at it then looked at Theo's details then gave me a slip of paper to sign. Behind me, the two businessmen were signing for the two girls.

'Have a nice holiday!' said the hostess to all of us.

It seemed a long way to walk down to baggage collection. Theo had a small backpack with him which he wanted to carry.

We reached the baggage carousel and stood waiting. He was level with my shoulder now.

'What bag do you have?'

'The black one. I'll show you.'

'How was the flight?'

'Good.'

'You weren't worried?'

'I've done it before heaps of times visiting my grandma.'

I should have remembered that he'd flown from Sydney to the north coast a couple of times a year while he was living in the mountains.

'Of course. I forgot about that. What did you do on the plane?'

'Played with my Game Boy.'

'Did you talk to the other kids?'

'Not really.'

'Did the hostess give you coloured pencils and books?'

'Yeah, they always do. But I played my Game Boy.'

'You've had your hair cut.' His dark brown curls had been shorn off. It made him look older.

'Yeah. Dad cut it.'

His luggage was taking ages. The two businessmen and their daughters had disappeared. A few other people were still waiting, leaning on their trolleys. I felt a faint stretching of space away from me, a sense I didn't quite fit as neatly in the air. I was loose, as if I might just as easily disappear and the air would flow back over where I had stood.

When we got to the car I studied the street directory – I hadn't driven back from the airport by myself before this and my brain didn't seem to be able to translate the route backwards from the way I had come. It was a cold, blustery day but I felt hot. Theo sat quietly and waited. He was almost always obliging. He didn't want to annoy anyone, give them any reason for abandoning him. His protests were still passive.

'I'm not quite sure of the way,' I explained.

'That's all right,' he said. 'I don't mind if we get lost.'

I looked at him. He was only ten years old and his eyes were sure.

'I do. But I suppose it doesn't matter, does it?'

'No, 'cos we can look at your map and find our way back. Nothing will happen to us.'

He was right of course. Being reassured by a motherless ten-year-old humbled me enough to see sense. We headed out of the airport, negotiating the maze of roads and construction work going on around it. We headed across the Princes Highway and through streets of shops emptied by shopping malls, and then up along the bustling streets of Campsie. I only had to stop once to consult the street directory, in Burwood Road, and realised I had discovered a more straightforward route anyway.

From here where I'm sitting at the table I can see a small handprint on the glass of the back door. It's only visible from here, the light catching the shape and making the chubby fingers distinct. It is evidence of others being here at the beach-house, probably on holiday, filling the rooms with laughter and sand and games. Of course it's impossible to tell whether it's the print of a little boy or girl but I decide it's a boy and that he was gazing out at the others playing on the verandah. Someone will wipe it away one day when they sit here at this same angle and see it marking the glass. Tears sting at the sight of the small sticky print for no reason except that it seems somehow to be part of Dina and Theo's story. I try to understand the labyrinthine workings of association, to understand how the print connects to Theo, to the reflections and shadows of having been in a particular place and time that is only ever made up of moments, and to the way everything changes, how transitory and fragile things are, how we can never call a halt and at best only briefly hold on to a sticky handprint. I know it means singing and telling stories might not last long or change anything, but it's all we have and we probably couldn't go on without them.

Chella swayed and clapped and the rest of us joined in, following her. Her body moved in a sinuous way, as if it were connected by ropes instead of bony joints. She started to stamp her foot every third beat and the choir stamped with her.

I watched her hands, her feet, her mouth. I still felt as if I must have been made with the part that remembers rhythm and pitch missing. One day I told Chella that she had whole hemispheres of her brain mapped that were entirely featureless in mine, that the neural pathways were not formed in my childhood and that is why I couldn't do it, but she smiled and said, you can do it.

'Ya ya-ya yahieee aa nah aaa aoooow.' She began to wail in time with the clapping and we wailed after her. It was too hard to remember the pattern of sounds *and* hit the notes *and* keep the rhythm. I forgot to clap altogther and Chella looked at me. I had become convinced that her whole body had the power of hearing, that her skin was an aural receptor. She knew what sound every person in the room was making individually.

'Sha sha sh-sha-sha ououou uh uh.' She sped up the rhythm and I tried to keep up with the patterns of sound.

'Ga ga ga ga gaarrrh,' she sang. It was a silly sound and she burst out laughing and the choir laughed too.

'Now you are laughing, you can sing,' she said. 'It is good to make silly sounds. And bad sounds. Try this.' She made a whinge-ing, complaining sound and everyone laughed again as they tried it.

'Everyone do it. Don't think about it. Just let it come out.'

Around the room, one by one, we created sound for the others to repeat – pleading, enraged, pathetic, fearful, defensive, accus-ing sounds. There were cries, roars, mutters, coughs, retches, screams, squeaks, giggling. My noise was a 'it's not my fault' petu-lant cry and I was surprised at the sound but not too embarrassed. We repeated sounds over each other, making a kind of dull roar.

Then something else started to happen. Without Chella saying anything, someone, the tall man with the sweet little son (not leaning on his leg any more but seated nearby silently listening), crowed loudly, like a rooster, and someone else, the neat-skirted woman, answered with a miaow. A stocky Dutch woman growled like a tiger and the Modigliani woman made pigeon-cooing noises. Blood rushed to my face. I didn't know what to do. Gradually the hall filled with growls, quacks, purrs, barks, bleats, twitterings, neighs, miaows, howls, brays, cluckings, crows, moos, hisses, squawks. I felt myself letting go into the sound, being inside it. Something else was needed. Softly, underneath, a magpie warbling began. It oddle-ardle-wardled under the menagerie of sound, a black and white bird with beady eyes and a sharp beak.

Chella was smiling and conducting. She waved her hands upwards indicating a crescendo and the magpie gave full throat to her song for a few seconds as the whole menagerie roared, and then Chella brought her hands down and outwards abruptly and we all finished together. Everyone was pink-skinned and smiling, our zoo blood racing.

'That was great!' Chella's eyes were shining. 'Now you can really sing!

It was quiet when we arrived back in the Mountains. Mani had left a note on the table – Gone down to Woodford Dam. See you later.' What was he doing down there in this weather? Theo looked disappointed but tried to rearrange his face so I didn't notice. It's Mani he wants to see, I suddenly realised, Mani who tumbled with him, played soccer with him, made him laugh uncontrollably with tickling and silly games. I was background, necessary so there wasn't a big blank in the landscape, but not the focus of the picture at all.

'What is there for me to do, then?'

He never used to ask that. He stood looking around, waiting for something to happen. Behind him on the kitchen noticeboard was a picture of his mother, wearing a black jacket and talking on the telephone. It had been taken at work and she looked elegant and competent. Theo didn't look at it. He'd seen it a hundred times before.

'Well, you can put your bag in your room for a start.'

'Mani's room, you mean.' He looked at me. Was he challenging me? Rebuffing?

'Mani's room and your room.' I held his gaze.

'Okay. Then what?'

I leaned against the sink and folded my arms. He was moving away from me into a world where I could not cuddle and kiss him any more, could not hold him in my arms for as long as we both wanted. He didn't come from my body but I still felt the pang of losing him. It reminded me that one year, sooner or later, my body would lose its ability to make boys. These strange departures of libido over the summer had been a forewarning of it. I felt a heavy thickness in my body again and knew now that it was a premonition of grief.

'Then we'll have a cup of tea.'

Then he will grow up, then he will be gone, he will fly from my nest, then I will be someone he once used to stay with in the school holidays when he was a kid.

'Have you got cake to have with it?' he asked.

Flying Away

'Ah – Ah – Ah, Ah'm goin' to fly away. Oh glory,' sang Chella.

It was another slave song about the soul fleeing to God. No nightingales in the cotton fields or slave-markets, only the human voice singing, saving its own soul.

The 'Oh glory' at the end of the line jumped up nearly an octave from 'away'. With weeks of practice I had learned to move from one note to the next, learning to trust that there was some connection between hearing and the voice box, but a leap like this was like leaping across a chasm. There was no guarantee that I'd land on the other side at all. And it was a note you needed to belt out. You can't 'Oh glory' in a quiet, retiring way.

'Just the altos', said Chella. 'Remember the leap at the end of the line.'

'I don't know where to land,' I muttered.

'That's all right. We never do. Just leap – that's all.' Chella smiled and I knew she was right. It was, is, when I'm afraid of taking the next step on the high-wire that I start wobbling. If there is faith that there will be something there – if not the wire then air to glide on – at least the next step can be taken. Sing the next note. Even if it sounds dreadful, even if I make a galah of myself.

We sang the first two lines and somehow I made the leap and hit the note. I could hear my voice melding in with the other altos. It still seemed like a matter of pure chance and although I was beginning to believe that I could do it with everyone else, match my voice to theirs, I knew I couldn't do it without them.

That's okay. I suddenly thought, that's okay. I cannot do it without them, but I can do it with them. That's something, isn't it? I sang more loudly, chest out, mouth open.

Oh Glory!

We were still in the kitchen. It was quiet except for our scrabbling voices. The house was warm and we had finished our tea and cake and we should have been comfortable. Without my cup of tea in my hands I didn't know where to put them.

'So, now what can I do?'

'Well, what about we walk up the hill together? To the shops. I have to do some posting,' I said. I'd been thinking about it while we had our tea.

'It's cold,' Theo said.

'Yeah, it is cold. I heard on the radio it's snowing further up the Mountains. We could sing to keep warm. I've been going to a choir for a while and I know a few songs now.'

'Can I have some pocket money if I go up to the shops with you?'

'Sure.'

We rugged up in our coats and gloves and headed out into the wintry cold. Our breath came in white puffs and the air had a painful bite. I tucked my scarf in around my neck. As we turned out of our street and walked up the hill we could see the brown snow clouds sitting heavily and blurrily in the western sky, making a yellowish light. The oaks up the hill were bare and smoke was curling out of narrow slow-combustion chimneys and drifting through stark branches. I could feel the cold of the ground through the thin leather soles of Dina's flowery boots.

A fine sleety snow, too wet to properly call snow, started to fall. Walking up the hill like we had so many times before, and the novelty of the snow falling, changed things between us. Theo looked up at me and grinned. His eyes sparkled with understanding. I knew from his shining face and the determined trudge of his step that he felt like a fierce and stubborn traveller. Me too. I felt a song we'd been learning at choir rise in my body. I knew the words and tunes of several songs by now, and whole lines of songs rose out of the middle of my body. I could feel them, pressing inside my chest and up my throat into my mouth.

'We are going, heaven knows where we are go-oing.
But we know within.'

'Can you sing now?' Theo's face was turned towards me.

'Well, I don't know. What do you reckon?'

'Yep. It sounds like it.' He smiled encouragingly. I knew he was being polite but I didn't mind. That he wanted to encourage me was enough.

'We will get there, heaven knows how we will ge-et there,
But we know we will.'

'That was a good song.' He said it thoughtfully, in that way he had of making you feel he knew exactly what he was talking about.

'Yes, I like it too. It's a gospel song. I think the slaves in America used to sing it in the olden days.'

It reminded me of 'Motherless Child', which we had been learning to sing as a 'round' with 'Wade in the Water'. I wondered if I ought to sing it.

'Sometimes I feel like a motherless child.' I sang it out loud. It needed a strong voice and I wavered.

'I don't feel like a motherless child,' said Theo.

'Don't you?' I was surprised and couldn't hide it.

'No. I don't feel like one, I *am* one.' He looked pleased with the way he'd caught me. It gleamed over the 'poor little boy' look he sometimes used. There was unshakeable grief in him, it permeated his being, but every now and then it was a selfconscious sorrow. He was aware of how he was seen.

'We are going,' I sang again.

'We are going,' sang Theo.

He joined in with me! My heart lifted – my ribs, lungs expanded. He joined in singing with me!

'You know this song?' I stopped and asked.

'Just from you, now.'

Oh my, someone is singing a song learned from me!

'I might not be singing it right,' I said humbly, proudly.

'That's all right,' Theo said.

'You're an angel,' I said. He smiled winningly. He knew what I meant.

We trudged up the hill together, singing in loud voices.

'We are going, heaven knows where we are go-o-oing
But we know within.'

Tears from the wind glittered in our eyes and we wiped them away with the backs of our hands.

Last night, in that half-state between waking and sleeping, when only the thinnest membrane separates wakefulness and unconsciousness, so thin you can hear mopokes calling outside, strange birds and beasts paraded through my mind. There were large ibis with long golden necks flying through aqua-coloured skies, and white zebras without stripes on a wide plain, and kangaroos with folded wings. It was night in there too, stars glittered and the sky was black, but I could see each creature clearly. They were streaming from the darkness, from the vault of metaphors and jokes and dreams buried in the cerebrum, simply, it seemed, for my entertainment. I don't know why the brain so busily creates such elaborate images and narratives; perhaps it's remembering its own evolution from fish and bird and beast; or perhaps the Vedas are right and the universe is created outwards from the mind, singing its own creation, its own illusion.

I don't know whether Dina's brain kept doing that for her, creating a sense of being in the world, or whether it left her in a hell of nothingness inside her tormented body. I can't know. The mystery of existing at all bumps up against me, an everyday mystery. Even mathematicians searching for a theory of everything have not found one single intrinsic reason in the universe why it should exist at all. Perhaps it does not matter. We are here set down and, like Damon in the highland village, must try to knock a few apples down to eat. Friends die young or grow old and die, and so will we all.

Today, though, I walk around the house singing. The words and tune are distinct, and the voice lifting and falling through the house is sometimes clear and strong, sometimes straining. There are some honeyed notes, warm and golden, appearing to melt into the light, to change form as they float through the air, some notes thin and flat as old dishwater, and sometimes the voice cracks and the singing stops. It starts again after a moment and the notes harmonise with the chairs, curtains, cupboards, for a few seconds seeming to flow around them like fragments of silk flung out around the room. Afternoon sun streams through the window, patterning bamboo on the walls and lighting the haphazard pile of books on the table. As I sing, my voice mingles with sun and shadows. No-one can hear me, but I'm singing with my mouth wide open, with my breath and flesh and bones.

Acknowledgments

The author and publisher are grateful to the following for permission to reproduce copyright material: Amanda Lohrey for lines (and inspiration) from *The Clear Voice Suddenly Singing*, in *Secrets* published by Pan Macmillan, Sydney, 1997; Pearson Educational Books for the extract *from Speech and Hearing Science: Anatomy and Physiology* by William R. Zemlin published by Prentice Hall Inc, New Jersey 1988; Penguin Books for the line from 'People' by Yevgeny Yevteshenko in *Selected Poems* published by Penguin Books, London, 1962 and also for the extract from *Tosca* by Isabel Allende in *The Stories of Eva Luna*, published by Penguin, London, 1991; Kelesi Woodhouse for a line from her song, 'Blessing'; Penguin Books Australia for lines from 'Littoral' by Gwen Harwood in *Selected Poems* published by A&R Modern Poets, Sydney, 1988, and for lines from 'The Crane is My Neighbour' by John Shaw Neilson in *Shaw Neilson: Selected Poems* published by A&R Modern Poets, edited by Robert Gray, Sydney 1993; and Allan Music Australia for lines from 'We'll Meet Again' written by Parker and Hughes. Acknowledgments are also due for a line from 'Bellbirds' by A.B. Paterson.

Thank you to all the people who answered my internet queries on singing: Alison Winkworth, Department of Speech Pathology and Audiology, University of Queensland; Janet Rodger, Pacific College of Music; and Kevin Robison, Pacific Conservatory of the Performing Arts. I also acknowledge medical information from various health sites on the internet.

Thank you to Peter Bishop of Varuna, who shook his head at the right time, to Jane Palfreyman and Jo Butler at Random House for their enthusiasm for my work and Jo Jarrah for her heart-lifting wonderful editing. Very special thanks are due to Anne Dunn for the beach-house writing sojourn that changed everything, and to Jean-Paul and Monique Delamotte for the use of the A.C.F.A. writing studio in Paris.

My heartfelt gratitude is offered to my past and present singing and choir teachers: Simon Chate, Kelesi Woodhouse, Ellie Franchmont, Rachael Hore and to Rachael's choir, Voiceworks, all of whom have helped me give in to singing.

Thanks also to the people whose stories I have retold and refashioned here: Suzanne Collum for Wilson Cadiogan's story, Maureen Williams. Terry Wiltshire, Daniel Soler, Lisa Lamey, Connie Fry and J.B. Thanks to everyone whose entries in the hospital book were used.

This book could not have been written without the extraordinary generosity of 'Kit' and 'Theo' – thank you for permitting me to tell some of the story of 'Dina'. I hope all of 'Dina's' many friends who were so much a part of those days will forgive the inaccuracies they might find in this story. It is only my variable memory of the time; also many names and incidental details have been changed to protect privacy.

Finally, and most of all, deepest thanks to Anthony Reeder, my best and dearest critic for his enduring faith in my journey.

About the Author

Patti Miller is the author of *Writing Your Life*, *The Last One Who Remembers* and *Child*. From 1984 to 1992 she was a lecturer in Writing and Literature, first at the University of Technology, Sydney, and then at the University of Western Sydney. Since 1991, when she founded the Life Stories Workshops, she has offered fiction and life-writing workshops at writers' centres, community centres and for Continuing Education courses at the University of Sydney.